The "How To"
Grants Manual

Other selected titles in the series:

The "How To" Grants Manual

Successful Grantseeking Techniques for Obtaining Public and Private Grants

Sixth Edition

David G. Bauer

Published in partnership with the

AMERICAN COUNCIL ON EDUCATION
® The Unifying Voice for Higher Education

Rowman & Littlefield Education
Lanham • New York • Toronto • Plymouth, UK

Published in partnership with the
American Council on Education

Published in the United States of America
by Rowman & Littlefield Education
A Division of Rowman & Littlefield Publishers, Inc.
A wholly owned subsidary of The Rowman & Littlefield Publishing Group, Inc.
4501 Forbes Boulevard, Suite 200, Lanham, Maryland 20706
www.rowmaneducation.com

Estover Road
Plymouth PL6 7PY
United Kingdom

British Library Cataloguing in Publication Information Available

Library of Congress Cataloging-in-Publication Data

Bauer, David G.
    The "how to" grants manual : successful grantseeking techniques for obtaining
public and private grants / David G. Bauer.—6th ed.
        p.   cm.—(ACE/Praeger series on higher education)
    Includes bibliographical references and index.
1. Fund raising.   2. Grants-in-aid.   3. Nonprofit organizations.   I. Title.
HG177.B38 2007
658.15′224—dc22   2007027877
4429   8767   9/10
ISBN: 978-0-275-99790-8 (cloth : alk. paper)
ISBN: 978-1-60709-554-5 (pbk. : alk. paper)
ISBN: 978-1-60709-555-2 (electronic)

CONTENTS

LIST OF EXHIBITS, FIGURES, AND TABLES

PREFACE

In each of the previous five editions of The "How To" Grants Manual, the changes in the grants marketplace eclipsed each prior edition in ways that challenged the imagination. The first edition made no mention of email, web sites, electronic database searches, or the Community of Science. I personally feel privileged to have been involved in the testing of the first database search system developed at the State University of New York (now known as SPIN) and to have witnessed and taken part in the monumental changes in the field of resource development that have made grantseeking more accessible to you.

The first few editions of this book instructed grantseekers on how to make preproposal contact by letter. Later editions mentioned making contact via fax and, eventually, email. Through all of these advancements one concept has remained the same—the importance of making personal contact to gather research on potential grantors. The means have experienced dramatic changes, but the principles have remained the same. Researching prospective grantors and incorporating means to meet their needs result in money to you.

The 2003 fifth edition addressed the impact the attack on the World Trade Center and our nation's search for Osama Bin Laden had on our nation's economy and our grant resources. Massive changes occurred in the portfolios of the nation's leading grantors, and there was a significant decline in the profits of our major granting corporations.

The economic picture has changed since then. Corporate profits, the DOW, and the NASDEX have surpassed previous highs. The private grants marketplace has been bolstered by the Bill & Melinda Gates Foundation's assets of over

$30 billion, its grants payouts of approximately $1.5 billion, and Warren Buffett's decision to add an additional $1.5 billion annually to the Gates's expenditures.

Sections in this edition will extol the virtues of the private foundations exhibited at the writing of this book. However, these must be balanced with the contractions in the federal marketplace brought on, in part, by the wars in Afghanistan and Iraq. The increase in the national deficit that will occur during the useful life span of this sixth edition (estimated to be from $3 trillion to $9 trillion) will have a significant impact on the federal grants marketplace, and on your chances of securing federal dollars for your projects, programs, and research for years to come.

Other forces have also affected the grants marketplace in unprecedented ways. For example, the use of congressional earmarking to secure funding has replaced the role of need, peer review, and research/project/program credibility with the congressional strength of your state's elected officials.

Although grantseeking is now seriously intertwined with politics, make no mistake that the focus of this sixth edition is not to further the author's political agenda. The purposes are to educate the grantseeker in the grants marketplace and to inform the grantseeker how to use it to his or her best avail by keeping up with its ever-changing face and maintaining a mix of its expanding and contracting segments.

INTRODUCTION

The sixth edition of this book, and the changes that are incorporated in it, stem from user feedback, the author's first-hand experience with hundreds of grantseekers, and the dramatic events occurring in the grants world. Independent evaluation of the fifth edition of the book on the Internet rated it 5 out of 5. The reviewers' comments reinforce the primary concept that each of the previous five editions have been based on—providing an easy-to-use, systematic approach that will help you determine which grantors will net you the greatest return for your investment of time and resources.

The advertisements for grants programs, products, and materials that promise quick and easy grants success have increased significantly over recent years. It is a shame that most of these advertisements are fraudulent and that many have led to misunderstanding and, in some instances, abuse in the grants marketplace. After viewing one of the advertisements, I wondered how an individual could get the federal government to pay for his or her free vacation to Europe, as promised by the person in the ad seen running up the steps of the Capitol with dollar bills attached all over his clothes. I looked into it and found out that the free trip turned out to be dependent on securing a Fulbright Scholarship. These awards are made to university faculty who are published icons in their fields. Most have received numerous government grants supporting their past research activity. I do not know about you, but to me that seems a bit optimistic for a novice grantseeker, and even for a successful government grantseeker like me.

Calls to my office from individuals looking for grants for their profit-making companies are becoming alarmingly frequent. These individuals' projects are best suited for a loan, and while they can investigate the possibility of securing

Small Business Innovative Research grants, the bulk of the $400 billion in federal grants referred to in this book is awarded to nonprofit organizations. What you will learn in this book is when and how to integrate partners, including in some cases profit-making companies, into your successful consortia.

The government cutbacks in grant programs force you to explore every technique possible to ensure a competitive edge. Federal granting agencies have already reported $7 billion in cuts and face a further rescission of 1.5 percent per agency. Even flat funding is really a grant's cut equal to the rate of inflation. The deficit spending related to the wars in Iraq and Afghanistan will force Congress to deal with hundreds of billions in costs even if and when the confrontations are reduced or eliminated due to increased health care for the wounded veterans and replacement of destroyed equipment. It is worthy to mention that 2007 is extraordinary in federal budget history. It is the only year our whole government was funded on a continuing resolution and not on a budget.

Congress, the president, and both of the political parties will have tough choices to make as they seek to balance the budget. Traditionally, domestic grants programs have not faired well during times of government cutbacks. Research and grants programs do not have a clearly focused voice like lobbyists, financial supporters of the corporate world, and groups that represent major constituencies such as the elderly (that is, AARP).

But please take note that in the past, I have seen some grantseekers overreact to news of federal cutbacks, and in some cases, the number of applications have actually gone down. This means that the astute grantseeker, equipped with the strategies presented in this book, can increase his or her success rates.

No new edition of this book could fail to include the effects of earmarking on the grants marketplace. For those colleges, universities, and other nonprofit organizations that have used political leverage, consultants, and the lure of noncompetitive earmarking (pork) to fund their programs, the new changes in Congress will affect them. While earmarking a bill to include funding has increased dramatically, this grants strategy has always presented a problem with post-pork continuation funding. Even though earmarking may seem like an expedient avenue to fund research, programs, centers, and institutes, the process bypasses competitive peer review. And while the peer-review process is not without some problems, avoiding it diminishes the need for federal program officers, which has its consequence. With earmarking now under scrutiny and criticism, many grantseekers will find that they must return to the peer-review process and to contact with the program staff that have been circumvented in the past. Because of this phenomenon, this sixth edition of The "How To" Grants Manual addresses how to rebuild relationships with program officers and improve the quality of your proposals as you compete at a higher level.

There are also many other new pressures on the research/grants enterprise at the federal level. Never before have we had to deal with federal researchers and program officers making two to three times their salaries as consultants to corporations, while purporting to maintain an objective viewpoint in their granting of awards by their agencies. The perception that federal researchers are not seeking the truth through their research, but rather what will make them the most money, has damaged the public's opinion of the grants mechanism. These factors, and the fact that many program officers and reviewers have left their granting agencies to set up consulting firms to assist grantseekers in getting grants from their past programs, all work against us in getting more federal grant funding.

The purpose of this book is to educate you on the politics, practices, and strategies to obtain the information you need to produce the highest scoring proposal. The quality represented in your proposal is a credit to those of us in the field that support peer review, candor, and professional ethics in our grantseeking.

PART ONE

....

Getting Ready to Seek Grant Support for Your Organization

CHAPTER 1

Motivating Yourself to Follow a Proactive, Success-Based Grants System

This book represents the author's best effort at providing you with a system of proven strategies for success in getting your proposals awarded. The overarching question is, "How can you get the greatest return in funding for your efforts?" The goal is always to increase your grants acceptance rate. Why? Because rejection wastes your time and your organization's resources and positions you negatively with grantor agency personnel and/or board members. Even reviewers remember your flawed, past submittals and will view your latest efforts with a jaundiced eye. The most frequent reason for a poorly developed proposal is that the writer did not have enough time to produce a quality effort before the deadline occurred.

The key to success is to be proactive and to initiate the proposal development process early, months, or even a year, before the deadline. By starting early and using the proactive strategies presented in this book, you can achieve a grants acceptance rate of over 75 percent. This brings up an important question. Will you actually employ these strategies to guarantee yourself a high success rate? Your response should be yes. But my experience with over 30,000 grants seminar participants tells me that you probably will not, until you fail so often that you decide you have to reflect on what you are doing wrong. My 30 years of experience in grantseeking, teaching, and writing have shown me that grantseekers must motivate themselves to set up my proven system for success. In other words, only you can do it!

Whether you are starting your career, restarting your career, looking to achieve tenure at a university, moving ahead in your nonprofit field, or having fun assisting your favorite charity, reflect on your goals, time commitments, and motivation. Successful grants procurement will have a dramatic, powerful, positive impact on your career. Few skills that I have developed have propelled my career as a researcher and educator more than grantseeking.

This chapter is all about you. Take a few minutes now to review why you are seeking grant funds and to determine how your actions and their results will influence your career plan and the mission of your organization. By doing this, you will be much more eager about using the proactive, reality-based system for grant success outlined in this book.

Your consideration of a career-enhancing grants strategy does not begin with a specific grantor and a looming deadline. If you are reading this chapter with perspiration dripping from your forehead because of a rapidly approaching deadline, stop! My first suggestion is to forego the application and read on since pursuing this grant will most likely result in rejection. You simply do not have enough time to take advantage of the proactive grants system suggested in this book. However, if this is impossible (because your supervisor, manager, or administrator is forcing you to apply, or for some other reason), skip the first eight chapters of this book and move on to those dedicated to proposal development. When your proposal is rejected, you can then read the first eight chapters to help you determine how best to approach a resubmittal.

The grants strategies in this book require you to use the same system each time you approach the grants marketplace for a research project or a program. The key to success is recognizing that you do not inherently know how to approach grantors or to write your proposals. The grants marketplace is based upon *change*. The very fact that grantors (be they federal, foundation, or corporate) solicit requests is based on their desire to fund *new* approaches, protocols, and solutions to problems.

This represents a planning dilemma. The strategy or approach that worked in the last proposal is not likely to work in the next one. It is in the past. Even the proactive grantseeking techniques we employed may need to be changed. To be successful we must constantly question the way we like or prefer to approach grantseeking and force ourselves to determine with each and every application/ proposal if the field has changed and, therefore, whether our approach must change.

Grantseeking should be thought of as the successful negotiation of a maze. We must be open to looking at various avenues and hope that we do not ultimately choose the wrong one, or a dead end. You may find the book *Who Moved My Cheese?*[1] as helpful as I have in this respect. The book is short and easy to read, and while the lessons are universal, they are particularly insightful with respect to negotiating the grants maze. Just the names of the characters should entice you into reading it. Two characters are mice named Sniff and Scurry.

(How many grantseekers have you seen sniffing for the money and scurrying after it?) The book's other two characters are little people named Hem and Haw. They successfully navigate the maze and find the cheese (grant money), but refuse to believe that their previously successful strategies are not working to find new cheese (more grants). They try nonproductive strategies over and over again hoping for different results. The book's main tenet is that you must be ready to change again and again because the cheese (a metaphor for what you want) is always being moved.

I understand totally why I sometimes fail at getting grantseekers to employ my suggested strategies. It is tough to manage one's time effectively and to act proactively when surrounded by constant change. However, this book will show you that by collecting grantor research before scurrying off to write a proposal, you will be able to uncover changes that have occurred and then be able to take these changes into account when developing your ever-evolving grants strategy.

DEVELOPING YOUR CAREER GRANTS PLAN

In a few chapters you will be moving through the maze to grants success. Each successful grants quest leads to more knowledge, but also to more questions and additional grant opportunities. Success gathers momentum. But beware that if money is your only goal, you may be propelled down a pathway that leads to areas where you have little professional interest, or may not want to spend a lifetime pursuing. Being forewarned is being forearmed. Once you succeed, publish, and speak at conferences and so forth, your grant interests can take on a life of their own.

In a survey of my grants seminar participants, less than 2 percent reported that they left graduate school with a five-year career plan, and none had considered how grantseeking could fit into a career plan. Exhibit 1.1 helps you determine your personal vision of where you want to be in five years and what role grantseeking will play in that vision. I have found that this visioning process, as outlined in Denis Waitley's classic book *The Psychology of Winning*,[2] is one of the keys to success. He states that to *achieve* something you must first *conceive* it and then *believe* it. Your first step is to conceive your grants plan and then to believe in it. It is important that you alone create a definition of success, for both yourself and your career. If you are an academic, or a nonprofit program manager, state your vision of success and define it. How much time will you devote to grants? to research? to teaching? to program management? to administration? Quantify each part of your vision.

Exhibit 1.1 helps you refine your vision by asking what resources you think you will need. For example, will you need special release time or time specifically allocated to your grant as opposed to your regular workload or schedule? If so, how much time will you need to achieve success? partial release time for your grant-funded project or full time? Remember, you cannot perform your current

1. Where do you want your career to be five years from now? What projects, programs, and research will you be performing? How do these projects, programs, and/or research fit into your vision of success in your field?

2. What percent of your time will be devoted to these projects/programs/research as opposed to your current job responsibilities? _____%

    Based on the percent of time you will be devoting to projects/programs/research, what is the estimated cost of your grant-related salary/wages including fringe benefits?

3. What personnel will you need to help you perform the tasks you would like to accomplish in the fifth year of your vision?

	Number	Estimated Cost
Project Coordinator(s)	_____	_____
Laboratory assistant(s)	_____	_____
Graduate assistant(s)	_____	_____
Work study student(s)	_____	_____
Other (please list)	_____	_____

4. What facilities will be required to house these individuals? In-house, on-campus, off-campus, etc.? What do you estimate the required square footage to be?

5. What new equipment (computers, software, machines, vehicles, etc.) will you and your staff need to accomplish the projected task?

Equipment Item	Equipment Cost
_____	_____
_____	_____

6. Will you submit
    *   Articles for publication? If yes, how many and in what journals?

    *   Books or chapters for publication? If yes, how many and under what titles?

    *   Requests for presentations? If yes, how many and at what conferences/meetings?

7. Based on salary/wages, personnel, and equipment, what is the total amount of resources needed in year 5? $ _____

    Of this total, how much will be needed from your organization/institution? $ _____
    How much will be needed in grants? $ _____

YOUR PERSONAL GRANTS PLAN

EXHIBIT 1.1

workload plus your grant workload unless you want to risk working 200 percent of your time! Continue to answer the questions regarding your five-year vision. What personnel will you require? project coordinator? lab assistants? support staff? work study students? graduate assistants, and so on? What software, equipment, transportation, and so on will you require? By estimating the cost of the components you need to fulfill your five-year plan you can come up with a total cost and then determine if any of the cost may be covered by your normal budget process. If so, subtract this amount from the total so that you can come up with a more accurate estimate of the amount you must procure through grants.

This visioning process is critical in that it will help you develop benchmarks to keep your five-year plan in focus as you start out toward your first-year goals. Your plan will provide you with a guide for success as defined by you, and it should be reviewed, updated, and changed on a yearly basis.

Exhibit 1.2 will help you break your five-year plan into a one-year plan and assist you in determining the immediate resources you will need. First, review your five-year plan and write down what initial steps are critical to begin movement toward your vision. What smaller steps must you take now to begin the process? What components will require grant funding? Second, determine who might be able to help you achieve the initial steps. Consider organizing a small group of individuals who are interested in your project or research area and have had experience working with you. Potential group members could include individuals from your undergraduate, graduate, and postgraduate work. Consider advisors, mentors, and colleagues as potential project consultants, co-investigators, or consortium partners.

DEVELOPING A PROACTIVE SYSTEM

Once you have your five-year grants plan written, you are ready to begin the process of developing grant support. Many well-intended grantseekers begin the process by creating a proposal and searching for a grantor, or they learn of grants with a rapidly approaching deadline and try to get a proposal completed quickly. However, this is called reactive grantseeking and results in high rates of rejection (80 to 90 percent).

By contrast, in proactive grantseeking you spend time researching a prospective grantor before writing and submitting a proposal. As a proactive grantseeker you will uncover information that will help you increase your chances of acceptance by

- determining what the grantor is really looking for (the grantor's hidden agenda),
- predicting your likelihood of success before investing additional time, and
- tailoring your proposal to the funding source's needs.

1. What steps can you take in the next 12 months to move you toward your five-year vision? (These steps could include procuring smaller start-up or initiation grants, needs assessment grants, grants to develop preliminary data, or grants for a minimal amount of essential equipment or software.)

2. What resources do you need to help you initiate these first steps? (These resources should include a list of potential advisors, mentors, colleagues, etc. with whom you can brainstorm your topic, enlist support, and/or develop a consortia approach.)

3. Whom will you contact, and when?

    Who   When

    _____   _____
    _____   _____
    _____   _____
    _____   _____

SETTING YOUR GOALS AND ENLISTING SUPPORT

EXHIBIT 1.2

The difference between reactive and proactive grantseekers is *when* and *how* they invest their time and how these variables influence their success rate. Proactive grantseekers put in small amounts of time *throughout* the grantseeking process. The reactive grantseeker invests a lot of time just prior to the deadline. This approach often results in last minute, general proposals that are designed to fit almost any possible grantor's guidelines, lack specificity, and are not targeted or tailored to the needs of the grantor. In addition, they are usually easily recognizable because of a preponderance of statements beginning with "We want," "We need," and "We propose to do" and contain little reference to why the grantor would want to fund the proposal.

Unfortunately, this self-focus has been aided by the use of computers for researching grantors. In many cases overzealous and self-focused grantseekers will secure printouts of all the grantors who have funded projects even remotely related to theirs and then send the same proposal to every grantor on the list. What these grantseekers overlook is that this shotgun approach results in high rates of rejection and negative positioning with funding sources.

Whenever your proposals (or those of your nonprofit organization) result in failure, you risk positioning your organization in a negative manner. Of course, grantseeking will always result in a certain percentage of rejection. That is bound to happen. But how much rejection can you, the grantseeker, and your organization afford before the very appearance of your name on a proposal elicits a negative reaction from grantors? What is the success rate you need to achieve to avoid negative positioning? Anything less than a 50-percent success rate results in negative positioning. An 80- or 90-percent failure rate could not possibly create a positive image for your organization with the grantor's staff or reviewers.

Embracing a proactive approach to grantseeking means starting the process early. This enables the grantseeker to employ quality assurance techniques to increase his or her chances of success and avoid negative positioning. A proactive grantseeker has enough time to conduct a quality circle exercise or mock review of his or her proposal before submittal, using the same review system that is to be used by the grantor. This technique helps to ensure that the submitted proposal represents the grantseeker's best effort. By starting early and finishing your proposal three to four weeks before the grantor's deadline, you will be able to have your proposal read and scored by friendly role players who can pick up any errors before your proposal is submitted for its real review. While chapters 14 and 23 provide details on how to use a grants quality circle to improve a proposal, the simple fact is that you will not have enough time to use this invaluable technique unless you become a proactive grantseeker!

Exhibit 1.3 shows what kinds of reviewer comments are likely to be received when proactive grantseeking is abandoned. Quickly put together, last-minute submissions often contain spelling, grammar, and punctuation errors, especially when they are submitted electronically on grantor web sites that do not provide tools such as spelling and grammar checks. You can be sure the staff and the reviewers will remember submissions like this, but for all the wrong reasons!

I quickly learned that the best strategy for winning grants was to tailor each and every proposal to the perspective of the potential grantor. After a reactive grantseeking failure, I remembered a theory I learned as a psychology major and applied it to grantseeking. Thirty years later, I can unequivocally say that this theory has helped me develop millions of dollars in successful projects and research for nonprofit organizations. I share this theory with you to help you approach grantseeking from the grantor's perspective and to provide you with the basis for developing a tailored proposal to each grantor.

APPLICATION NUMBER

Technology Innovation Challenge Grant Program
Individual Technical Review Form - Tier 1

SUMMARY ASSESSMENT

Please summarize your overall thoughts about the application in light of your previous
comments on "significance" and "feasibility," and mention any important points on
which the application is unclear so that these points can be raised with the applicant.

*The conversational style was welcome and easy reading. For once there was an absence
of educational "buzz words." However, watch out for too much informal style (e.g., the phrase
"parents don't have a clue").*

*Don't forget to identify acronyms; GSAMS was identified only in a letterhead in the
appendix.*

*It is extremely important to proofread your application. There were no less than nineteen
grammar and punctuation errors. If simple details like these are not corrected as a matter of
professionalism, can one reasonably be expected to properly manage several million dollars?*

OVERALL GRADE ___B___
A=high, B=medium, C=low

SAMPLE REVIEWER'S COMMENTS

EXHIBIT 1.3

FESTINGER'S THEORY OF COGNITIVE DISSONANCE

Dr. Leon Festinger developed the theory of cognitive dissonance[3] while performing research on cognitive development and the assimilation of new information.
In summary, Festinger found that preconceived ideas and constructs have a fil-
tering effect on newly presented information. If the new information does not
support preexisting concepts, students react negatively to learning and to assimi-
lating the new data. Festinger labeled this resistance to new information as "dissonance." According to his theory, individuals do not view new data with an
open mind, and that which does not match their preexisting constructs creates
static or dissonance. In essence, we want to maintain homeostasis, and we tend
to see and hear that which reinforces our existing beliefs and omit that which
does not.

In my first attempt to write a proposal, I remembered Festinger's work and
wanted to be sure my proposal would be "seen" by the reviewers. In fact, I con-
cluded that to truly be read and understood, I needed to know more about the

way the grantor viewed the world. The first grants seminar I attended dedicated hours on how to write clearly. And while I believe that writing clearly is very important, I was more intrigued by the idea of creating consonance rather than dissonance. At that point I remembered my high school English teacher's mantra—write from the point of view of the reader. That is when I realized how important it was that I understood how my prospective grantor saw the world and the way in which his or her grant funding impacted and changed it. That is when I realized how important it was for me to do my grantor homework.

VALUES-BASED GRANTSEEKING

By expanding Festinger's theory, I developed the values glasses theory and the concepts of values-based grantseeking. A common mistake of grantseekers is to write their proposals based on their own values. They assume that their prospective grantors have similar values to themselves and that they will read their proposals from their (the grantseekers') point of view. This is a mistake. Using a proposal to try to change the values of a grantor or to show that the funding source's granting pattern is unenlightened is another mistake that usually results in dissonance and rejection. Some grantseekers also make the mistake of using their own vocabulary in proposals, forgetting that grantors will read and react to proposals based upon their (the grantors') vocabulary.

Figure 1.1 illustrates the grantseeker's predicament. As a proactive, values-based grantseeker he or she must strive to get the facts through the lenses (filters) of the grantor over to the brain of the grantor that controls the hand, arm, and money (check) the grantseeker wants.

The ensuing chapters are all based on uncovering the information you need to understand the values of the grantor so that your proposal can be written and presented in such a way that it reinforces your prospective grantor's values. Values-based grantseeking entails uncovering information about the grantor that will help you develop an appreciation and understanding of the grantor's values glasses. Once you have this information, you can use it as a guide to your approach, helping you select the right needs data and vocabulary to include in your proposal and ensuring that you present a compelling case for funding.

Successful grantseekers avoid jeopardizing their chances at being funded by remaining sensitive to the values of the grantor. They do not pander to the reviewer, or wrap a wolf in sheep's clothing, but their approach to proposal preparation does reflect their knowledge of the grantor and, ultimately, respect for the grantor's values.

If you follow this theory through, it will be obvious to your prospective grantor that you know what the grantor values and that rejecting your proposal would be a repudiation of his or her (the grantor's) own values. In fact, not funding you would be unpleasant, create internal static, and produce dissonance!

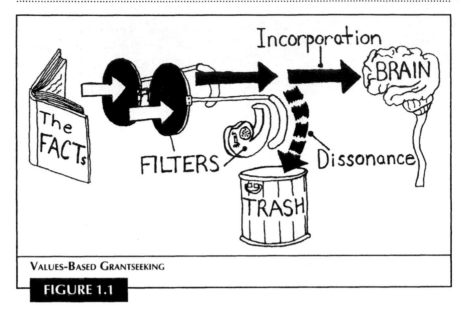

VALUES-BASED GRANTSEEKING

FIGURE 1.1

This theory does not apply just to private funding sources (foundations and corporations). Proposals to federal and state grantors are read by staff and peer reviewers who are also likely to give the best scores to proposals tailored to their beliefs. In fact, reviewers selected by government bureaucrats are likely to be professionals who have perspectives and values similar to those of the government bureaucrats.

To be truly successful, your proactive grants system should be based on a triple win—meeting the needs of the grantor, your organization, and you, the proposal developer. You need not invest more time in the process than the reactive grant-seeker; you just need to invest your time earlier and more wisely. Instead of a 72-hour, last minute, Herculean proposal effort, invest 10 hours per month for seven months. This will give you plenty of time to research the grantor, make prepro-posal contact, and construct a tailored proposal—all without the stress of a last-minute effort!

Now that you know some of the advantages of proactive grantseeking, you have come to your first major grantseeking crossroads. Yogi Berra once said, "When you come to a fork in the road, take it,"[4] and you will. I have always pre-ferred having a plan and have told all my students that if you do not have a plan, any road will get you there. The only problem is you will not know when you are there. I hope you have a plan and are ready to move into the next phase of suc-cessful grantseeking. The projects, programs, and research you propose are important to you, your career, and to the fields you will impact.

If there is one lesson that grantseeking has taught me in the millions of dollars of grant-funded projects I have completed in my 30-year career, it is that you can make a living doing a lot of things, but what is truly important is making a living while making a difference. If the strategies outlined in the following chapters help you move toward your vision, then I have reached my goal in writing this book.

NOTES

1. Spencer Johnson, M.D., *Who Moved My Cheese?* (New York: G.P. Putnam's Sons, 2002).

2. Denis Waitley, *The Psychology of Winning* (New York: Berkley Books, 1984).

3. Leon Festinger, *A Theory of Cognitive Dissonance* (Stanford, CA: Stanford University Press, 1962).

4. Yogi Berra, *The Yogi Book* (New York: Workman Publishing, 1999), p. 48.

CHAPTER 2

Searching the Literature to Document Your Project's Statement of Need

Creating an Urgent and Compelling Case

Whenever I am afforded the chance to interact with government or private grant personnel, I ask, "What are the most common mistakes that grantseekers make in their proposals?" It turns out that the most common mistake is not following instructions. The second most common mistake is not developing a credible statement of the need to be addressed or the problem they are attempting to solve.

In their zeal and enthusiasm to get money and to get started, proposal writers often present their project methods or protocols before even establishing the *need* for a solution. While this rush to action is understandable—grantseekers are, after all, action-oriented "doers"—this jump to the solution assumes that the grantor knows the importance of addressing the need/problem. By making this assumption, you forfeit your opportunity to

- demonstrate your command of the latest research in the field,
- reinforce your credibility as an expert in the field, and
- show confidence in a thorough knowledge of the need/problem that will reinforce an exemplary solution.

Take a moment now to focus on the need/problem that your project seeks to impact. Develop a three- or four-sentence description that summarizes the need/problem that your proposal (and the grantor's money) will address. Review your need/problem statement to be sure that it *does not* contain or present a solution. That proposal component will come later.

14

To ensure that your need/problem description is clear and concise, present it to a colleague whose level of expertise is similar to that of your prospective grantor (its reviewers, board members, or staff members). If your test elicits a response that indicates that he or she sees the problem, you are on the right track. Too much jargon or the use of vocabulary that requires an advanced understanding is not good. Trying to be too complex to impress your reader will introduce confusion. Remember, even the National Science Foundation cautions you to write for a scientifically literate lay reader.

Many grantseekers make a fatal error when attempting to provide evidence of the need or the problem by documenting the *means* to an end, rather than the end. For example, a prospective grantee who desires a building might try to show evidence of need by providing architecture plans and the documentation of a leaky roof and the presence of asbestos in the existing building. These are not reasons enough for a grantor to fund a building. What the grantseeker should document is the difference between what can be done in the existing facility and what more a new facility would enable the organization to do. In other words, the grantseeker should let the prospective grantor know how a new building would facilitate increased research, programs and services, or better solve the problems of the organization's clients. The building (or lack of it) is not the problem. It is the means to an end, and the end is what needs to be documented.

Researchers are faced with a similar dilemma. The need is not the research they propose to accomplish but, rather, the benefits of their research and the problems it can be used to solve. Even pure bench research must seek to close a gap of knowledge in the field. The documentation of the need must include a cohesive explanation of how current research has driven the researcher to ask additional questions, seek to test other relationships, and advance the field so that new and even more poignant questions can be asked.

After you are satisfied with the quality and appropriateness of your description of the need/problem, place it under question 1 on the Needs Assessment Worksheet (exhibit 2.1).

DOCUMENTING THE NEED/PROBLEM

The way to demonstrate that the need/problem *really* exists, and is not just your opinion, is to collect and organize a search of the relevant and latest literature in the field. This literature search is a *must* for every type of grant be it research, demonstration, or project. How do you know that there is a need? How do you know this is a problem? What has been explored to date? Who has done work on solving the problem, and what has their work left unanswered?

At this point you should collect all the information you can on the need/problem. This includes information on past attempts that have failed to solve the problem and successful attempts that have reduced the problem somewhat, or moved the field ahead to its current position. Use the Internet in your search,

1.   What is the problem?

2.   What data do we have to document the problem? (What exists now?)

3.   What information do we need to create a compelling and accurate assessment of the problem?

4.   What information do we have to provide a clear picture of the desired state of affairs that should or could exist? (What ought to be in the future?)

5.   What will happen in the field if the problem is not addressed in a timely manner? (The urgency and motivation)

NEEDS ASSESSMENT WORKSHEET

EXHIBIT 2.1

as well as known journals and other major publications in your field. Since you have not decided on a particular grantor yet, collect international, national, regional, and local data. This way you will be prepared irrespective of your potential grantor's geographic focus. Enter several of your most significant examples of data that document the problem under question 2 on the Needs Assessment Worksheet (exhibit 2.1).

As you consider the literature that exists, you will begin to make observations about the data you wish you had to make a more thorough case. List the information you need to create a more compelling and accurate assessment of the problem under question 3 in exhibit 2.1. If your completion of exhibit 2.1 demonstrates that you are weak in the area of needs documentation, or if it becomes difficult to locate studies, literature, or data to document the problem you seek funds to solve, you may find that you need to attract a small foundation or corporate needs assessment grant to help you. For example, if data or studies exist on a *national* level only, you may decide to prepare a proposal to develop knowledge on the *local* problem. Yes, it may be possible to locate a local or regional grantor that will value the fact that its modest investment may help you document the problem where it "lives" and ultimately make it possible for you to attract larger grants from other funding sources for conducting your project. A needs assessment grant also can help to position you as the resident expert in your field and provide you with valuable insights into the problem. It may also provide you with an improved tool to use in the measurement of the need. See chapter 20 for information on how to locate potential, private funding sources for small needs assessment grants.

CREATING A GAP BETWEEN WHAT EXISTS NOW IN THE FIELD AND WHAT COULD OR SHOULD BE

Being selected as a grant recipient is based upon several variables, many of which will be addressed later in this book. The most important variable is how well you provide a clear and documented statement of the problem. Grantors are motivated by a desire to alter or impact a problem. Their motivation is enhanced when proposal developers reinforce the importance of their (the grantors) commitment for change. Grantseekers can do this by creating a discernible gap between what exists now (based on their search of the literature) and what could or should be.

As you search the literature, be on the lookout for statements or quotes from influential granting officials, corporate executives, foundation directors, or field experts concerning the importance or relevance of solving or reducing the problem. These types of statements or quotes serve as documentation of the gap between what we know now and what would, could, should, or ought to be. What or whom can you quote that documents the value of knowing, proving, or reducing the problem and what ought to be in the future? Record information you gather on the desired state of affairs on the Needs Assessment Worksheet (exhibit 2.1, question 4).

The first edition of this book over 20 years ago warned the proposal writer to avoid suggesting the *value* of the results of his or her proposal. At that time, this was seen as researcher bias and suggested that the researcher had previous knowledge of the results of the research, and thus the outcomes of testing his or her hypothesis. Much has changed since then as corporations and government agencies have moved from viewing research as a way of expanding knowledge to viewing it for application possibilities and what it can be worth. Even basic researchers must document how their research will move the field forward, save time and money, and expand knowledge that another scientist will use to apply to unique solutions. The focus has changed to application.

In addition, all proposal developers, including researchers, need to identify the possible impact of not addressing the problem *immediately*. It is imperative that they provide grantors with a futuristic reference to why the problem needs to be addressed *now*. Since your proposal will be evaluated against hundreds of others, and grantors will often have to address multiple gaps in one field, your needs documentation must be compelling. What will continue to happen that is counterproductive in your field, or cannot happen, if this question is not answered? How is time and money wasted if we do not "know"? Use exhibit 2.1, question 5 to record your thoughts on this question.

TYPES OF NEEDS ASSESSMENT

The two basic grants marketplaces—public (federal, state, and local government agencies) and private (foundations and corporations)—rely on very different forms of needs assessment. However, at this point in the grants process you need not know for certain which marketplace you are pursuing, or which specific grantor or grant program you will be approaching. Therefore, you will need to revisit this section on needs assessment to select the documentation best suited to win your grant *after* you have completed the process of developing solutions, redefining your project, and conducting a thorough search and analysis of possible grantors. When you are ready, use the Statistically Based Needs Documentation Table (table 2.1) and the Needs Assessment Table (table 2.2) to help you decide which approach to adopt for your project.

Since you do not know at this point which type of grantor you will be pursuing, you might be wise to search for and record needs documentation data that you might normally overlook because it is not scientifically valid. (Remember, many grantseekers who assume they will be approaching only federal grant sources discover that they could benefit from a small needs assessment grant from a local foundation or corporate grantor to strengthen their larger federal proposal.)

Most researchers and innovative program and project developers seeking government (federal and state) grants and sizable grants from larger foundations will search for and record information derived from the three sources outlined in the Statistically Based Needs Documentation Table (table 2.1)—statistical analysis, survey, and studies. These types of grantors have educated and professional staff, utilize a peer-review process that is based on their knowledge of the major contributors in the field and their work, and prefer needs statements based on facts and studies. Use the information outlined in table 2.1 to categorize and evaluate the data you have collected. Are there problems with the data and/or the approach?

Researchers should be wary of becoming so impassioned in the documentation of their project that they run the risk of being perceived as arrogant or disrespectful of their fellow scientists. Imagine you are writing a proposal for a research project, and you have decided to document the need by citing relevant research in the field. Besides making sure that your references document both

TABLE 2.1		
STATISTICALLY BASED NEEDS DOCUMENTATION TABLE		
METHOD	POSITIVES	NEGATIVES
Statistical Analysis—Most funders like to see a few well-chosen statistics. With this approach you use existing data to develop a statistical picture of the needs population: • Census data/records • Government studies/report • Reports and research articles	• There is an abundance of studies and data. • Little cost to access data. • Allows for flexibility in drawing and developing conclusions. • Analysis of data is catalytic in producing more projects and proposals as staff "sees" the need.	• Can be very time-consuming. • Bias of staff shows up in studies quoted. • Belief on funder's part that anything can be proven with statistics. • If original data have questionable validity, your extrapolation will be inaccurate.
Survey—Very commonly used approach to gathering data on the needs population. This approach is useful even when the survey is carried out with volunteers and has limited statistical validity. Accurate surveys may entail control groups, random samples, computers, and statistical analysis. However, acknowledging that the results of your survey cannot be extrapolated beyond the sample group will prove more than adequate in most situations.	• High credibility with funders. • Excellent flexibility in design of survey to get at problem areas and document exactly what you want to document. • Demonstrates local need. • Provides proof of your concern for the problem well in advance of proposal preparation. • Small sample size and identified needs population provide for an inexpensive means of assessment.	• Takes time to conduct the survey properly. • Small sample size and nonrandom sample make it impossible to extrapolate to the entire needs population.
Studies—Citing of relevant research in the field or area of need. Commonly used approach to document the gap between what is and what ought to be for research projects, as well as model projects. The literature	• Citing studies demonstrates the proposal developer's thoroughness and expertise in the area and command of the subject data. • Studies provide an unbiased approach to documentation of need.	• Unless properly organized, the literature search may seem disjointed and overwhelming to the reader. • Time-consuming.

(continued)

TABLE 2.1 *(continued)*

METHOD	POSITIVES	NEGATIVES
search should focus on articles, books, papers, etc. that resulted from a controlled study or use of a scientific approach		

the urgency of the problem and your command of the current knowledge in the field, be certain not to include statements about the citations that minimize the work of other contributors or researchers or make them appear ignorant because they did not understand the importance of reducing or eliminating the problem. Remember that the researchers quoted in your citations, or one of their graduate students, doctoral students, or friends, may be on your prospective grantor's review committee. Keep sight of the fact that the last thing you want to do is cause dissonance in the reviewers.

Be aware also that you could cause dissonance by citing references, research-ers, or data that the reviewers do not favor. While the reviewers' reactions to specific information are not totally in your control, the more you know about the values and background of the reviewers and decision makers, the better able you will be to avoid this problem.

Most foundations and corporations do not have professional staff. Nor do they use outside reviewers or formal scoring systems to evaluate proposals. They are generally interested in reviewing a few references concerning the current research in the field, but are more concerned with the local or regional impact of the proposed work. In fact, the use of a statistically driven needs assessment may prove counterproductive in helping these types of grantors *visualize* the need. Corporate and foundation grantors usually respond best to case studies or examples of the human side of the need. Review the Needs Assessment Table (table 2.2) for some ideas on how you might collect some less statistically based, but motivating, data. While the strategies outlined in table 2.2 do not hold up well under scientific review, they do help at getting the grantor to *see* the problem.

After reviewing exhibit 2.1 and tables 2.1 and 2.2 you may be thinking of what additional needs assessment tools might be required to make a compelling case to the grantor, or how you can combine the different techniques to make the greatest impact. I have seen a federal review group react very positively to the placement of a case study in a very statistically and scientifically based pro-posal. The fact that the project initiators took the time to interview clients put a very real human side to their proposal. Whatever the case may be, by having a variety of needs assessment techniques at your disposal, you will enhance your ability to tailor your proposal to your specific grantor.

TABLE 2.2

NEEDS ASSESSMENT TABLE

METHOD	POSITIVES	NEGATIVES
Key Informant—Solicit information from individuals whose testimony or description of what exists for the client population or state of affairs is credible because of their experience and/or expertise. This includes elected officials, agency heads, police chiefs, delinquency case workers, parole officers, and so forth. Funders may value their opinions and insights.	• Easy to design. • Costs very little. • You control input by what you ask and whom. • Excellent way to position your organization with important people (shows you are working on common problems/concerns.	• Most funding sources recognize that you have selected and included comments from those individuals sympathetic to your cause and that you may be leaving out parts of the population who feel differently.
Community Forum—Host or sponsor public meetings. You publicize the opportunity to present views of the populace and invite key individuals to speak.	• Easy to arrange. • Costs very little. • Increases your visibility in the community. • Promotes active involvement of the populace. • Funder may like the grassroots image it creates.	• Site of forum has profound effect on amount and type of representation. • You can lose control of the group and have a small vocal minority slant that turns the meeting into a forum for complaints.
Case Studies—An excellent way to assist the funder in appreciating what representative members of the client population are up against. Select individuals from the needs population or client group, and provide an analytical, realistic description of their problem/situation, need for services, and so forth.	• Easy to arrange. • Costs very little. • Increases sensitivity to the client's "real world." • Very moving and motivating.	• Your selection of a "typical" client may be biased and represent a minority of cases. • You must describe one "real" person, not a composite of several. The anonymity of the person must be ensured.

After you, the grantseeker, document a need, ask yourself the following question: Would you dedicate your own money to closing this gap between what we know now and what we could know or do? Many grantseekers say no to this question, but they are happy to take someone else's money. Compelling and motivating proposals come from grantseekers who truly believe that their project is critical to closing the gap and would use their own money if they had it.

CHAPTER 3

Developing a Proactive Grants System

Finding the Time to Organize for Grants Success

The two major obstacles to successful grantseeking are finding the time to get involved in the process and developing a proactive approach. Grantseekers must deal with deadlines, and this makes many feel as if the proposal development process is a ticking time bomb. Because time is their enemy, they end up preparing proposals hurriedly and at the last minute, which results in poor-quality proposals, negative positioning with grantors, and rejection.

In most cases, proposal developers are expected or encouraged to perform grantseeking activities in addition to their normal job responsibilities and in their *spare* time. In the college and university setting, grantseeking is done after preparing course work, teaching, advising, and participating in committee assignments. Seldom are faculty members or staff given release time to *prepare* grant proposals. Even when individuals are expected to attract outside funding for tenure or advancement, they rarely get release time to write their proposals. The goal, they are told, is to work extra hard to prepare a proposal and get it funded, so that they can get release time from their normal duties to carry it out. Then, while carrying it out, the successful grantseeker is expected to find the time to create yet another proposal! If one is to add "having a life" to all of this, then there is precious little time left for grantseeking.

Rarely are there personnel at nonprofit organizations, including colleges and universities, whose main job responsibility is to write grants for other staff members, faculty, and so on. While there are some job descriptions that include proposal preparation as one of the job responsibilities, these are usually jobs in state or regional government agencies, where federal grant moneys are passed through to local grantseekers. And the fact of the matter is that even individuals hired solely as grant writers often do not have enough time to fulfill their duties.

Many grantseekers are overwhelmed by the *total* amount of work involved in proposal preparation. Because of this, they procrastinate and avoid approaching proposal development until it is too late to do an adequate job. Yet, they still do it; because they are driven, creative, and value the contributions they may have the possibility of making in their fields.

How can you break this cycle and get ahead of the curve? How can you find more time for grantseeking? How can you make the proposal preparation process less overwhelming, more controllable, and not as much of a hassle?

While struggling with this dilemma several years ago, I attended a seminar on time management. The concepts I learned at this seminar, and my adaptation of them to grantseeking, have enabled me to use my time more efficiently throughout my career, and more importantly, to develop a sense of control over what to some seems like grants insanity.

Alan Lakein, an early leader in time management, suggests in his book *How to Get Control of Your Time and Your Life*[1] that when you face a large, complex task that cannot be accomplished in a short time span, you divide it into smaller, less overwhelming parts. In his book, a mouse is faced with its dream—a huge piece of cheese. However the mouse must move this large, heavy chunk of cheese. Instead of putting off the task because it feels overwhelmed, the mouse decides to turn the solid block of cheese into Swiss cheese by eating small pieces at a time. Basically, the mouse divides the chore into manageable parts so the final task of carrying the cheese away is less onerous (see figure 3.1).

Lakein's example of a mouse confronted by the job of carrying away a huge piece of cheese is analogous to a grantseeker presented with the prospect of creating a grant proposal. While preparing and getting your proposal funded may seem like a overwhelming, crushing task, you can eat holes through the process and break it into smaller, controllable parts by strategically employing a number of logical steps (the scope) in a particular order (the sequence). The secret is not to dwell on the *whole* proposal preparation process. By accomplishing the smaller steps that lead up to the desired end, you can maintain a sense of control, or as I often refer to it, a sense of order in the universe.

I have applied Lakein's concept to grantseeking and developed what I call a Swiss cheese book (referred to professionally as the proposal development workbook; see exhibit 3.1). The Swiss cheese book consists of a set of tabs that can be placed in a three-ring binder dedicated to a problem area that you, the proposal developer, have selected to seek grants to impact. I have divided the task of developing a proposal into steps, with each step corresponding to one tab in

THE SWISS CHEESE CONCEPT

FIGURE 3.1

the Swiss cheese book. The tabs also correspond to the chapters in the manual. The binder is labeled with the problem, and the steps that are accomplished are recorded in their respective sections. The worksheets, letters, emails, forms, and tables in each chapter have been designed to be completed and placed behind the corresponding tabbed sections. Please note that all of these materials can also be found on the CD-ROM that accompanies this book. The exhibits can be printed off of the CD, completed, three-hole punched, and then filed behind the appropriate tabs.

As a case in point, if you came across a research study particularly relevant to your problem, you would make a copy of the article and place it under the tab for "Introduction & Documenting the Need." Or you could place a copy of just the article's summary or abstract under the tab, but include with it a complete article citation and a reference to where you have the whole article filed. This Swiss cheese book system will also work for filing and retaining possible solutions, advisory committee notes, grantor research, preproposal contact results, and so forth.

Exhibit 3.1 provides you with tab 1 of the Swiss cheese book—Introduction & Documenting the Need. Review the following list of suggested Swiss cheese tabs.

PROPOSAL DEVELOPMENT WORKBOOK
(SWISS CHEESE BOOK)

INTRODUCTION & DOCUMENTING THE NEED

Introduction

The Proposal Development Workbook is based upon a systematic approach to grantseeking described by David G. Bauer in his book *The "How To" Grants Manual* (Westport, Connecticut: ACE/Praeger Series on Higher Education, 2007). The following set of tabs has been designed to help you use the concepts presented in this text for organizing and streamlining the grantseeking process.

Many individuals find the grantseeking process complex, tedious, and overwhelming. Figure 3.1 in *The "How To" Grants Manual* demonstrates one way to manage and simplify the task. As the Swiss cheese concept suggests, a mouse confronted with a block of cheese does not attempt to eat the cheese in one large piece. Instead, it eats holes in the cheese, devouring a little at a time until it is all gone. The same concept can be applied to grantseeking. Approach each part of the grantseeking process a little at a time and before you know it, the process will be completed.

Each tab or section of the workbook represents a step in the grantseeking process. Place the workbook in a three-ring binder and label the binder with the problem you are seeking to solve or reduce. Start a proposal development workbook for each major area in which you are developing projects that you want to finance through the grants mechanism. Place behind each tab data aimed at helping you complete each step. A description of the step and instructions on how to proceed are printed on the face of each tab. The worksheets suggested in each section are explained in greater detail in *The "How To" Grants Manual* and can be reprinted from the CD-ROM that accompanies the book. (Permission has been granted by ACE for individual use.)

You are now ready to begin grantseeking proactively by organizing the materials that will make up your proposal.

Documenting the Need

Many well-intended grantseekers want to move immediately to what they want to do before documenting that something needs to be done. The purpose of this section is to document the problem, not offer the solution. Some work on this step of the process should be done before you even develop your solution, and all of it should be done in advance of either contacting your prospective funding source or writing your proposal.

The documentation you accumulate in this first section of the workbook should provide an accurate and compelling picture of a need that must be addressed now. Start by printing out and completing exhibit 2.1 from *The "How To" Grants Manual* (Needs Assessment Worksheet).

TAB 1—INTRODUCTION AND DOCUMENTING THE NEED

EXHIBIT 3.1

- Tab 1—Introduction and Documenting the Need
    Chapter 1
    Chapter 2
- Tab 2—Developing Solutions and Redefining Ideas
    Chapter 4
    Chapter 5

- Tab 15—Submission and Follow-Up Private (Corporate)
  Chapter 28

You will find that the Swiss cheese concept and the creation of proposal development workbooks will provide you with an organized approach to proposal preparation, and a more effective use of your time. In addition, this approach will help you improve your organization's image with funding sources by enabling you to present your project as well planned and thought-out. Grantors are favorably impressed during pre-proposal contact with an organized grantseeker who can reference and substantiate the important points he or she may explore in an interview. They want to fund a project director or principal investigator who will be as organized in carrying out the proposal as he or she is in introducing and discussing it with them.

The same techniques employed in a *hard copy* version of the Swiss cheese book could also be employed *electronically*. You could create a computer file for each of your proposal development tabs, scan pertinent information like relevant literature into your lap top, and place the information under the appropriate automated file. But, please note that while some may prefer to do this, a computer CD may be difficult to use with a potential funding source during a visit. Therefore, a hard copy will still be necessary.

No matter which form of the Swiss cheese book you employ, hard copy or electronic, you will still need to set aside some time for grantseeking. However, by employing the Swiss cheese concept you can set aside *small* segments of time which may otherwise have been wasted. For instance, use the 15 minutes from 11:45 to your 12:00 lunch appointment to go to your Swiss cheese book, select a specific step (like emailing an associate an invitation to participate on your advisory group), and accomplish it.

If you are willing to dedicate one hour per week to your grantseeking, in one year these 52 hours will equate to six or seven days of work that will most likely result in a well-constructed proposal that is ultimately funded. If you use six or seven consecutive days right before a deadline in a reactive effort to produce a hastily written proposal, you will have much less chance of success.

Once the Swiss cheese approach is initiated, I am sure you will find it invaluable for promoting the development of project ideas, locating funding sources, writing proposals, and impressing prospective funders. I personally have found it a great help in making the grants process more understandable, manageable, and time efficient. The construction of a proposal development workbook is a proactive process that I *know* can work for you and your organization!

NOTE

1. Alan Lakein, *How to Get Control of Your Time and Your Life* (New York: American Library, 1974).

CHAPTER 4

The Grant-Winning Approach

Expanding Your Possible Solutions

From the preceding chapters you can already deduce that the winning solution is not based on which approach *you* favor. It is based on the one that the grantor or the reviewer thinks is the best. Since *best* is a values-based term, the strategy suggested in this chapter is to review the problem and to develop a number of approaches that could be used to solve it without introducing your own biases or values. Since you have not identified all of your prospective grantors at this point and researched what they want, keep an open mind and generate a variety of solutions that could appeal to that unknown, but perfect grantor.

The scientific method would propose that you review the literature first, develop solutions, and then evaluate them to identify the best choices. The truth is that most grantseekers display their own biases by deciding on an approach, intervention, or solution first and then identifying data that reinforce it. Essentially, their values glasses use selective discrimination to view only the data that validate their selected approach.

I urge you not to succumb to this very natural tendency because it may keep you from uncovering unique, and sometimes, grant-winning solutions. Try as best you can to be impartial and to explore at least several of the possible solutions. In my seminars I like to remind myself, as well as my participants, of Joyce Cary's (1888–1957) quote, "It is the tragedy of the world that no one knows what he doesn't know—and the less a man knows, the more sure he is that he knows everything."[1]

In addition to appearing open-minded, this approach will generate many possible solutions that can be used with grantors in preproposal discussions to elicit their feedback and to uncover the criteria they may be using to select their grant recipients. The grantseeker who approaches a potential grantor with only one solution to the problem not only demonstrates a myopic viewpoint, but also has little to fall back on if the grantor is not interested in that particular approach or indicates that that approach has already been tried with poor results. Your research/project is important enough that in these cases you will be sure to have several "backup" solutions, protocols, or approaches to present.

In addition, it is crucial to recognize the fact that granting agencies, their staffs, and their reviewers all have their own values glasses that they use to view and evaluate ideas and approaches. By having several solutions ready, you will have a much better chance of hitting the grantor's hot spot. To develop and present the approach that you believe will be the grant winner, you must uncover the variables that the grantor will consider in making its selection. Will it see the *best* approach as the one that

- is the most cost-efficient?
- is the most reliable and valid?
- will have the greatest impact in the field?
- is likely to lead to applications in the field?

The strategies for gathering grantor research that are presented in chapters 11, 12, 20, 21, 25, and 26 will help you determine the variables considered by your prospective grantor. But, at this point you need to come up with a variety of solutions and to develop a system you will eventually employ to evaluate them.

BRAINSTORMING MORE FUNDABLE IDEAS

One of the most productive techniques for developing a wide variety of alternative solutions to problems is to organize a brainstorming session. Ask a small group of colleagues who have some related knowledge or interest in your problem area to join you in exploring unique and creative approaches to solving or reducing the problem. Whether this exercise is accomplished in a small face-to-face group setting, through a conference call, or over the Internet, inviting others to share in idea generation taps the collective genius of the group and builds support for your proposal. In fact, the brainstorming process can even promote the feeling that your project is all-inclusive and everyone's project. This way colleagues and volunteers will be more willing and eager to work at night and on weekends in our effort to promote a proactive approach that exceeds the deadline. This initial group may even form the nucleus of a project team, advisory group, or consortia (more on this in chapter 7).

Care should be taken to explain the purpose of the brainstorming session to the group. At this point, you will just be exploring possible alternative solutions to the problem. However, many researchers are reluctant to share their ideas and creative solutions because they fear that they will be stolen by colleagues. In the majority of cases this fear is unwarranted. Most colleagues can be trusted, and discussing proposal ideas and solutions with them can help eliminate the development of narrow, self-focused grant ideas. In addition, more and more grantors are interested in sponsoring consortium grants, and brainstorming ideas can provide an ideal way to foster the development of joint funding. Since you may be employing this technique as a vehicle to create partners and consortia, it is critical that you share ideas in a noncompetitive forum. However, if any concerns should arise related to the ownership of the ideas as intellectual property or as part of a noncompetitive agreement, they should be addressed immediately. Universities can provide intellectual property agreements, noncompetitive agreements, and patent/copyright forms if necessary.

Brainstorming is a simple technique for quickly generating a long list of creative ideas. To obtain maximum benefit from the process, provide your group participants with Rules to Successful Brainstorming (exhibit 4.1).

COST-BENEFIT ANALYSIS

An important aspect of any fundable idea is its economic feasibility. Funding sources want to know that you have chosen methods that will produce the best results for the least amount of money. The Cost-Benefit Analysis Worksheet (exhibit 4.2) will help you demonstrate economic accountability.

Column 1. Place brief descriptions of each approach you are considering in column 1. For example, a project to feed senior citizens could range from a meals-on-wheels program, to group meals, to a food cooperative of the elderly. Choose two or three possible approaches that will meet the goals of the project from your brainstormed list of ideas.

Column 2. Record the estimated price or cost of each idea or set of methods in column 2. This figure can be taken off of your preproposal summary and approval form (see exhibit 5.1 in chapter 5) and is intended to be an estimate of the cost of the approach, not a final budget. One way to ensure variety in the approaches and in the amount of funds required is to select the approach you favor and determine how you would have to alter it if you could have only one-half of the amount requested.

Column 3. Use columns 3 and 4 only if your project involves subjects. For evaluating research protocols, go directly to column 5. Use column 3 to estimate the number of people who will be affected by a particular approach. Remember to roll out the benefits over several years and over the life of the equipment.

Column 4. Enter the estimated cost per person or client served. This is essential, since funding sources are apprehensive about sponsoring projects that possess an unrealistic cost per individual served. Projects with a high cost per person are considered a waste of money by many funders, so grantseekers

1. Break your participants into groups of five to eight.

2. Appoint a neutral group leader to facilitate the process (encouraging and prodding other members, checking the time, etc.).

3. Appoint a recorder.

4. Set a time limit (10 minutes will be plenty).

5. State one question or problem (e.g., reducing the number of high school dropouts, nutritional needs of pregnant adolescents, reducing alcoholism in the elderly, increasing awareness of wildlife preservation).

6. Ask group members to generate and present as many possible solutions to the problem as they can within the time limit.

7. Encourage group members to piggyback on each other's ideas (suggesting a new idea that adds to one already given).

8. Record all answers, combining those that are similar.

9. Avoid any evaluation or discussion of ideas until the process is over; this rule is critical for productive brainstorming. The recorder can ask to have an idea repeated but should allow no comments, negative or positive (e.g., "We can't do that!" "That's stupid!" or "I love your thinking.") from others.

RULES TO SUCCESSFUL BRAINSTORMING

EXHIBIT 4.1

may have great difficulty securing continued or follow-up funding for such projects.

Column 5. Summarize the advantages of each idea or set of methods in this column. By having this information on hand, some funders may actually consider supporting a more costly approach because they can see how the outlined advantages outweigh the expense.

Column 6. In this column, outline the disadvantages or drawbacks to each approach. This demonstrates your honesty, which will increase both your credibility with funders and their confidence in you. Funders know that each approach has pitfalls or variables that must be controlled.

Use this worksheet each time you refine your project ideas, and bring completed cost-benefit analysis worksheets to preliminary meetings with funding officials. They will be impressed by the fact that you considered their financial interest while designing your project.

Executives of profit-making companies are very sensitive about maintaining cost efficiency in all of the investments they make, whether they are corporate or grants related to their work with nonprofits. By taking costs into account

1 Summary of Idea and Methodology	2 Cost	3 No. of Persons Served	4 Cost per Person Served	5 Positive Points	6 Negative Points

COST-BENEFIT ANALYSIS WORKSHEET

EXHIBIT 4.2

when refining your project ideas, you will win more grants. By brainstorming
more approaches to solving problems you will not only appear to be open to considering more solutions, you will also initiate a process that can lead to uncovering more potential grantors.

NOTE

1. http://www.brainyquote.com.

CHAPTER 5

Developing Key Search Terms
to Identify the Best Grantor(s)

Redefining Your Project and Improving Your
Research/Grants Profile to Get the Right Hits

The secret to tapping into the $449 billion in federal, foundation, and corporate grant funds is to find the right grantor for your research/project. And the first step to finding the right grantor is to determine the best key words or terms to use in your funding source database searches. Grants databases allow you to enter *key search terms* into their systems, which they then match to similar words in their database, and then to funding sources with interest in that area. The key search words contained in the databases are either selected by the grantors represented in the database or by the best efforts of data input personnel. A match between a key word and a grantor is frequently referred to as a "hit."

Online databases are getting better every day. They are faster and contain more helpful information than ever to assist you in matching your proposal to the most appropriate grantor(s). But your success still relies on your development and use of the *right* key words for your search. Grantors and database managers look at the world through their own values glasses and unique lenses. And the key words they use may be quite different than the key search terms you would initially use to define your research/project. That is why it is so important when developing key search terms to think about your project from a grantor's perspective and how others might describe it and its benefits. Unfortunately, the more zealous you are as a grantseeker, the harder it sometimes is to look at your project and its benefits with flexibility and an open mind. For example, when working with an organization assisting the blind, the grantseekers initially

34

did not want to use the term *blind* as a search term. They felt it was an old and somewhat discriminatory term. I suggested using *visually impaired, visually challenged,* and/or *visually handicapped.* But they did not like any of these either. They preferred *people without sight.* However, when they used *people without sight* as their key search term, they did not get any hits. When they used *blind* and *visually impaired* they uncovered many opportunities. They decided that the use of these words was not so bad after all as long as it helped them find the money and the right grantor for their project. The moral of the story is to be wary of how your own "values" glasses may keep you from recognizing and using the right key search words or terms.

Before you begin the process of determining your key words, review the literature in the field. What are the terms used in the literature, and what is their frequency of use? What are the terms commonly used in related news releases and presentations? Are there related terms that are consistently used throughout these sources? Are the terms changing and evolving?

Many of the grants databases let you review the terms they use to categorize grants interests. The secret is to use several terms and see which combination meets with what appears to be the most interested grantors. Also, take into consideration that most of the electronic databases allow you to place quotation marks around phrases to perform a more precise search. For example, if you searched using *higher education* without quotation marks, the database's use of bouillon logic would search under *higher* and under *education* and then both higher education and education higher. But by placing quotation marks around the two-word phase, it would search only for grantors whose interest area was *higher education.*

REDEFINING YOUR PROJECT

Obviously, the more key words you can use to define your research/project and its benefits, the more grantors you may be able to uncover who could see how your research/project relates to their needs. By redefining your project you can develop more search terms and thus increase the likelihood of relating your project to new and different grantors. However, project redefinition calls for more flexibility than just identifying different terms. Redefinition requires that you look carefully at your project/research and ask how you could change it slightly to make it and its contributions valuable to other constituency groups, causes, or interest areas, thereby expanding the universe of your potential grantors.

For example, a project I know of that was aimed at developing the writing skills of sixth-grade students was cleverly redefined to look at how the Internet could be used to increase reading and writing skills. In fact, the grantseeker (teacher) used the Internet to connect sixth graders to elderly individuals at a local senior center and residential facility who became their adopted grandparents and communicated with them via email. Through email the students strengthened their reading and writing skills and actually got writing tips from their adopted grandmothers and grandfathers. The high school computer club also got involved by training the students and the elderly on how to use email to connect with one another. This example of redefinition moved the project from benefiting the sixth grade to a much larger world, allowed the grantseeker to expand her search words to include several relevant fields (that is, seniors, elderly, and so on), and ultimately enabled her to uncover more potential grantors.

Research grant ideas can also be redefined by extrapolating to other areas and fields. The focus of the research could be slightly changed, and/or others involved in similar projects with a slightly different approach could be invited to participate in a consortium grant. As with the generation of project grant ideas, you are limited only by your own level of creativeness.

While the goal is to uncover the less than obvious grantors, the process of redefinition is not intended to take you off track from your grants plan or to turn you into a grants mercenary who will do anything for money regardless of where it takes you and/or your organization. If you do not like the direction redefinition takes you, do not go there. But if redefinition allows you to locate even partial funding for a related project that keeps you, your career, and your grants plan operational, you may want to pursue it rather than be a purist with no funding.

To uncover your most operant terms complete the Redefinition/Key Search Terms Worksheet (exhibit 5.1). This worksheet should be used to help develop key search terms for identifying potential government funding sources, as well as foundation grantors. However, I suggest you use a different worksheet (exhibit 5.2) to help you develop corporate key search terms.

Searching for corporate grantors requires a special focus because of the unique way they (corporate grantors) view the grants process and its benefits. When searching for corporate grantors, you must take into consideration that corporations usually prefer to support where they "live" and like to fund projects that can be related to their profits, products, and workers. Use the Corporate Redefinition Worksheet (exhibit 5.2) to develop search terms associated with the following:

- hiring, retaining, educating, or training today's workforce as well as the future's,
- employee benefits and resulting corporate benefits, and
- positioning of the corporation as a concerned partner in the field and in your geographic area.

In addition, consider whether there is or could be a direct benefit between your project and increasing corporate profits through

- possible patents or new product development,
- product enhancement, redesign, or reengineering, and
- product position/sales.

1. **Values**: What would a funding source need to value in order to support your project?

2. **Subject Areas**: Subject areas such as employment, environment, mental health, child development, etc. are used as key search terms in many of the electronic grantor databases. List the subject areas that your project can be related to and/or impacts.

3. **Other Potentially Relevant Fields**: How could you change the focus of your project so that it could be potentially related to more subject areas/fields, and what would these areas/fields be?

4. **Constituency Groups**: Many government and private funding sources focus their grant priorities by the constituency groups they want to impact, such as children, at-risk youth, elderly, economically disadvantaged, etc. What constituency group(s) would a funding source have to care about to support your project?

5. **Project Location**: What is the geographic location for your project, and how could you redefine it to better appeal to a grantor's geographic perspective?

_____

_____

City/Community	County/Borough/Parish	State
Regional	National	International

6. **Type of Grant**: What type of grant support are you looking for, and how could you redefine you project to attract grantors interested in different types of support?

_____

_____

Model/Demonstration Project	Research Project	Needs Assessment Grant
Planning Grant	Training Grant	Discretionary
Unsolicited Proposal	Contract	Other

7. **Consortia Partners**: What potential partners/collaborators could you involve to assist in redefining your project and enhancing your funding perspective?

Potential Partner/Collaborator: _____

Advantage: _____

REDEFINITION/KEY SEARCH TERMS WORKSHEET

EXHIBIT 5.1

1. How does your intended project/research relate to the concerns of corporate (for profit) grantors? What are your shared values?

2. Does or can your project/research provide benefits to corporations in the areas of:

   - employee development/skill enhancement?
     If so, how?

   - employee benefits (including health, quality of life, low costs or risks)?
     If so, how?

   - public relations (promotion of a concerned and responsible image in the community)?
     If so, how?

3. Can you redefine your project so that it increases corporate profits by:

   - promoting a lead to new product development (possible patents, etc.)?
     If so, explain.

   - enhancing current products through new application, redesign, etc.?
     If so, explain.

   - increasing sales though product positioning with clients, students, etc.?
     If so, explain.

CORPORATE REDEFINITION WORKSHEET

EXHIBIT 5.2

DEVELOPING YOUR RESEARCH/GRANTS PROFILE

Many of the databases you encounter will encourage you to provide them with a profile consisting of your search terms so that a constant search for new potential grantors can be carried out automatically and sent to you by email. This search component is available on several free, as well as subscription only, electronic funding databases. These databases will be discussed in greater detail in chapters 11, 20, and 25.

The success of all of these systems relies on your development of key words. The time to develop and redefine your project for the key words is when the need and the innovative solutions are fresh in your mind. After you have read this chapter and completed the accompanying exhibits you will begin to understand how you could conduct a database search for grantors that could be as specific as what grantor(s) funded projects related to these key search terms in the following zip codes!

CHAPTER 6

Why Grant Funds to You and Your Organization?

Capitalizing on Your Capabilities

Why would a funding source select your organization and you, as the project director or principal investigator, to grant funds to? If your response is, "Because we thought up a fabulous project," you are not looking at your proposal from the grantor's perspective. Even if your approach to solving the problem is creative and dynamic, the grantor's ultimate decision is based on who it believes can best carry out the project. While grantors expect creativity and superior ideas, they make their final decision based on the grantee's *capability* to complete the project.

While the criteria used to evaluate federal applications vary from department to department, office to office, and program to program, most government grant applications will include review criteria that specifically address the capabilities of the project's key personnel and the extent to which the grantee's own resources can support the proposed project. For example, the Department of Education commonly refers to these selection criteria as "Quality of the Project Personnel" and "Adequacy of Resources." In terms of quality of the project personnel, the Department of Education wants to know the qualifications, including relevant training and experiences, of the project director/principal investigator, and other key personnel. Often, they are also interested in knowing the extent to which the applicant encourages applications for employment from persons who are members of groups that have been traditionally underrepresented based on race, color, national origin, gender, age, or disability.

40

The National Science Foundation (NSF) evaluates these two variables under its general review criteria entitled "intellectual merit of the proposed activity." Proposals to the NSF will be evaluated in part on how well qualified the proposer (individual or team) is to conduct the project, the quality of the proposer's prior work (when applicable), and if there is sufficient access to resources at the grantee's organization to support the project.

Many federal agencies and departments allocate points to each of the review criteria they select. Others rank them on a scale. While the scoring method used to evaluate the quality of key personnel and the adequacy of resources will vary with each program, you will be asked repeatedly to document why your organization's resources and your and your partners' skills and background make you the perfect choice to carry out the proposal and how you have planned for the provision of supplanting any areas of weakness.

When considering the quality of your key personnel, ask yourself the following questions:

- Do your job descriptions adequately reflect the skills needed to make the project work?
- Are the duties of personnel clearly defined?
- What relevant qualifications do the proposed personnel possess, especially the project director? (Focus on their experience and training in fields related to the objectives of the project, though other information may be considered.)
- Will proposed personnel need to be trained for the project?
- How much time will the proposed personnel actually devote to the project?
- To what extent do you encourage employment applications from members of traditionally underrepresented groups?

When evaluating your adequacy of resources, determine if

- your budget is adequate to support the proposed project,
- the proposed facilities and equipment are adequate for your project purposes, and
- you have access to any special sources of experience or expertise.

The importance of this documentation is even more evident when you compete for government contracts. In this very competitive process of bidding on the completion of a well-defined deliverable, you must actually include a capability statement that documents your capacity, resources, and related experience in producing the desired end product. Even if you are the lowest bidder for the contract, you can be passed over for a higher, but more capable, bidder.

In many instances, making a grantor's first cut means that you are now on a *short* list of potential grantees, which includes hundreds as opposed to thousands of applications. What can you do to enhance your proposal in such a way that it makes the final award list?

Fearful of appearing arrogant or boastful, many well-intended grantseekers are hesitant to enhance their proposals by emphasizing their unique qualifications. This is unfortunate. While you should not create falsehoods or downgrade your competition, you do need to analyze your institution's capabilities and the characteristics that differentiate you from the other applicants. Your prospective grantor needs to know that your proposal has a greater likelihood of success because of your and your collaborator's personal capabilities and your institution's distinct advantages. These advantages are not hypothetical, but rather the actual resources involved in the successful completion of the activities and methods that your project or research will utilize.

Every funding source will want to know why you are its best choice for funding, and developing a list of your organization's special qualities or uniquenesses will go a long way toward convincing a grantor that yours is the right organization to fund.

WHEN TO USE SIMILARITY AS A UNIQUENESS

In model or demonstration grants, as opposed to research proposals, you may need to consider varying the uniqueness approach slightly. If one of the desired outcomes of the grant is to develop a model that can be applied to other organizations, institutions, or colleges, then you need to demonstrate your similarity to others in your field that face the same problem. You do not want to highlight the *unique* qualities of your institution that are critical to the model's successful implementation. This would only weaken your case for the model's replicability. Instead, you want to identify the variables you share with others and focus on the uniquenesses that allow you and your organization/institution to develop, test, and produce materials that will be useful to those who will follow the results of your work or replicate your model.

Many government grant applications include "project significance" as a selection criterion. These funding opportunities are interested in knowing the importance or magnitude of the results or outcomes likely to be attained by the proposed proposal, and the broader impacts of the proposed activity. Exhibit 6.1 outlines some of the variables that may be of particular interest to them. As you can see, several of the items are related to the future use of project products, extrapolation of results, replicability, and so on. With these criteria in mind, a successful grants strategy would entail convincing the reviewer that while your organization/institution shares the similarity of the problem and its inherent variables with others, it has unique qualities that enable it to create valid approaches from which others can benefit. These might include special capabilities in the areas of testing, model development, evaluation, training, and dissemination, as well as past success in these areas.

Significance

The following is a list of factors to take into consideration when determining the significance of your proposed project/research.

- National and/or international significance
- Likelihood that the project will result in system change or improvement
- Potential of project to contribute to development and advancement of theory, knowledge, and practice in its own field and/or across different fields
- Likelihood of project to yield findings that may be used by other appropriate agencies and organizations
- Likelihood of project to build local capacity to provide, improve, or expand services that address the needs of the target population
- Extent to which the project involves the development or demonstration of promising new strategies that build on or are alternatives to existing strategies
- Effective use of product resulting from the project (i.e., information, materials, processes, techniques, etc.)
- Dissemination of results in a manner that will enhance understanding and allow others to use the information or strategies
- Potential replicability of the project or strategies
- Potential to enhance the infrastructure for research and education, such as facilities, instrumentation, networks, and partnerships

SELECTION CRITERIA—SIGNIFICANCE

EXHIBIT 6.1

Most foundations and corporations do not have as well a defined or documented review process as public funding sources. But they still have the same question in mind: "Why should they fund you and your organization to do this project?" Later, in parts 2, 3, and 4, you will learn where to include these important credibility builders (uniquenesses) in your proposal. But why wait to identify them until you are filling out your application? Consider developing a list you can use with many grant opportunities. Start now and be one step ahead of the game!

UNIQUENESS EXERCISE

Use the following brainstorming exercise to develop a data bank of your organization's unique features. This exercise will add a little excitement and flavor to meetings and can be done with a variety of groups such as staff, volunteers, clients, board members, and grants advisory committee members. Keep the information you develop in your proposal development workbook, where it will be ready for use in proposals, endorsement letters, and preproposal contact.

Please note that you may encounter some initial reluctance to this exercise because some individuals think it promotes bragging. However, these same individuals probably believe that humility and occasional begging will move grantors to take pity on your organization and fund your proposals. They are wrong! From the grantor's point of view, the humble, woe-are-we approach does not highlight the reasons a prospective grantee should be funded and may actually do the opposite.

To combat this problem, just remind all those participating in the exercise of its positive results. After the exercise, you will have a list of factors that make your organization a strong contender—a list from which you will be able to select those uniquenesses that may appeal to a particular funding source. Also, the exercise will refocus those participating in the activity on the positive attributes of your organization and away from the negative.

1. Distribute the uniqueness worksheet (see exhibit 6.2) to the group, remind the group of the rules for brainstorming (outlined in chapter 4), and set a time limit for brainstorming.
2. Record the group's answers to questions 1 and 2.
3. Ask the group to rank the order of the responses to the questions from a potential grantor's perspective with rank number 1 being the most positive uniqueness or qualification.
4. Have the group select the top three answers for both questions and combine them to develop a list of your organization's most positive uniquenesses/qualifications with respect to the adequacy of your institutional resources and the quality of your project personnel.

If your institution has a computer or decision lab, have the group meet there so you are in close proximity to the hardware and software necessary to provide instant rank ordering and frequency distributions.

Use the final list to select uniquenesses that will convince funders that their money will go further with you than with any other prospective grantee. For example, a particular funding source may be impressed with your total number of years of staff experience, central location of buildings, special equipment, and broad needs populations and geographic coverage.

Your uniquenesses list will also prove valuable in

- selecting consortia partners or additional team members who can fill personnel voids and/or improve your capabilities;
- recruiting and training staff, board members, and volunteers;
- developing case statements; and
- using other fund-raising techniques such as direct mail and wills and bequests.

Do not forget to include yourself, the proposal initiator, project director, or principal investigator, as a uniqueness. Your previous work, publications, collaborative efforts, awards, and recognition are important components of your organization's overall uniqueness.

Federal and state proposal applications will require information on your organization's ability to perform the tasks you outline in your proposal. Your unique qualities or attributes are what enable you to perform these tasks. The sections of government applications that require this information are sometimes referred to as Adequacy of Institutional Resources and Quality of Project Personnel.

On government applications these sections may be assigned a point value. While these components may not be mandatory on foundation and corporate proposals, the information they contain is equally important in convincing private funding sources that your organization is the right grantee for them.

What makes your organization uniquely suited to carry out the work outlined in your proposal and provides the grantor with the assurance it will receive a job well done?

1. **Adequacy of Institutional Resources**: Please list the positive qualities and uniquenesses that your organization/institution possesses that will ensure a grantor that you are the best place to do the job. When applicable, include factors such as:

   - relevance of purpose and mission
   - geographic location
   - relationship and availability to subject population
   - presence of animal laboratories
   - data analysis capabilities

   - _____
   - _____
   - _____
   - _____

2. **Quality of Project Personnel**: Please list the unique qualifications of your project personnel. Take into consideration factors such as:

   - years of related experience
   - number of publications and presentations
   - awards and special recognition
   - number and dollar amounts of grants and contracts successfully carried out

   - _____
   - _____
   - _____
   - _____

UNIQUENESS WORKSHEET

EXHIBIT 6.2

One culminating activity is to have half of your group role-play a grantor and the other half role-play a prospective grantee. Review one of the problems or needs your organization is planning to address and your organization's proposed solution. Then have the individuals playing the grantor ask those playing the prospective grantee why the grant seeker's organization should be the one selected to implement the proposed solution. Have the grantee group start by saying, "Our organization is particularly suited to implement this solution because...."

USING YOUR ORGANIZATION'S CASE/MISSION STATEMENT TO SUPPORT YOUR PROPOSAL

Your case or mission statement is another key ingredient in convincing the grantor that your organization should be selected for funding. When you submit your application for funding, your approach should be based on the following three important factors:

1. There is a compelling need for the project.
2. Your organization is uniquely suited to carry out the project.
3. The project supports your organization's stated purpose or mission and fits with what you are currently doing or planning to do.

The third factor is especially important. Your case/mission statement should demonstrate your organization's predetermined concern for the project area. If yours is a joint or consortia proposal, the mission or case statements of all the participating organizations should provide a documentable concern for the problem you will address. In short, this statement should give the funding source written documentation that the purpose of your organization (its reasons for existing), your project, and the grantor's values and concerns are a perfect match.

USING YOUR EXISTING CASE/MISSION STATEMENT

Most nonprofit organizations have an existing case or mission statement. Educational organizations use it to provide the foundation for accreditation, and in faculty and staff recruitment. While an institution's case/mission statement can provide the framework for a college, division, department, institute, or center, even the lowest level of the organization should be able to state its case for existence and inclusion in the future of the organization.

Grantors do not want their grant funding to influence what your organization becomes. Instead, they want you to tell them where your organization wants to go, and how your proposal will help move it toward that goal.

If you have a case/mission statement, use it to convince the grantor of your purpose. If you do not have a case/mission statement, or if the one you have is no longer accurate or too long, consider updating it, editing it to one concise page, or developing a new one tailored to the grants marketplace.

ELEMENTS OF A CASE/MISSION STATEMENT

Your case/mission statement should consist of how and why your organization got started, what your organization is doing today, and where your organization is going in the future.

How and Why Your Organization Got Started. Explain the original societal problems or needs that resulted in the formation of your organization. Most funding sources will find societal need today more important than the number of years your organization has been in existence. In fact, some funding sources actually have the greatest doubts about those nonprofit organizations that have been around the longest. These funders believe that such organizations generally are bureaucratic, have a tendency to lose sight of their mission, and have more so-called deadwood on their payrolls than younger nonprofit organizations.

What Your Organization Is Doing Today. Describe your organization's activities. What are its current priorities, programs, resources, and uniquenesses? Who are its clients? How has the passage of time affected its original mission and reason for being?

Where Your Organization Is Going in the Future. Because funding sources look at their support as an investment, they want to be sure they invest in organizations that will be around when their funding runs out. In other words, they want the organizations they invest in to have a five-year, ten-year, or even longer plan for operation. By demonstrating to funding sources that your organization has a long-range plan and the ability to secure future funding, you will show grantors that you are worthy of their funding and that the project they invest in will continue to benefit people for many years to come.

Use the case/mission statement worksheet (see exhibit 6.3) to determine what should be included in your case statement.

Remember, most potential grantors are more interested in how funding your proposal will move both of your organizations (theirs and yours) toward each of your missions than in your actual project methods. Funding sources consistently work to separate applicants who sought them out simply as a source of money from applicants who can demonstrate that the direction outlined in their proposal is predetermined and an important component of their organization's overall mission.

In a funded proposal to the BellSouth Foundation for over $250,000, the successful grantee told BellSouth that it was that organization's goal and priority to approach the very same problem that the BellSouth funding was designed to impact. In fact, the successful grantee told BellSouth it could show over five years' worth of meeting minutes and budget expenditures that demonstrated its commitment to dealing with the problem. The grantee also went so far as to suggest that it would be committed to the same course of action even without Bell-South's grant. Yes, the grantee told BellSouth that this course of action was so much a part of its goals, priorities, and case that the organization would move ahead with the project anyway! Naturally the grantee also let BellSouth know

This worksheet can be completed based on the broad definition of your organization, college, or university, or on a smaller subunit such as your center, institute, school, department, or program.

1. **How and Why Your Organization Got Started:** _____

   _____

   Year: ____ Primary Movers/Founders: _____
   Original Mission: _____
   _____

2. **Today – Where Your Organization Is Now:** _____

   _____

   Changes from the Original Mission: _____
   _____

   Societal Need – Changes in Clients/Students: _____
   _____

   Current Priorities: _____
   _____

   Clients: _____
   Staff: _____
   Buildings: _____

3. **Future – Where Your Organization Will Be Five Years From Now:** _____

   _____
   Anticipated Changes in Mission: _____
   _____
   Anticipated Changes in Need: _____
   Resulting Changes in Facilities and Staff: _____
   _____

4. **Existing or New Opportunities That Will Be Present to Move Your Organization toward Its Plans/Goals:** _____
   _____

CASE/MISSION STATEMENT WORKSHEET

EXHIBIT 6.3

the project would take ten years without BellSouth's money instead of three years with it. The BellSouth money would be the catalyst in the equation for change. It would hasten the result.

The importance of relating your proposal to your organization's mission cannot be overemphasized. Before soliciting a potential grantor, be sure to ask yourself whether you are going to the funder just because you heard it had money and you want some or because your proposal can serve the missions you both value.

CHAPTER 7

Creating Grant-Winning Teams and Consortia

Involving Volunteers through Advisory Committees and Advocacy Groups

The success of a proposal and the completion of a project rely on the incorporation of a complex mixture of supporting partners and expertise. How this combined effort is created and maintained is fast becoming one of the most critical elements in attracting grant and contract support from government sources, as well as private foundations and corporations. In most cases the creation of these critically important relationships has been left to chance and luck. However, by employing the science of group dynamics and team interaction, you can move your grant-related groups away from relying on chance and toward increased efficiency and accountability.

The following suggestions for improving your grants success by increasing the effectiveness of your grant-related groups come from my work and experience with grants professionals who have taken part in my effective grant team-building workshop. Participants of this workshop have been eager to improve how they function in groups and to work on developing more productive approaches to increase their group's effectiveness. I believe their positive responses to increasing personal and group effectiveness is a function of the difficulties they have encountered when attempting to work on proposal development with experts from interdisciplinary fields—something they are asked to do more and more frequently.

In today's grants marketplace, it is rare to find a project director or principal investigator who possesses *all* the expertise needed to complete a grant-funded project in any area, and research projects frequently depend on expertise in several disciplines that may have previously been thought to be unrelated. These interdisciplinary projects must now be completed by cooperating professionals who may think about and approach problems from radically different viewpoints. Even demonstration grants and model projects require community integration and support from partners who just a few years ago would not have been approached but now must provide board resolutions and letters of support and endorsement.

An informal survey of 200 of my proposal development seminar participants revealed that only 5 percent had received formal training in group/team functioning or leadership skills. Except for those in technology areas such as software development, team functioning was not a part of their undergraduate or graduate education. However, from volunteers on your advisory committees and advocacy groups to colleagues who must commit to be part of your project, the ability to organize and coordinate an effective group or team is *now* a necessary skill.

Consider the following suggestions for evaluating and improving your own personal group skills and the team skills of your grant-related groups such as advisory committees, advocacy groups, proposal development teams, centers of excellence, multidisciplinary groups, consortia partners, and so on.

RECOGNIZING THE ROLES THAT COMPRISE AN EFFECTIVE TEAM

There are many theories and much research on effective team formation and development in the corporate world. Applying successful techniques to the nonprofit world and colleges and universities has just begun. However, after helping several universities develop more effective grant-related volunteer groups and development teams, I believe the basic element to group success and team building is the role that individuals take in a group and how well the varying roles interact with one another to maximize strengths.

As you select the members for your grant-related group or analyze the makeup of your existing group or proposal development team, take into consideration the roles that must be assumed to assure effective group functioning. While there are a variety of techniques and materials that can be used to assist team members in developing awareness of the roles involved in a productive team, one simple and easy to use system is the *Team Dimensions Profile* by Inscape Publishing (order through David G. Bauer Associates, Inc. at $15.50 each). This profile or survey helps individuals understand and value the contribution they make to successful innovation teams or groups by allowing them to determine their personal approach to thinking and behavior (conceptual, spontaneous, normative, or methodical) and their role on the team/group (creator, advancer, facilitator, refiner, or executor).

As you review the four basic approaches to thinking and behavior, consider which one best describes the approach you use in the team innovation process and the approaches taken by those with whom you work. Keep in mind that many individuals use more than one approach and, in essence, develop their own unique team and task orientation.

- Conceptual Approach—The individual who takes a conceptual approach is the idea developer who likes to brainstorm alternatives, focus on the future, and develop new theories.
- Spontaneous Approach—Those who take a spontaneous approach are free thinkers with little respect for tradition or rules. They move from one subject to another, focus on many things at once, and are sometimes impatient.
- Normative Approach—The individuals who take this approach want to see consequences before acting, prefer the norm or the familiar, and rely on past experiences and expectations.
- Methodical Approach—Those who take a methodical approach like order in the universe. They are rational, follow scientific methods and step-by-step processes, and prefer to focus on details that make everything fit together.

After reflecting on these different types of approaches, you can understand why many grant-related teams/groups fail. The mix is critical. For example, if you are part of a team with five conceptual approach investigators and three spontaneous approach investigators you will get a lot of ideas generated, but no follow-up and little chance of developing a detailed proposal.

Research by Allen N. Fahden and Srinivasan Namakkal[1] on these four approaches to innovation focuses on how the individual approaches work together in a group and how the various combinations of these approaches affect the completion of the work inherent in successful group/team projects. Their research resulted in their identification of five roles that must be present in a team or group to achieve project success—the creator, the advancer, the facilitator, the refiner, and the executor. The four basic approaches to innovation naturally predispose individuals to accepting some of these roles with relative ease. The key to group success is to determine who prefers to take on the needed roles, who has certain of the skills inherent in the roles, and/or who will take on the role simply for the good of the group.

The theory is that in a well-functioning team all of the five roles are present and that the individual team members can hand tasks back and forth, utilizing the strengths that each role provides. Subgroups are developed when the team has more than one member who can function in each role and, therefore, can share tasks.

- Creator—Grant-winning solutions must be innovative and fresh and often require team members to think outside of the box. The creator does just that. This individual helps generate new and unusual concepts, ideas, and solutions to the problem and then passes them on to the advancer. Creators become bored discussing and explaining their new ideas (which to them are getting old) and can upset the group by coming up with newer and greater ideas before the team has completed working through the previous task. Creators will create grant proposal idea number 2 before number 1 is written. If not thoughtfully enjoined with the challenges and creativity of making idea number 1 work, they have a tendency to loose interest and skip group meetings.

- Advancer—In this role, the individual sees great ideas, solutions, or approaches and develops ways to promote them. The advancer develops objectives and plans by the most direct and efficient means. On grants teams advancers talk others through a new idea or concept, get the other team members on board, and keep them excited about the project. In addition, they are usually good at making preproposal contact with potential grantors.

- Facilitator—This is the group manager's role. This person monitors the proposal development process and work task distribution. This is a critical role for efficient proposal preparation and group productivity. When problems occur with the proposed protocol or solution, the facilitator hands tasks back to the responsible parties for their input and clarification.

- Refiner—This is the group's "devil's advocate." Refiners challenge, analyze, and follow a methodical process to detect process flaws or leaps in logic or process that creators sometimes make in brainstorming new approaches. They pass ideas and plans back to the facilitator to take to the creator and advancer.

- Executor—Executors are the workhorses of the group. They may not enjoy the more visible leadership roles. Their fun is in making the process an orderly and efficient one. Not only are they critical for developing the solution and proposal implementation plan, they are also essential in carrying out the proposal after it is funded. They pay attention to details and insist on quality.

On a successful team, the facilitator ensures that tasks are handed off from the creator to the advancer, from the advancer to the refiner, and from the refiner to the executor. You can probably see yourself in one or more of these roles, and now understand why some of your group efforts have failed—one or more of the five team roles—creator, advancer, refiner, executor, and/or facilitator—were missing and no one recognized this or was willing to assume the missing role(s).

While working with an innovative interdisciplinary team seeking to develop federal proposals I discovered that five out of the seven team members were creators. The group had been meeting together for one year, had brainstormed several unique approaches to problems, and was enjoying each other's company. The problem was that they never developed one completed proposal. The two noncreator types expressed exasperation with the group's inability to come to a consensus and develop a plan. The group's main problem was that the majority of its members assumed the role of creator—always generating new concepts and ideas. Unfortunately, they also needed individuals in the group who could

- give some structure toward the implementation of these new concepts and ideas (advancers),
- work through the concept's/idea's problems (refiners), and
- assume the responsibility of final implementation (executors).

Poor team performance will result when there is an excess of team members assuming similar roles or coming from comparable orientations. A solid functioning group or team identifies the approaches and roles of its members, defines tasks, and hands them off from one role to another, allowing group members to focus on their strengths in the process. It also recognizes what roles are missing from the group. With awareness, the group can either add additional team members with the necessary orientation and skills, or the existing members can consciously take on the roles that are lacking and assume the subsequent tasks.

Higher education and nonprofit organizations are plagued by poorly functioning groups. From the dreaded committee assignments to proposal development teams, we have witnessed legendary failures.

The for-profit world has assumed the lead in seeking to develop highly successful teams at all levels, from the shop floor to top management. In his book *Teamwork Is an Individual Skill: Getting Your Work Done When Sharing Responsibility*,[2] Christopher Avery suggests that the first step to developing successful teams is to rid ourselves of the misconceptions we have about teamwork. One misconception we need to discard is that team members need to love each other. Believe it or not, we do not necessarily need to appreciate each other's personality to operate successfully. What we need to do is appreciate each group member's specific approach and to understand how it helps to get the job done. The second misconception we must eliminate is that our own personalities and individual orientation do not count and that we should leave our personal needs at the door of each group meeting. In actuality, being a team player does not mean you that you cannot be yourself or that you cannot expect something back from the group for your time. The key to group success is to be yourself, act normally but responsibly, and recognize and appreciate what each group member naturally brings to the table. This knowledge will help you develop teams comprised of individuals with the mix of approaches and orientations necessary to achieve success.

LEGAL GUIDANCE FOR THOSE INVOLVED IN YOUR PROJECT/RESEARCH

While I do not want to raise your concern to a level of paranoia over individuals who may steal your ideas and projects, you must consider how to protect yourself and your collaborators from this type of problem. In order to keep your professional and personal relationships on a positive, trustworthy basis it is necessary to discuss the professional expectations and ethical standards you expect from each other.

Consortia partners, team members, and advisory group members should be briefed concerning your expectations related to the following:

- Conflicts of interest—Does working with your group conflict with their own research or grant-related projects or other groups in which they are an active member?

- Nondisclosure agreements—It is not uncommon to be asked to sign an agreement that assures the group (project initiators) that you will not inform other people or groups about the project, its protocols, or the ideas that are brainstormed and discussed.

- Noncompetition agreements—This upfront agreement acknowledges that all parties will work together and that one partner will not split from the consortia/group and submit a proposal that competes with the team's proposal.

- Patent/copyright agreement—If the project in question could result in a product, approach, article, book, or theory it is recommended that the grounds for ownership and the sharing of any of these be spelled out in advance.

For readers who are part of a college or university, the vice president for research will usually have an Office of Intellectual Property that will supply forms, agreements, and guidance on how to approach your partners and retain the necessary records. In some instances this office will even apply for copyrights and patents for you. For those of you in a nonprofit organization, I suggest that you recruit an individual from higher education to be on your advisory committee and ask him or her to get any agreements/forms you may need from his or her institution. Then you can tailor these agreement/forms to fit your needs.

INVOLVING VOLUNTEERS

One of the most important resources in a successful grants effort is the involvement of volunteers. When grantors are faced with volunteers who believe so strongly in a project that they are willing to work to further it with no personal benefit, the credibility of your project and the lead applicants' organization is greatly enhanced.

Involving others in increasing your potential to attract funding suggests that *who* you know may be more valuable than *what* you know and how you write your proposal. But a poorly developed idea and proposal will need much more than just friends and the suggestions presented here. If you have a great idea or proposal, however, you owe it to yourself to take advantage of every possible edge in your quest for funding. This includes involving individuals who can help ensure that your proposal receives the attention it deserves. One foundation director told me that approximately one-third of her foundation's grants went to the board members' favorite organizations and projects, one-third to the board members' friends' favorite projects, and the remaining one-third to the most skilled grant seekers.

While this may sound like politics, hold your condemnation just one more minute. The politics of grantseeking is a fascinating area that spells M-O-N-E-Y for those who master the art. Do not be frightened or disgusted by the word *politics*. The politics of grantseeking is a very understandable process that enables individuals to become advocates for what they value and believe in.

Those people who know your organization and identify with your cause or mission deserve to know how they can be of service to you and the cause or field you represent. When asked to become advocates for your project, individuals are free to say no or that they are too busy, but you should not make this decision for them by assuming that they would not want to be involved. There is no harm in asking, and you will be surprised by how many individuals welcome your invitation.

Consider exploring the area of advocacy and how you can help others help you. The worksheets in this chapter will assist you in determining who your advocates are and how they can best serve you. You will probably discover that there are more supporters for your project than you realized.

GRANTS ADVISORY COMMITTEES

One highly effective method for involving volunteers in your grants quest is to develop an advisory committee focused on the need or problem your grant proposal will address. For example, while working for a university-affiliated hospital, I initiated one advisory committee on health promotion and wellness for children and another on research for children's diseases with different individuals on each committee. Even though you should think of your advisory committee as an informal affiliation of individuals you invite to take part in attracting grants to the problem area you have chosen, you may be able to recruit more members and support if you leave the word *grant* out of the committee's title. Include the problem instead. For example, I called one of the groups I initiated the Committee for Promoting Research on Children's Diseases instead of the Grants Committee for Promoting Research on Children's Diseases.

Invite fellow professionals, individuals from other organizations and the community, and corporate members who are interested in the area you have identified. By inviting a cross section of individuals to join your committee, you develop a wider base from which to draw support. Ask yourself who would care if you developed grants resources to solve a particular problem. The one common denominator for all the committee members should be their concern for positive change in the identified area of need. Develop a list of individuals, groups, and organizations you think would volunteer a little of their time to be instrumental in making progress in the problem area. Be sure to include

- individuals who might know foundation, government, or corporate grantors and
- colleagues who may have previously prepared a proposal for the grantor you will be approaching or who may have acted as grant reviewers.

Also consider current and past employees, board of trustee members, and former clients.

GRANT RESOURCES

After you have identified individuals or groups that would be interested in seeing change in the area identified, make a list of skills and resources that would be helpful in developing your proposal. Match these with the types of individuals who might possess them. Your list of skills and resources may give you some ideas about whom you should recruit for your grants advisory committee. Consider the skills and resources and the types of individuals that could be useful in

- preparing your proposal (writers, experts in evaluation design or statistics, and individuals with computer programming skills),
- making preproposal contact (individuals with sales and marketing skills and people who travel frequently—especially to Washington, D.C.), and
- developing consortia or cooperative relationships and subcontracts (individuals who belong to other nonprofit groups with similar concerns).

All volunteers, including your advisory committee members, should be asked to review the Grant Resources Inventory (exhibit 7.1) and to indicate those resources they are willing to contribute. Tailor the list to include only what you need, and if you know of specific assets possessed by your volunteers, do not be afraid to ask.

Please indicate the resource areas you would be willing to help with. At the end of the list, provide more detailed information. In addition, if you are willing to meet with funding sources please list the geographic areas you travel to frequently.

___ Evaluation of Projects
___ Computer Equipment
___ Computer Programming
___ Spreadsheets on Methods & Protocols
___ Objectives, Hypothesis, Specific Aims
___ Budgeting, Accounting, Developing Cash Flow Forecasts, Auditing
___ Audiovisual Assistance (Equipment, DVDs, etc.)
___ Web Site Development
___ Travel to Make Contact with Grantors
___ Writing, Editing, Submission
___ Searching for Funding Sources
___ Equipment/Materials
___ Space for Program/Research
___ Other:

_____

_____

Description of Resources:
_____
_____
_____

Areas Frequently Visited:
_____
_____
_____

GRANT RESOURCES INVENTORY

EXHIBIT 7.1

HOW TO INCORPORATE ADVOCATES TO INCREASE GRANTS SUCCESS

Specific activities to consider in relation to advocacy roles of individuals on your list are

- writing endorsement letters,
- talking to funding sources for you and setting up appointments,
- providing expertise in particular areas (finance, marketing, and so on), and
- accompanying you to meetings with potential funders or even visiting a funding source for you.

Use the advocacy planning sheet (exhibit 7.2) to organize your approach.

Project Title: _____

Project Director: _____

Select from the following list of techniques you can suggest your advocates employ to advance your project.

- Endorsement letters
- Testimonials
- Letters of introduction to grantors
- Set appointments with granting officials
- Accompany you to see funding sources
- Go to see grantors for you

Techniques for This Project	Advocate to Be Used	Who Will Contact Advocate & When	Desired Outcome	Date Completed

ADVOCACY PLANNING SHEET

EXHIBIT 7.2

Endorsement Letters

One very effective way to use advocates is to request that they write endorsement letters related to your organization's credibility and accomplishments. Without guidance, however, many advocates will develop endorsement letters that focus on inappropriate aspects of your project or organization. To prevent this, spell out what you are looking for. Provide advocates with a draft endorsement letter that suggests what you would like them to consider including in their letters, such as

- pertinent facts or statistics that you may then quote or use in your proposal,
- the length of time they have worked with you and/or your organization (for example, number of hours, consortia, or cooperative work relationships), and
- a summary of their committee work and their major accomplishments.

Advocates should almost be able to retype your draft on their stationery and sign it. If the grantor has any special requirements concerning endorsement letters, make sure they are followed.

Contacts

Another way to involve your advocates is to present them with the names of potential grantors and their board members and to ask whether they know any of the grantors' key individuals. This approach is particularly useful if your advocates are reluctant to reveal all of their contacts and are holding back to see how serious you are in researching potential grantors.

If your advocates are trusting, you can ask them outright for a comprehensive list of their contacts. This includes asking your grants advisory committee members to reflect on their ability to contact a variety of potential grantors that may be helpful in your grants effort. To take this proactive approach, follow these steps:

1. Explain the advocacy concept to the individuals you have identified and how the information they provide will be used. Ask each participant to complete an advocacy webbing worksheet (exhibit 7.3) and return it to you. Some organizations find they have better results in introducing the advocacy concept when they relate the concept to a major project of the organization that has widespread support.
2. Distribute the advocacy webbing worksheet to the individuals you have identified as possible advocates. This may be done in a group or individually.
3. Input the advocacy information you collect from the completed worksheets in your computer, or file it.
4. When a match between a potential funder and an advocate is made, call your advocate and discuss the possibility of having him or her arrange a meeting for you with the funding source. Ask the advocate to attend the meeting with you to add credibility to your presentation.

Keep all completed advocacy webbing worksheets on file and update them periodically. This is a good activity for volunteers. Be aware, however, that care should be taken to safeguard advocacy data. Advocacy data should be considered

Our organization's ability to attract grant funds is increased substantially if we can talk informally with a funding official (or board member) before we submit our formal proposal. However, it is sometimes difficult to help make preproposal contact without having a link to the funding source. We need your help. By completing this worksheet, you will identify any links that you may have with potential grantors and increase our grants success dramatically.

If you have a link with a funding source that our research indicates may be interested in supporting one of our projects, we will contact you to explain the project and discuss possible ways you could help us. For example, you could write an endorsement letter, arrange an appointment, or accompany us to see the funding source. Even a simple phone call could result in our proposal actually being read and not just left in a pile. No matter what the case may be, you can rest assured that we will obtain your complete approval before any action is taken and that we will never use your name or link without your consent.

Links to foundations, corporations, and government funding sources are worth hundreds of thousands of dollars per year, and your assistance can ultimately help us continue our vital mission. Thank you for your cooperation.

Your Name: _____
Your Phone No. _____ Your Email: _____
Your Address: _____
_____

1. What foundations or corporate boards are you, your spouse, or close friends on?

2. Do you know anyone who is on a foundation or corporate board? If so, who and what board?

3. Does your spouse know anyone on a foundation or corporate board? If so, who and what board?

4. Have you served on any government committees? If so, please list.

5. Do you know any government funding contacts? If so, please list.

ADVOCACY WEBBING WORKSHEET

EXHIBIT 7.3

personal information that is privileged; you must not allow open access to the data or you will be violating your advocates' trust. Using a large central computing facility to store this information greatly reduces security. Instead, use a small personal computer system, and store a copy of your program in a safe place. This approach will ensure the privacy of this confidential information. When a potential funding source is identified, search your advocacy database to determine whether any of your advocates have a relationship to the potential funding source.

You may have an advocate who

- is a member of both your organization and the funding source's board,
- can arrange an appointment to get you in to talk to the funder,
- can write a letter to a "friend" on the funding source's board, and/or
- has worked for the grantor or been a reviewer for the funder's grant program.

Community Support

Advocacy can also play a valuable role in developing and documenting community support for your project. Some funding sources require that you demonstrate community support in the form of advisory committee resolutions and copies of the minutes of meetings, and more grantors are encouraging the development of consortia when applying for funding. Whether you are looking at a joint submittal for your proposal or just endorsement and support, it is important to start the process of applying for a grant early so that deadlines do not interfere with your ability to document your advisory committee's involvement and valuable work. To deal creatively with the area of community support,

- put together a proposal development workbook (see chapter 3) to focus on your problem area;
- organize an advisory committee to examine the problem area; and/or
- involve the advisory committee in brainstorming project ideas, examining needs assessment techniques, writing letters of endorsement, and providing links to funders.

Review the worksheet on developing community support (see exhibit 7.4) to help you determine how to use community support to increase your fundability.

Organize your supporters and maximize your chances for success by working through and with your volunteers. Involve those individuals who can be of service to your cause, from enhancing your resources to helping identify links to funders.

INVOLVING EXISTING BOARDS, ADVISORY GROUPS, VOLUNTEERS, AND STAFF

Do not overlook the advantages of using the linkages that your organization's existing groups, volunteers, and staff may already have. These individuals and groups have already demonstrated an affinity for your organization and your

#	Techniques	Applicability of the Techniques to This Project	Who Will Call Meeting	Members of Committee	Dates
1	Use advisory committee to brainstorm uniquenesses of your organization				
2	Use advisory committee to work on setting up needs assessment				
3	Use advisory committee to brainstorm project ideas				
4	Use advisory committee to develop a public relations package and to produce it (printing, etc.) including newspaper coverage for your organization (press releases, interviews) and television coverage (public service announcements, talk shows)				
5	Have an artist perform or have an open house for key people in the community				
6	Other				

DEVELOPING COMMUNITY SUPPORT WORKSHEET

EXHIBIT 7.4

programs. Participation in this opportunity should be voluntary, and while some administrators may express concern over asking paid staff to contribute names of friends and relatives who have connections to funding sources, they will be surprised at the voluntary response they receive. Involve your employee associations and unions, and initiate the idea by relating it to strong needs and well-accepted programs and projects that many people want to see developed or expanded.

Many nonprofit organizations already have boards and standing committees that can be invited to become involved in this webbing and linkage process. Most corporate people will be happy that they have been asked to participate in a game that the corporate world plays all the time. From my experience at universities, I have also found that department chairs, deans, and members of boards of institutes and centers usually respond favorably to the concept.

The key to acceptance of the webbing and linkage process is to assure those participating that linkages will not be contacted without their knowledge or approval and, in most cases, their assistance.

HOW TO USE WEBBING AND LINKAGE INFORMATION

To help you get the most out of your newly discovered linkages, list them by linkage type. For example, foundation, corporate, federal, state, and so forth. Then use the funding source research tools described in chapters 11, 20, and 25 to look up the interest areas of the grantors to which you have a link. Review your organization's needs and projects and look for potential matches with the grantors. When a match is found, make preproposal contact through your linkage.

NOTES

1. Allen N. Fahden and Srinivasan Namakkal, *Team Dimensions Profile* (Minneapolis, MN: Inscape Publishing, Inc., 1995).

2. Christopher M. Avery, with Meri Aaron Walker and Erin O'Toole Murphy, *Teamwork Is an Individual Skill: Getting Your Work Done When Sharing Responsibility* (San Francisco: Berrett-Koehler Publishers, Inc., 2001).

CHAPTER 8

Selecting the Right
Marketplace for Your Project

The two main sources of support for universities and nonprofit organizations and their grant requests are public and private philanthropy. Each marketplace and its subcategories are very different from one another in whom they fund, what they fund, the amount of support they provide, and what they will require of you and your organization.

Not only are there vast differences between the various types of grantors in each of the marketplaces, there are also differences in how the marketplaces are viewed in terms of prestige and credibility. When determining which grants marketplace is right for you and your project/research, you must take into consideration your career plan and how it may be affected by the grants marketplace hierarchy.

Whether you are using research grant funding to build your rationale for gaining tenure at a university or for a promotion in a nonprofit organization, peer-reviewed grant awards are viewed as the most prestigious and credible. Except for earmarked pork grants, most competitive federal grants (research and model projects) are peer reviewed and carry the highest regard in the grants world. Other peer-reviewed grants from state agencies, counties, and cities follow in a descending order.

Foundation grant awards are usually considered less prestigious than peer-reviewed government awards because most are decided by internal staff and board members. Some decision makers may be knowledgeable in the field, but true peer review is used only by a very select few. The few that use peer review are considered more prestigious, but the system is much less refined than federal peer-reviewed grants. Being able to say you were funded by a foundation like the Robert Wood Johnson Foundation is more noteworthy than saying you were funded by a community foundation.

Grants made by nonprofit organizations, professional societies, service clubs, membership associations, and national and international groups in your field are viewed by many as the next most prestigious because they are reviewed and selected for funding by your peers. While these awards are usually for small amounts, they *are* credibility builders.

Corporate grants are the lowest on the scale since they are viewed by many as pay or remuneration for services, research, or knowledge wanted by the grantor. With more and more university/corporate alliances, this formally clear demarcation has become blurred. How a corporate grant is viewed in terms of credibility and prestige is linked to the project's objectivity and whether the research conducted was free from bias.

So, as you look at the major marketplaces you must consider your career, your research/project, and your position in your field. Breaking through the glass ceiling to get a highly coveted federal grant may mean starting with a grant from a less prestigious marketplace sector, such as a foundation. This funding will allow you to gather preliminary data, test hypotheses, publish in journals, and build a track record that improves your image as well as that of your organization. Remember, where you work and the letterhead on your stationery *will* make a difference with each grantor segment.

Now that you have assessed in a broad sense how the different grants marketplace must be integrated into your career plan, it is time to get down to specifics. Start by reviewing the distinct characteristics of each marketplace, where the money is, and who your competition is.

GENERAL GRANTS MARKETPLACE INFORMATION

I have administered a grants marketplace quiz as a pretest assessment instrument to over 30,000 grantseekers since 1975. These grantseekers attended one of my training seminars and, therefore, were not randomly selected and may not represent all grantseekers. However, they do vary widely in grants expertise and background. What is interesting and surprising is that more incorrect answers are given to the quiz today than 30 years ago. Why is this, when today's grantseekers are exposed to an abundance of information about grants and funding sources through the general media, professional journals, newsletters, conferences, grant databases, and email alerts? I believe that improved grants information may, in fact, contribute to current misconceptions about the grants marketplace and, consequently, to faulty grant strategies.

Grantseekers, and the administrators they work for, read announcements about nonprofit groups that attract large, above-average grant awards, but these awards that make the news are usually exceptions to the rule. These awards unfortunately are often interpreted by well-meaning, motivated grantseekers and their administrators as the norm or average. Nonprofit leaders use these larger awards to shape their view of the marketplace. Judging the marketplace by larger grants that make headlines thus creates and reinforces misconceptions about grant making and influences unrealistic expectations about the level of grant support from each sector of the marketplace. As a result, many grant-seekers end up basing their strategic grants decision making on fantasy or wishful thinking rather than on fact.

To choose the correct marketplace for your proposal, you need to base your choice on knowledge. In the public arena, the decrease in government grant funding in the mid-1980s created an initial overreaction on the part of colleges, universities, and other nonprofit organizations. Because many grantseekers knew that government funding was cut, they did not even bother to apply for government funds, and the applications for government grants declined substan-tially. (Therefore, those that did apply were rewarded.) The same phenomenon reoccurred in the mid-1990s. Well-publicized cuts in a few government programs resulted in minimal increases in applications to federal sources and large increases in requests to foundations and corporations. The astute grantseeker will not make false and potentially costly assumptions, but will look beyond the latest news and inquire into how changes in appropriations will affect spe-cific federal grant programs.

The late 1990s saw a historic event—the balance of the federal budget. In pre-vious years, when budget cuts had to be made, the only place to cut was the grants area. This is partly because most budget allocations are for fixed areas of expendi-tures such as social security and Medicare with yearly cost of living raises, and no politician or federal bureaucrat wants to be associated with cuts to these programs. The general grants and research area does not have a unified political action com-mittee or strong lobby. The grants area has experienced cuts or no increases for many years, and only a few professional organizations appealed for no cuts or more funding. But with the balancing of the budget and then the actual 1998 budget surplus, politicians increased grant dollars to popular programs. However, because of the federal deficit and the cost of the wars in Iraq and Afghanistan, this has all changed and grant appropriations will continue to be cut.

Answer the following questions to help develop your insight into who your competition is and where the money is—two critical areas to assist you in choos-ing the correct grants marketplace.

1. In the United States, approximately how many nonprofit organizations are eligible to receive gifts and grants?

   a. 58,000

   b. 525,000

     c. 1,400,000

     d. 900,000

2. What was the total amount of private money (nongovernment) donated to these nonprofit organizations (see question 1) as tax-deductible gifts in 2006?

     a. $10 billion

     b. $26 billion

     c. $133 billion

     d. $295 billion

3. The total amount of private money donated to nonprofit organizations came from the following four basic sources. Indicate the percentage attributed to each source.

Foundation grants	____%
Corporate grants	____%
Bequests	____%
Individual giving	____%

4. How much grant funding came from the federal marketplace in 2006?

     a. $75 billion

     b. $100 billion

     c. $200 billion

     d. $400 billion

Turn to the end of this chapter for the correct answers.

If taking this quiz reaffirmed what you already knew to be true, that is great. If your answers were incorrect, be thankful that you now know the correct answers and can avoid approaching the wrong marketplace and experiencing unnecessary rejection.

Most of my seminar participants guess that foundation grants account for 40 to 50 percent of the $295 billion donated in private money, with corporate grants at 30 to 35 percent, and bequests and individuals representing the balance of 15 to 30 percent.

I wish these misconceptions were correct. That would mean that foundations and corporations would have more grant funding than the federal government. However, wishful thinking will not get you a grant. Knowledge and a sound grants strategy will pay off in the end with a funded project.

The fact is that the foundation and corporate marketplace provides over $49 billion in grants, and their funding of projects can provide a catalyst in attracting the more plentiful government grant funds. However, these private grantors complain about the wild ideas and inappropriate monetary requests presented to them by grantseekers who have not done their homework and know little about the grants marketplace. To avoid this, I suggest you approach the marketplace in the following manner.

First, research the sector of the grants marketplace with the greatest amount of funds—the government marketplace (federal, state, county, and city). In order to approach these potentially valuable partners with knowledge and conviction, read through the government funding section (part 2) that follows. Take time to log on to the appropriate web sites and do a search. Talking to a federal program official will often provide you with valuable insights into what you need to do to make you and your project more competitive and fundable.

Then approach the smaller marketplace after you can demonstrate that you have searched the government grants area and can show why the private marketplace (foundations, corporations, nonprofit organizations, membership groups, professional societies, and service clubs) provides you with your best opportunity. Keep in mind that foundations and corporations may provide valuable startup funding to develop preliminary data, test hypotheses, and develop your consortia that will eventually result in larger grants from the government. See parts 3 and 4 of this book for a more detailed discussion of private funding opportunities.

Remember, if you can recognize when you have identified an inappropriate grantor for your proposal and/or when you are requesting an inordinate amount of funding and you do not apply, you avoid positioning your institution and yourself negatively, and you keep your grants success rate up. Learning about each of the marketplaces and developing your strategies from the information provided in this book is bound to pay off for you.

QUESTION	CORRECT ANSWER
1. In the United States, approximately how many nonprofit organizations are eligible to receive gifts and grants?	1d. 900,000
2. What was the total amount of private money (nongoverment) donated to these nonprofit organizations (see question 1) as tax-deductible gifts in 2006?	2d. $295 billion
3. The total amount of private money donated to nonprofit organizations came from the following four basic sources. Indicate the percentage attributed to each source.	Foundation grants 12.4% ($36.5 B) Corporate grants 4.3% ($12.8 B) Bequests 7.8% ($22.9 B) Individual giving 75.5% ($222.9 B)
4. How much grant funding came from the federal marketplace in 2006?	4d. $400 billion

CHAPTER

Documenting Organizational
Support for Your Proposal
Preproposal Summary and Approval

B efore you launch into your grantor search, you need to consider whether your application will be supported and approved by your sponsoring organization. While almost all colleges, universities, and other nonprofits have a sign-off procedure for proposals, few have a sign-on requirement. The following preproposal summary and approval form (see exhibit 9.1) has been designed to help you with this issue. Exhibit 9.1 could be subtitled "The Grant-seeker's Insurance Policy." When you have an idea you would like to seek funding for, fill out this form before writing your full-scale proposal. Then have the form reviewed by your proposal review committee, staff, or administrators, and have it returned to you with their criticisms and suggestions. Many organizations find it useful to make the preproposal summary and approval form available electronically to the appropriate individuals as an email attachment.

The purpose of the preproposal summary and approval form is to elicit comments from your organization's leaders and to have them endorse your solution. The form actually provides a vehicle to test the acceptance of your idea or project with your superiors. This is important because they should agree on the use of institutional resources before you invest hours of your time on proposal development.

There are many benefits to using the preproposal summary and approval form at this point in the process. Since proposal developers have not yet invested a great deal of time writing their proposals, they are less defensive when their

1. Proposed Proposal Director/Project Director:

2. Statement of the Problem:

3. Brief Statement of the Solution:

4. How the Project Relates to Our Mission/Goals:

5. Suggested Grantor:

    Special Grantor Requirements:
    ___ Matching Funds
    ___ Other

6. Estimated Cost of Project:

7. <u>Proposed Project Personnel</u>   <u>Released Time/New Employee</u>

    _____   _____
    _____   _____
    _____   _____

8. Facilities Required:
    Square Feet: _____   Desired Location: _____

9. Equipment Needed for Project (Note if equipment is on hand or is to be
    provided by grant, and if any special maintenance will be required):

10. Signature/Approval (Your signature represents approval of any institutional
    support outlined above): _____

11. Conditional Signature/Approval: _____
    Approval to proceed with full proposal development as long as the proposal
    developer meets the following conditions:

    Attach a brief summary/concept paper to this approval form and a list of
    potential/probable funding sources.

PREPROPOSAL SUMMARY AND APPROVAL FORM

EXHIBIT 9.1

project summary is criticized, suggested improvements are easier to make, and if
necessary, plans to deal with a lack of support can be developed.

Using this form can also be beneficial when proposals *must* be approved
before they are submitted. Make sure the form is reviewed by those people who
will be signing the final proposal. This way these individuals will know in

advance that the proposed project is coming. Have these key people comment on the areas they question or have a problem supporting. If they have no problems, they can endorse your idea by signing at number 10 of the exhibit. If they have a condition that must be met first, they can list the condition under number 11 of the exhibit and provide their conditional signature. This ensures that the time, money, and resources spent in your proposal preparation process will not be met with a negative response internally and result in failure to have your proposal signed when ready for submittal.

This preproposal summary and review process also enables decision makers to be made aware of important issues and the potential grantor's specific requirements and gives them an opportunity to comment on them. This includes, but is not limited to, the following:

- released time of project director/principal investigator to work on the grant when funded;
- matching funds commitment; and
- space, equipment, support personnel, and other resource allocations.

Because the form is generic and allows for the inclusion of the suggested grantor's specific requirements, it can be used with all of the grants marketplaces and with any grantor you uncover in the next three sections of this book.

Your grantseeking efforts are more likely to receive support and to provide a basis for matching funds and other resource allocations when you apprise your administration of your entrepreneurial grants effort and seek its endorsement in advance of submittal. This will reduce the chances of getting a grantor excited about your project and then not being able to submit your proposal because of internal problems and a refusal to sign off later by your administration.

PART TWO

. . . .

Public/Government Funding Opportunities

CHAPTER 10

Understanding the Government Grants Marketplace

THE HISTORY OF FEDERAL AND STATE GRANTS

The concept of transferring large tracts of land by making a grant predates our U.S. Constitution. Our founding fathers granted land to states to set up systems of higher education. The colleges and universities set up within these systems were referred to as land grant institutions. The concept evolved from the transfer of land to the transfer of money as the chief means to focus on a specific problem that federal and state governments wanted to impact. The public works projects from the Great Depression era used federal grants for funding. Educating farmers to end the dust bowl through the use of modern farming techniques was largely accomplished though a Department of Agriculture grant program to states to initiate a youth education program known as 4-H.

While the use of a government grants mechanism was established early on in our country's history, the mechanism we twenty-first-century grantseekers know really took off in the 1940s, particularly during World War II. During the war the government stepped up grants primarily to deal with medical and scientific problems created by the war. These grants resulted in many advances, including the discovery of penicillin.

The 1950s witnessed the creation of the National Science Foundation and grants to close the gap in science created by the Soviet launching of *Sputnik*. The federal government expanded the use of the grants mechanism from health and science to education. Presidents began to utilize the grants mechanism to push for changes in their chosen areas of interest, and in many ways these grant programs became synonymous with their legacies. For example, President John F. Kennedy's New Frontier Initiative and President Lyndon B. Johnson's Great Society Initiative were both driven through a grants mechanism to improve education, health, and social programs. Historically, when there is a national problem the grants mechanism has been used to come up with a solution. For instance, the 1970s' recession gave birth to the Comprehensive Employment Training Act, a grant program to retrain and upgrade worker skills and increase employment.

Both Republican and Democratic administrations and Congress have used grant-related initiatives to create change and make a direct and often immediate impact on our cultural, social, health, education, and scientific/research infrastructure. An example is President George W. Bush's Faith-Based Initiative that allows religious-based organizations to apply for federal grants. The former separation of church and state requirements have been lifted and in some government grant programs religiously affiliated groups actually get preferential treatment when competing with other nonprofit organizations. This is a dramatic departure from previous administrations' use of the grants mechanism.

While both Democrats and Republicans have utilized the grants mechanism, there are underlying philosophical differences as to the type of mechanisms that each group prefers. Republicans tend to favor local, regional, and state distribution of federal government grant dollars. Democrats tend to prefer national programs directed from Washington.

In the 1970s a growing trend developed on how to allocate federal grant dollars. The trend was based on federalism or the belief that the federal government should give funds back to state and local governments for them to distribute. The notion was that states should have the right to set their own agendas.

President Ronald Reagan utilized this new federalism or revenue sharing to cut and eliminate funding for programs that were previously controlled by federal agencies. Federal funds for categorical grants aimed at specific problems or areas were reduced, eliminated, or combined in an effort to support the administration's philosophy of "the government governs best which governs the least."

The idea of allowing states to grant funding to their priorities still has a lot of support. However, the concept is not tenable in the areas of research and model or demonstration grants. Even staunch conservatives agree that we must have a federal controlling management system for these types of grants or a wasteful duplication of efforts will occur.

The next section of this chapter describes the various mechanisms for distributing grants in more detail. It is important that you, the grantseeker, are familiar with these different types of mechanisms so that you can develop your grant strategies accordingly and recognize when to shift your grants research away from federal agencies and to state or local government agencies that control the moneys you desire.

CATEGORICAL GRANTS

As previously mentioned, categorical grants are designed to promote proposals within very specific, well-defined areas of interest. These grant opportunities address a specific area with which a federal program is concerned, such as arts, humanities, drug abuse, dropout prevention, nutrition for the elderly, or research on certain types of diseases and scientific advances. The government, through hearings, selects the problems to be addressed, appropriates funds, and encourages prospective grantees to design approaches to solve or reduce the problem, or to increase knowledge in the area through research.

Project and research grants are awarded by various agencies under these congressionally authorized programs. Ideally, grants are awarded to the organizations (and individuals) whose proposals most clearly match the announced program guidelines. Most federal grant programs use nongovernmental review panels (often referred to as peer-review panels) to evaluate the projects. Peer review helps ensure that the best proposals are selected for funding. Because project design is left to the grantseekers, there is room for a wide variety of creative solutions, making the project and research grant approach very popular among grantseekers.

Government granting agencies usually require grantseekers to complete detailed applications. As categorical grants have increased, each federal agency that controls funds has developed its own grants system. Grants applications and the administration of grants differ in format from agency to agency, and sometimes from program to program within the same agency. Even with the use of online creation and submittal through Grants.gov, the applications are tedious, complicated, and time-consuming to complete. It is a challenge to tailor your proposal content to meet the requirements of the granting agency as well as your own needs. There is usually a three-to-six-month review process, which may include an internal staff review by federal agency personnel and a peer review. Successful grantees are required to submit frequent reports, maintain accurate project records, and agree to federal audits and site visits by government staff.

To be successful in research and project grants, grantseekers must be mindful of the constant changes in emphasis and appropriations. Hidden agendas and shifts in focus result from the funding agency's prerogative to interpret and be sensitive to changes in the field of interest, and to what Congress accepts from each year's appropriations. Be mindful that while presidents may set priorities, Congress appropriates the funds. The federal budget changes dramatically from what the president presents, and generally, Congress likes the control that categorical grants provide.

EARMARKED GRANTS

The use of grants earmarking, more commonly referred to as pork legislation, increased so significantly from 2000 to 2006 that the 2007 Congress is considering legislation to eliminate the practice, or shed so much public scrutiny on it that it is drastically reduced. In earmarking, a project bypasses federal agency oversight and is placed in a bill that Congress is likely to pass. This can currently be accomplished without the name of the project sponsor (the congressperson or senator) even appearing on the earmarked bill.

Bills that are popular or necessary to our country may have a number of very specific projects attached to them, projects that have little or nothing to do with the bills themselves. When passed, these specific projects do not have to go through an internal (agency) or peer-review process. Once approved, the project must be handled by a federal agency (usually the most logical categorical program) that cannot question or alter the approved, funded project.

This process has become so widespread that most colleges, universities, local governments, and major national nonprofit organizations spend billions each year to retain special lobbyists in Washington, D.C., to assist them in getting senators and congresspeople from their states to insert earmarks for them in federal legislation. The practice is so pervasive that while working with a college to assist in getting federal funding for a researcher, I had to wait for permission from the university's earmarking consultant before I could contact a program officer to pursue competitive, peer-reviewed grant sources.

If not curtailed, the earmarking mechanism could eliminate entire categorical federal grants programs, especially since earmarked funding is frequently taken from the budgets of categorical programs. For example, in a recent year the Fund for the Improvement of Postsecondary Education had *all* its appropriated funds earmarked for special projects.

There will be no internal staff or peer reviews to evaluate and select the highest quality projects and research. The only ones to be funded will be those with the ability to push the other pigs out of their way at the federal grants trough. It is easy to see how this practice could be used to fund inferior research, poor model and demonstration grants, and devastate the peer-reviewed grants system, and why it is publicly criticized for funding wasteful projects such as the "bridge to nowhere in Alaska."

Even with the new emphasis on reducing earmarking and promoting transparency by requiring the sponsor's name, it will be difficult to stop the pork process now that it has reached the current level. While earmarking appears at first to be very inviting (and easy), there is a disadvantage to consider. Many of the federal officers whose jobs entail administering grant programs, ensuring that their programs accomplish their goals, and organizing peer reviews, see earmarking as a threat. Earmarking threatens their agency's credibility since they are the ones who will get blamed when these often ill-conceived projects are publicized. This is particularly frustrating since they have nothing to do with the choice of the grantee or the funding of the grant, but still have to administer it and send out the funds. Interviews with some program officers have revealed a lot of irritation with grantees who are subverting the grants system through earmarking. As a result, earmarked grantees can experience great difficulty in moving from a pork grant back to a peer-reviewed grant within the same agency and program.

Since control of the House and the Senate has moved to the Democrats, earmarking has been in the spotlight and has been reduced. Only time will tell if this trend prevails. Like the other types of grants mechanisms, you need to understand earmarking so that you can determine the ramification involved in using it.

FORMULA GRANTS

The term *formula grants* refers to granting programs under which funds are allocated according to a set of criteria (or a formula). The criteria for allocation of these grant funds may be census data, unemployment figures, number of individuals below the poverty level, number of people with disabilities, and the like, for a state, city, or region. Formula grant programs are generally specific to a problem area or geographic region and historically have been used to support training programs in the fields of health, criminal justice, and employment. They are rarely encountered in research areas, but have been used to distribute funds for research equipment.

The formula grant funds must pass through an intermediary, such as a state, city, or county government, or a commission, before reaching the grantee. The formula grants mechanism is another example of the New Federalism that started developing in the early 1970s. While the general guidelines for formula grants are developed at the federal level, the rules are open to interpretation, and local input can significantly alter the intent of the original federal program. To encourage local control and input into how federal funds are spent, the formula grants mechanism requires a mandated review by local officials but usually very little accountability or evaluation of the actual impact of the funds. Because of this, it is difficult to substantiate the results of these programs at subsequent congressional appropriation hearings, which means that they (the programs placed in formula grant formats) are often easy targets for elimination.

BLOCK GRANTS

The block grant concept was founded on the premise that it was not the purview of the federal government to force the states to follow categorical grant program priorities. Similar categorical grant programs were blocked, or synthesized into groups of related programs, and the federal funds were sent directly to the states. The states could set their priorities and grant the federal funds to the high-priority areas and projects they saw fit.

The block grant mechanism allowed the federal government to reduce staff formerly used to administer categorical grant programs. Decreases in staff were limited, however, because the federal government still had to direct the research component of categorical programs to avoid duplication and to coordinate research efforts.

Because of the federal government's continued involvement in the administration of grants (especially research grants), and Congress's desire to deal with problems in education, employment, and crime, the late 1980s marked the decline of the block grant mania of the early Reagan years, and the use of categorical funding mechanisms increased. Virtually all of the new grant programs introduced in the late 1990s were categorical grant programs designed to impact long existing or new problems. The conservative agenda of George W. Bush's administration, current and projected tax cuts, increased defense costs, and the deficit could result in more budget reductions, the blocking of more federal grant programs and, in general, fewer grant dollars.

CONTRACTS

No discussion of federal support would be complete without a discussion of government contracts. In recent years, the differences between a grant and a contract have become harder to discern. Indeed, after hours of negotiation with a federal agency on your grant, you may end up having to finalize your budget with a contract officer.

While there are several types of contracts, including fixed cost, cost reimbursable, and those that allow the contractor to add additional costs incurred during the contract, the basic difference between a grant and a contract is that a contract outlines precisely what the government wants done. You are supplied with detailed specifications, you propose a procedure to produce what the government agency has specified, and the contract is usually awarded on a lowest-bid basis. With a contract, there is decidedly less flexibility in creating the approach to the problem. To be successful in this arena, you must be able to convince the federal contracting agency that you can perform the contract at an acceptable level of competency and at the lowest bid. Contracts are also published or advertised in different ways than grants. Grants opportunities can be found in the *Catalog of Federal Domestic Assistance* and on Grants.gov, while contracts are advertised in Federal Business Opportunities (FedBizOpps.gov). These resources will be explained in chapter 11.

The $400 billion in federal grants quoted in question 4 of the quiz in chapter 8 does not include government contract moneys. One reason that contact moneys are not included in federal grant statistics has to do with rollovers. Grant funds are appropriated and awarded in the federal budget year, which runs from October 1 to September 30. Grants awarded on a one-year time frame from award date may allow for a small, no-cost extension, but even multiyear grants contain a caveat that future funding is dependent on yearly budget allocations. While grantees can usually obtain an extension on expending their awarded grant funds beyond the end of their grant period, rollovers of unexpended federal agency funds are prohibited. Unexpended grant funds revert back to the federal treasury, except for federal contracts. For example, the Department of Defense may accrue rollover funds in certain contract areas for several years. The rollover variable makes it virtually impossible to estimate how much total contract funding is available from all of the federal agencies in any one year. However, it is safe to say that the variety, number, and dollar value of government contracts are staggering and go far beyond the $400 billion in government grants cited in chapter 8 and could be in the trillions of dollars.

Contracts have been increasingly pursued by nonprofit groups in recent years. For example, shifts away from domestic grant program funds have led some nonprofit organizations to look at Defense Department contract opportunities for implementation of their programs and research. However, the contracts game requires a successful track record and documentable expertise. The best way to break into this marketplace is to identify a successful bidder and inquire as to whether you can work for them as a subcontractor. This way, you gain experience, confidence, and contacts with the contractor.

Many nonprofit groups have found that they can reduce the problems they routinely encounter in bidding contracts by developing separate profit and nonprofit entities for dealing with such issues as security agreements, academic freedom, patents, and copyrights. In addition, changes in the contracts area have been made to simplify government purchasing and to reduce paperwork. These changes, brought on by scandals over inflated prices for parts, have alleviated some of the problems associated with the administration of contract bids. Still, bidding on government contracts is a task for the experienced grantseekers only.

STATE GOVERNMENT GRANTS

The astute grantseeker will be ready to act discovering a federal grant opportunity in which the eligible recipient must be a state agency. In these cases, federal funds have been passed on for dissemination to the state agency that the state designates as best suited to do so. The federal program officers will know where the funds were directed in each state. States also place their own funds into state grant programs. Information on all federal funding must be accessible to the public and, therefore, are listed in the public grants database Grants.gov (to be explained in detail in chapter 11). Most states do not have a similar public database. To discover state grant opportunities you will need to look at state agency web sites and talk to state officials. Many states appropriate grant funds to programs and projects that their elected officials value. For example, states that have secured funding from the tobacco company settlement can use these funds as their legislature and executives see fit. One state used the funds for grant opportunities related to the expansion of opportunities and employment in the technology sector, while a number of other states have used the funds to develop antismoking programs.

It is difficult to estimate how many grant dollars are awarded through individual state program initiatives. Many states develop their own initiatives in the social welfare and health areas, while few states deal in research funding. In most states, the majority of state grant funds are federal funds that must pass through the state to you, the grantseeker.

There are some grantseeker advantages to state control of grants. State-controlled grants funded by the federal government are easier to access than federal grants. They require less long-distance travel and allow you to use state and local politicians to make your case heard. These advantages are counterbalanced, however, by the fact that some states develop their own priorities for these pass-through federal funds. States may add additional restrictions and use a review system similar to the federal peer-review system, or use a system made up of state bureaucrats and political appointees. Although states have their own moneys, granting programs, and rules, if they distribute grant moneys obtained from the federal government, they must guarantee that the eventual recipient of those funds will follow all federal rules and circulars.

Many of the federal government grantseeking techniques found in the preceding chapters of this book also apply to accessing state grant funds. However, to determine which of the government sectors (federal or state) is best for your proposal, you must first learn how to research the government marketplace.

CHAPTER 11

Researching the Government Marketplace

THE FEDERAL GRANTS SYSTEM

Federal grants programs are created by Congress, and federal funding is appropriated each year. Many federal grant programs are initiated as acts of Congress (for example, Higher Education Act). While the acts may create programs that legally exist for a set number of years before they are reviewed, the funding for all government grant agencies and their programs is currently limited to one year. The federal budget year runs from October 1 to the following September 30.

The current federal grants calendar is referred to as the 2008–2009 budget year (October 1, 2008 through September 30, 2009). The president submits his preferred budget items to Congress in the spring for the new fall budget year. Recent years have witnessed a Congress and a president that could not agree on the budget. When the budget does not get passed before the end of the fiscal year, Congress usually passes a continuing resolution that keeps the federal government operating while the parties work out their differences on what to cut and what to add. Continuing resolutions may call for the level funding, reduction, or increase within any given program.

The 2006–2007 budget operated on a continuing resolution from October 1, 2006, until February 2007 when Congress decided to avoid voting on a budget and to maintain the continuing resolution as the budget. This is the first time in U.S. history that a continuing resolution funded our government, and it speaks to the problems we face at the federal level.

The key for you to remember is that a multiyear funded grant award is not guaranteed. Each year of that award is subject to changes based upon the agency's appropriation by Congress. Each yearly award is guaranteed for that year only.

To make matters more confusing, you may receive your grant award notice in June for a one-year grant. In this case, even though the federal fiscal year in which you were awarded will end on September 30, you would be given an extension from October to the following May to complete your research/project.

The federal grants system operates on a very strict timeline that requires the public to have an opportunity to make comments on each federal program and how and what it funds with the tax dollars of U.S. citizens. Novice grantseekers who are not familiar with the federal grants system get started at the last minute and get caught in reactive grantseeking. If you know what you are going to look for before you start your federal program grants search, you will be way ahead of the game and able to take advantage of preproposal contact (see chapter 12) with federal officials.

FEDERAL GRANTS RESEARCH FORM

The key to providing your organization with federal funding is a combination of determination, hard work, and homework. The homework consists of systematic research, record keeping, and follow-up. The federal grants research form (see exhibit 11.1) will allow you to keep track of the grant programs you investigate (that is, those that seem like your most logical grant sources) and will prevent your contacts and projects from being lost. Load this form in your computer or print out the form from the CD in the back of this book so that your data gathering will be consistent and complete.

As you look at examples of the resources available on funding opportunities, you will see that information necessary to complete the federal grants research form is usually readily available. In instances when it is not available on agency web sites or program announcements, you can request it during preproposal contact. Do not stop with the first few funding sources that sound or look good. Remember, your goal is to locate the best funding sources for your project. Complete your research, then review and rate those funding sources you have identified using the past grantees analysis worksheet in chapter 12 (see exhibit 12.2).

FEDERAL RESEARCH TOOLS

How do you research and track federal grant opportunities? Federal law requires the availability of public knowledge and opportunity for input regarding government grants. As such, there are several tools to help you find federal funding sources for your projects/research. By employing these tools you, the grantseeker, can proceed proactively, make intelligent preproposal contact, and take control of the deadline and submittal process. The federal research

For (Your Project Reference or Title): _____

CFDA No. _____ GRANTS.GOV Funding No. _____

Program Title: _____

Gov't Agency: _____ Deadline Date(s): _____

Create a file for each program you are researching and place all information you gather on this program in the file. Use this Federal Grants Research Form to:

- keep a record of the information you have gathered
- maintain a log of all contact made with the federal program

Agency Address: _____

Agency Director: _____ Program Director: _____

Name/Title of Contact Person: _____

Telephone Number: _____ Fax Number: _____

Email: _____

In order to prepare a professional proposal you need to gather the information listed below. Place a check mark next to the information you have gathered and placed in the file.

___ Program description from *CFDA*

___ Synopsis from GRANTS.GOV

___ Subscription for automatic email alert/notification for up-to-date program info.

___ Copy of full announcement (link on GRANTS.GOV)

___ List of last year's grantees

___ List of last year's reviewers

___ Background information on last year's reviewers

___ Instructions on how to apply/submittal instructions (link on GRANTS.GOV)

___ Log on/sign on code

___ Name and contact information for your Authorized Organization Representative (GRANTS.GOV AOR)

___ Comments on rules/final rules from *Federal Register* or agency publication

___ Notices of rules for evaluation from *Federal Register* or agency publication

___ Grant scoring system

___ Sample funded proposal

___ Federal Funding Source Staff Profile (exhibit 12.5)

___ Summary of each contact made (provide below and/or attach to Form)

_____

_____

_____

_____

_____

FEDERAL GRANTS RESEARCH FORM

EXHIBIT 11.1

tools table (see table 11.1) outlines some of the more useful resources for locating government funds.

Grants.gov

Grants.gov is a central storehouse for information on over 1,000 grant programs and access to approximately $400 billion in annual awards. By registering once

TABLE 11.1

FEDERAL RESEARCH TOOLS TABLE

NAME	DESCRIPTION	WHERE TO GET IT
Grants.gov	Central storehouse for information on over 1,000 federal grant programs and access to $400 billion in annual awards (see sample entry)	Free online access at http://www.grants.gov.
Catalog of Federal Domestic Assistance (CFDA)	A database of all federal programs created by law (see sample entry)	Free online access at http://www.cfda.gov. If you wish to purchase a hard copy, call the Superintendent of Documents at (202) 512-1800 in the DC metro area or toll-free at (866) 212-1800, or order from the Government Printing Office's (GPO's) online bookstore at http://bookstore.gpo.gov. A hard copy can also be found at federal depository libraries throughout the United States (see below).
Federal Register	Official news publication for the federal government; makes public all meetings, announcements of granting programs, regulations, and deadlines (see sample entry)	Free online access at http://www.gpoaccess.gov/fr/index.html. A hard copy can be found at federal depository libraries throughout the United States (see below).
FedBizOpps (Federal Business Opportunities)	This government database lists notices of proposed government procurement actions, contract awards, sales of government property, and other procurement information over $25,000.	Free online access at http://www.fedbizopps.gov.

NAME	DESCRIPTION	WHERE TO GET IT
Congressional Record	Day-to-day proceedings and debates of the Senate and the House of Representatives, including all grant program money appropriated by Congress. Published daily when Congress is in session.	Free online access at http://www.gpoaccess.gov/crecord/index.html. If you wish to purchase a hard copy, annual subscription, you can do so by calling the Superintendent of Documents at (202) 512-1800 in the DC metro area or toll-free at (866) 212-1800, or order from GPO's online bookstore at http://bookstore.gpo.gov. Hard copy is also available at federal depository libraries (see below).
Federal Depository Libraries	Public and university libraries that allow free access to government publications like the CFDA, *Federal Register*, and the Congressional Record.	To locate a library near you, visit http://www.gpoaccess.gov/libraries.html.
Federal Directory	Directory providing nearly 52,000 names, titles, telephone numbers, and email addresses of senior and mid-level government officials in the executive office of the president, all 15 cabinet-level federal departments, quasi-governmental agencies, U.S. Congress, and the federal court system.	Fee-based print subscription available—4 issues per year Contact: Carroll Publishing 4701 Sangamore Rd., Suite S-155 Bethesda, MD 20816 (800) 336-4240 Fax: (301) 263-9801 Or order hard copy online at http://www.carrollpub.com/directories.asp.
Agency Newsletters, Publications, RFPS, and Guidelines	Many federal agencies publish newsletters to inform you about the availability of funds and program accomplishments. You may also request application materials, guidelines, and so on.	Usually free online availability from agency. See "Regulations, Guidelines, and Literature" in the CFDA entry.

on this site, your organization can apply for grants from 26 federal agencies that offer grant programs in 21 categories.

Grants.gov allows you to electronically find and apply for grant opportunities, as well as track your application. The web site also offers free subscriptions for email notifications of new grant postings.

You do not have to register with Grants.gov if you want only to find grant opportunities. However, if you want to apply for a grant, you and your organization must complete the Grants.gov registration process, which takes three to five business days to complete. Most colleges and universities are registered on Grants.gov and have an Authorized Organization Representative (AOR). There may be more than one AOR for an organization. Check with your institution's grants office before beginning the registration process.

Once you have gained access to Grants.gov's home page (http://www. grants.gov), click "Find Grant Opportunities" to perform a search. Then click "Search Opportunities" and follow the instructions on the screen. A basic search can be conducted using keywords, the funding opportunity number, or the CFDA number. In the sample search (exhibit 11.2), the grantseeker performed a basic keyword search for programs related to literacy. Search results are shown in exhibit 11.3. By clicking one of the programs listed on the search results, the grantseeker can retrieve a synopsis of the grant opportunity (see exhibit 11.4), as well as

- links to the full announcement contained in either the *Federal Register* or one of the grant-making agency's publications, and
- application instructions.

In this particular example, clicking on "Full Announcement" will bring you to the full text announcement in the *Federal Register*. The synopsis (see exhibit 11.4) also contains a link to the announcement in the *Catalog of Federal Domestic Assistance*.

Catalog of Federal Domestic Assistance

The *Catalog of Federal Domestic Assistance* (CFDA) is another valuable resource for searching through available competitive and discretionary grant opportunities. The primary purpose of the *Catalog* is to assist users in identifying programs that meet specific objectives of the potential applicant and to obtain general information on federal assistance programs.

The Internet web site http://www.cfda.gov is the primary means of disseminating the *Catalog*. However, the Government Printing Office continues to print and sell hard copies of the CFDA to interested buyers. For information about purchasing the CFDA from the GPO, call the Superintendent of Documents at (202) 512-1800 or toll-free at (866) 512-1800, or you may reach the GPO's online bookstore at http://bookstore.gpo.gov.

GRANTS.GOV™

Home > Find Grant Opportunities > Search Grant Opportunities

Search Grant Opportunities

Basic Search Browse by Category Browse by Agency Advanced Search Search Tips

APPLICANTS

About Federal Grants
Get Registered
Find Grant Opportunities
 Search Opportunities
  Basic Search
  Browse by Category
  Browse by Agency
  Advanced Search
  Email Subscription
Apply for Grants
Track My Application
Applicant Help

ABOUT GRANTS.GOV

FOR AGENCIES

RESOURCES

HELP

CONTACT US

SITE MAP

To perform a **basic search** for a grant, complete the "Keyword Search"; the "Search by Funding Opportunity Number"; **OR** the "Search by CFDA Number" field; and then click the "Search" button below.

Access Search Tips for helpful search strategies, or click the Help button in the upper right corner to get help with this screen.

Keyword Search:

literacy

Search by Funding Opportunity Number:

Search by CFDA Number:

Search   Clear Form

SEARCHING GRANTS.GOV ONLINE

EXHIBIT 11.2

GRANTS.GOV™

For Applicants   About Grants.gov   Resources   For Agencies

Contact Us   SiteMap   Help   Home

Home > Find Grant Opportunities > Search Grant Opportunities > Search Results

Search Results

Sort: Relevance, Descending

Sort by Open Date   Sort by Relevance

New Search

Results 1-9 of 9

APPLICANTS

About Federal Grants

Get Registered

Find Grant Opportunities

Search Opportunities

Basic Search

Browse by Category

Browse by Agency

Advanced Search

Email Subscription

Apply for Grants

Track My Application

Applicant Help

ABOUT GRANTS.GOV

FOR AGENCIES

RESOURCES

HELP

CONTACT US

SITE MAP

Close Date	Opportunity Title	Agency	Funding Number
03/01/2006	Environmental Literacy Grants	National Oceanic and Atmospheric Administration	SEC-OED-2006-2000467
03/21/2007	Environmental Literacy Grants for Free-Choice Learning	National Oceanic and Atmospheric Administration	SEC-OED-2007-2000859
04/11/2006	Improving Literacy Through School Libraries Program	U.S. Department of Education	ED-GRANTS-021006-001
	Understanding and Promoting Health Literacy (R01)	National Institutes of Health	PAR-07-020
04/02/2007	Improving Literacy Through School Libraries Program CFDA 84.364A	U.S. Department of Education	ED-GRANTS-021607-001
	Understanding and Promoting Health Literacy (R03)	National Institutes of Health	PAR-07-019
	Understanding and Promoting Health Literacy (R21)	National Institutes of Health	PAR-07-018
03/21/2007	Environmental Literacy Grants for Forral K-12 Education	National Oceanic and Atmospheric Administration	SEC-OED-2007-2000863
05/01/2007	Native American Library Services: Enhancement Grants	Institute of Museum and Library Services	NAG-ENHANCEMENT-FY07
05/15/2007	Native Hawaiian Library Services	Institute of Museum	NAG-HAWAIIAN-

GRANTS.GOV SEARCH RESULTS

EXHIBIT 11.3

GRANTS.GOV™

Home > Find Grant Opportunities > Search Grant Opportunities > Search Results > Synopsis

APPLICANTS

About Federal Grants

Get Registered

Find Grant Opportunities

  Search Opportunities

    Basic Search

    Browse by Category

    Browse by Agency

    Advanced Search

  Email Subscription

Apply for Grants

Track My Application

Applicant Help

ABOUT GRANTS.GOV

FOR AGENCIES

RESOURCES

HELP

CONTACT US

SITE MAP

Improving Literacy Through School Libraries Program CFDA 84.364A

Synopsis | Full Announcement | How to Apply

The synopsis for this grant opportunity is detailed below, following this paragraph. This synopsis contains all of the updates to this document that have been posted as of **02/16/2007**. If updates have been made to the opportunity synopsis, update information is provided below the synopsis.

If you would like to receive notifications of changes to the grant opportunity click send me change notification emails. The only thing you need to provide for this service is your email address. No other information is requested.

Any inconsistency between the original printed document and the disk or electronic document shall be resolved by giving precedence to the printed document.

Document Type:	Grants Notice
Funding Opportunity Number:	ED-GRANTS-021607-001
Opportunity Category:	Discretionary
Posted Date:	Feb 16, 2007
Creation Date:	Feb 16, 2007
Original Closing Date for Applications:	Apr 02, 2007 Applications Available: February 16, 2007. Deadline for Transmittal of Applications: April 2, 2007.
Current Closing Date for Applications:	Apr 02, 2007 Applications Available: February 16, 2007. Deadline for Transmittal of Applications: April 2, 2007.
Archive Date:	May 02, 2007
Funding Instrument Type:	Grant
Category of Funding Activity:	Education
Category Explanation:	
Expected Number of Awards:	100

GRANTS.GOV OPPORTUNITY SYNOPSIS

EXHIBIT 11.4

The *Catalog* contains five indexes that can be used to help you identify your specific areas of program interest more efficiently. They are as follows:

- Functional Index: Groups programs into 20 broad categories, such as agriculture, education, health, and so on, and 176 subcategories that identify specific areas of interest.

Estimated Total Program Funding: $19,486,000
Award Ceiling:
Award Floor:
CFDA Number: 84.364 -- Literacy
                                      through School Libraries
Cost Sharing or Matching Requirement: No

Eligible Applicants

Others (see text field entitled "Additional Information on Eligibility"
for clarification)

Additional Information on Eligibility:

Eligible Applicants: Local educational agencies (LEAs) in which at
least 20 percent of the students served by the LEA are from
families with incomes below the poverty line based on the most
recent satisfactory data available from the U.S. Census Bureau at
the time this notice is published. These data are Small Area
Income and Poverty Estimates for school districts for income year
2004. A list of LEAs with their family poverty rates (based on these
Census Bureau data) is posted on our Web site at:
http://www.ed.gov/programs/lsl/eligibility.html.

Agency Name

U.S. Department of Education

Description

•Note: Each funding opportunity description is a synopsis of
information in the Federal Register application notice. For specific
information about eligibility, please see the official application
notice. The official version of this document is the document
published in the Federal Register. Free Internet access to the
official edition of the Federal Register and the Code of Federal
Regulations is available on GPO Access at:
http://www.access.gpo.gov/nara/index.html. Please review the
official application notice for pre-application and application
requirements, application submission information, performance
measures, priorities and program contact information. Purpose of
Program: The purpose of this program is to improve student
reading skills and academic achievement by providing students
with increased access to up-to-date school library materials; well-
equipped, technologically advanced school library media centers;
and well-trained, professionally certified school library media
specialists. Catalog of Federal Domestic Assistance (CFDA)
Number: 84.364A. Applications for grants under the Improving
Literacy Through School Libraries program, CFDA Number 84.364A
must be submitted electronically using the Governmentwide
Grants.gov Apply site at http//http://www.Grants.gov. Through
this site, you will be able to download a copy of the application
package, complete it offline, and then upload and submit your
application. You may not e-mail an electronic copy of a grant
application to us. You may access the electronic grant application
for the Improving Literacy Through School Libraries program at
http://www.Grants.gov. You must search for the downloadable
application package for this program by the CFDA number. Do not

GRANTS.GOV OPPORTUNITY SYNOPSIS *(continued)*

EXHIBIT 11.4

- Subject Index: The most commonly used index, since most people express their interests according to subject.
- Applicant Index: Allows you to look up a program to see whether you are eligible to apply. Because you must already know of the program to use this index, it is not a great help in identifying sources.

include the CFDA number's alpha suffix in your search (e.g., search for 84.364, not 84.364A). THe telephone number for the Grants.gov Helpdesk is 1-800-518-4726.

Link to Full Announcement

Improving Literacy Through School Libraries Program CFDA 84.364A: Notice Inviting Applications for New Awards for Fiscal Year (FY) 2007

If you have difficulty accessing the full announcement electronically, please contact:

Julius Cotton
ED Grants.gov FIND System Admin.
Phone (202) 245-6140
julius.cotton@ed.gov
Program Managers:
Irene Harwarth
U.S. Department of Education
400 Maryland Avenue, SW., room 3W227
Washington, DC 20202-6200
Telephone: (202) 401-3751 or by e-mail: Irene.Harwarth@ed.gov, or
Miriam Lund
U.S. Department of Education
400 Maryland Avenue, SW., room 3W258
Washington, DC 20202-6200
Telephone: (202) 401-2871 e-Mail: Program Manager

Synopsis Modification History

There are currently no modifications for this opportunity.

GRANTS.GOV OPPORTUNITY SYNOPSIS *(continued)*

EXHIBIT 11.4

- Deadlines Index: Enables you to look up the deadline dates for programs to see whether the programs have a single or multiple deadline system.
- Authorization Index: Indexes the laws creating the funding.

Users should also be aware of the other sections of the *Catalog* that provide valuable information, such as

- Programs added and deleted since the last edition of the *Catalog*,
- A crosswalk of program numbers and title changes,
- Regional and local offices,
- Intergovernmental review requirements,
- Definitions of the types of assistance under which programs are administered, and
- Proposal Writing.

Using the CFDA on the Internet: Once you have gained access to the CFDA's web site, click "Find Assistance Programs" to perform a search. Then follow the instructions on the screen. In the sample search (exhibit 11.5), the grantseeker performed a keyword search again for programs related to literacy.

Search results are shown in exhibit 11.6. By clicking on one of the programs listed on the search results, the grantseeker can retrieve a *CFDA* entry describing the program.

Reading the CFDA: A sample *CFDA* entry (see exhibit 11.7) has been included to show the information provided in this valuable resource. All program descriptions/entries contain the following basic information:

Program Number and Title

Federal Agency: This is the branch of government administering the program, which is not much help to you except as general knowledge or for looking up programs and agencies in the *United States Government Manual*.

Authorization: You need this information to fill out some program applications and/or to look up the testimony and laws creating the funding (for the hard-core researcher and grantseeker only).

Objectives: Compare these general program objectives to your project. Do not give up if you are off the mark slightly; contact with the funding source may uncover new programs, changes, or hidden agendas.

Types of Assistance: Review and record the general type of support from this source, and then compare the information to your project definition.

CFDA
The Catalog of Federal
Domestic Assistance

Skip Navigation
Home | FAQ | Privacy | Feedback | About The CFDA Website | Search Tips

Query Options
Keyword literacy

General Options
Output Format HTML

Search

General Services Administration
Office of Chief Acquisition Officer
Regulatory and Federal Assistance Division (VIR)

SEARCHING THE *CATALOG OF FEDERAL DOMESTIC ASSISTANCE*

EXHIBIT 11.5

CFDA
The Catalog of Federal
Domestic Assistance

Search Results

Program Description		Score (in %)
84.002 - Adult Education_State Grant Program	**Abstract** 84.002 Adult Education State Grant Program FEDERAL AGENCY: OFFICE OF VOCATIONAL AND ADULT EDUCATION, DEPARTMENT OF EDUCATION AUTHORIZATION: Adult Education and Family Literacy Act, Chapter 2, Public Law 105-220, and Workforce Investment Act, Section 503, 20 U.S.C. 1201 et seq.	49
84.371 - Striving Readers	**Abstract** 84.371 Striving Readers FEDERAL AGENCY: OFFICE OF ELEMENTARY AND SECONDARY EDUCATION, DEPARTMENT OF EDUCATION AUTHORIZATION: Title I, Part E, Section 1502 of the Elementary and Secondary Education Act of 1965 as amended.	49
47.070 - Computer and Information Science and Engineering	**Abstract** 47.070 Computer and Information Science and Engineering (CISE) FEDERAL AGENCY: NATIONAL SCIENCE FOUNDATION AUTHORIZATION: National Science Foundation Act of 1950, as amended, Public Law 107-368, 42 U.S.C. 1861 et seq.	36
84.362 - Native Hawaiian Education	**Abstract** 84.362 Native Hawaiian Education FEDERAL AGENCY: OFFICE OF ELEMENTARY AND SECONDARY EDUCATION, DEPARTMENT OF EDUCATION AUTHORIZATION: Elementary and Secondary Education Act, as amended, Title VII, Part B, Public Law 107-110.	12
84.364 - Literacy through School Libraries	**Abstract** 84.364 Literacy through School Libraries FEDERAL AGENCY: OFFICE OF ELEMENTARY AND SECONDARY EDUCATION, DEPARTMENT OF EDUCATION AUTHORIZATION: Elementary and Secondary Education Act of 1965, as amended, Title I, Part B, Subpart 4, Public Law 107-110.	12
84.365 - English Language Acquisition Grants	**Abstract** 84.365 English Language Acquisition Grants FEDERAL AGENCY: OFFICE OF ELEMENTARY AND SECONDARY EDUCATION, DEPARTMENT OF EDUCATION AUTHORIZATION: Elementary and Secondary Education Act (ESEA), as amended, Title III, Part A, Sections 3101, 3129	12
93.142 - NIEHS Hazardous Waste Worker Health and Safety Training	**Abstract** 93.142 NIEHS Hazardous Waste Worker Health and Safety Training (Superfund Worker Training Program) FEDERAL AGENCY: NATIONAL INSTITUTES OF HEALTH, DEPARTMENT OF HEALTH AND HUMAN SERVICES AUTHORIZATION: Superfund Amendments and Reauthorization Act of 1986, as amended, Title I, Section 126, Public Law 99-499; Public Health Service Act, Section 405(b)(1)(C), as amended, Public Law 99-158.	12
93.577 - Early Learning Fund	**Abstract** 93.577 Early Learning Fund (Early Learning Opportunities Act) FEDERAL AGENCY: ADMINISTRATION FOR CHILDREN AND FAMILIES, DEPARTMENT OF HEALTH AND HUMAN SERVICES AUTHORIZATION: Public Law 106-554, Early Learning Opportunities Act of 2001, Title VIII, Section 801	12
93.600 - Head Start	**Abstract** 93.600 Head Start FEDERAL AGENCY: ADMINISTRATION FOR CHILDREN AND FAMILIES, DEPARTMENT OF HEALTH AND HUMAN SERVICES AUTHORIZATION: Community Opportunities, Accountability, Training, and Educational Services Act of 1998, Title I, Sections 101-119, Public Law 105-285.	12
94.011 - Foster Grandparent Program	**Abstract** 94.011 Foster Grandparent Program (FGP) FEDERAL AGENCY: CORPORATION FOR NATIONAL AND COMMUNITY SERVICE AUTHORIZATION: Domestic Volunteer Service Act of 1973, as amended, Title II, Part B, Section 211, Public Law 93-113, 42 U.S.C. 5011, as amended; National and Community Service Trust Act of 1993, Public Law 103-82.	12

CFDA Search Results

EXHIBIT 11.6

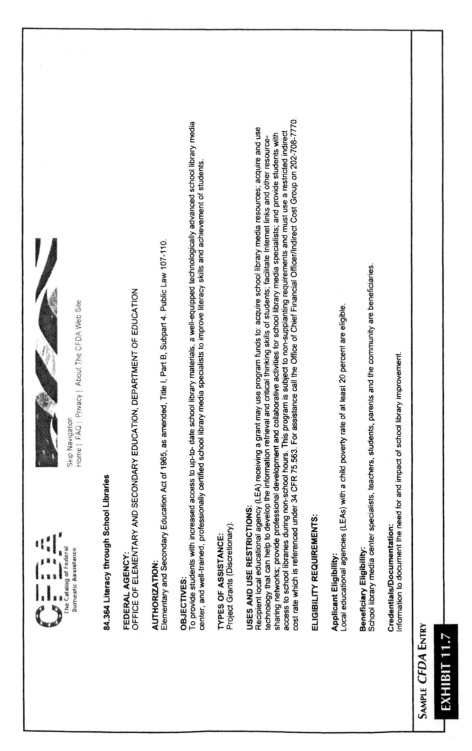

CFDA
The Catalog of Federal
Domestic Assistance

Skip Navigation
Home | FAQ | Privacy | About The CFDA Web Site

84.364 Literacy through School Libraries

FEDERAL AGENCY:
OFFICE OF ELEMENTARY AND SECONDARY EDUCATION, DEPARTMENT OF EDUCATION

AUTHORIZATION:
Elementary and Secondary Education Act of 1965, as amended, Title I, Part B, Subpart 4. Public Law 107-110.

OBJECTIVES:
To provide students with increased access to up-to-date school library materials, a well-equipped technologically advanced school library media center, and well-trained, professionally certified school library media specialists to improve literacy skills and achievement of students.

TYPES OF ASSISTANCE:
Project Grants (Discretionary).

USES AND USE RESTRICTIONS:
Recipient local educational agency (LEA) receiving a grant may use program funds to: acquire school library media resources; acquire and use technology that can help to develop the information retrieval and critical thinking skills of students; facilitate Internet links and other resource-sharing networks; provide professional development and collaborative activities for school library media specialists; and provide students with access to school libraries during non-school hours. This program is subject to non-supplanting requirements and must use a restricted indirect cost rate which is referenced under 34 CFR 75.563. For assistance call the Office of Chief Financial Officer/Indirect Cost Group on 202-708-7770.

ELIGIBILITY REQUIREMENTS:

Applicant Eligibility:
Local educational agencies (LEAs) with a child poverty rate of at least 20 percent are eligible.

Beneficiary Eligibility:
School library media center specialists, teachers, students, parents and the community are beneficiaries.

Credentials/Documentation:
Information to document the need for and impact of school library improvement.

SAMPLE *CFDA* ENTRY

EXHIBIT 11.7

96

APPLICATION AND AWARD PROCESS:

Preapplication Coordination:
None. This program is excluded from coverage under E.O. 12372.

Application Procedure:
Applications must be prepared and submitted in accordance with the notice published in the Federal Register. By the due date, eligible applicants must submit to the U.S. Department of Education, Application Control Center, a complete application that addresses the purposes of the program, the selection criteria, the absolute priority included in the application notice, and includes all required assurances and signatures. Required assurances and certifications include: Group Application Certification (if applicable); Assurances for Non-Construction Programs (SF 422B); Certification regarding Lobbying, Debarment, Suspension and Other Responsibility Matter, and Drug-Free Workplace Requirements (ED Form 80- 0013); Disclosure of Lobbying Activities (SF LLL) (if applicable); Response to Notice to All Applicants (Section 427, GEPA). Applications should also include a Cover Page (SF422A); the required Budget Form (ED Form 524); an itemized budget and other budget information; proof of eligibility; a project abstract; and a program narrative that includes responses to selection criteria. Applicants are encouraged to submit (1) one original and (2) copies of their application. This program is eligible for coverage under E.O. 12372, "Intergovernmental Review of Federal Programs." An applicant should consult the office or official designated as the single point of contact in his or her State for more information on the process the State requires to be followed in applying for assistance, if the State has selected the program for review.

Award Procedure:
Applications are reviewed and ranked by a panel of outside readers. The Department of Education notifies successful applicants of awards and negotiates the final award documents.

Deadlines:
Deadlines are published in the Federal Register.

Range of Approval/Disapproval Time:
Generally 60 to 120 days after the deadline for applications.

Appeals:
None.

Renewals:
None.

ASSISTANCE CONSIDERATIONS:

Formula and Matching Requirements:
None.

Length and Time Phasing of Assistance:
Grants are awarded for a period of not more than 12 months.

Sample *CFDA* Entry *(continued)*

EXHIBIT 11.7

97

POST ASSISTANCE REQUIREMENTS:

Reports:
Grantees must submit a final performance reports within 90 days after the end of the grant award period documenting how the funds were used and the how school library media centers were improved.

Audits:
In accordance with the provisions of OMB Circular No. A-133 (Revised June 27, 2003), Audits of States, Local Governments, and Nonprofit Organizations, nonfederal entities that receive financial assistance of $500,000 or more in Federal awards will have a single or program-specific audit conducted for that year. Nonfederal entities that expend less than $500,000 a year in Federal awards are exempt from Federal audit requirements for that year, except as noted in Circular No. A-133.

Records:
Records must be maintained for three years after the fiscal year in which the expenditure was made by the grantee, or until the grantee is notified of the completion of the Federal fiscal audit. In all cases of audit questions, records must be maintained until resolution has occurred.

FINANCIAL INFORMATION:

Account Identification:
91-0900-0-1-501.

Obligations:
(Grants) FY 05 $19,683,000; FY 06 est $19,486,000; and FY 07 est $19,486,000.

Range and Average of Financial Assistance:
In fiscal year 2005 approximately 85 awards were made; the average award was $100,000.

PROGRAM ACCOMPLISHMENTS:
In fiscal year 2005, approximately 85 awards were made.

REGULATIONS, GUIDELINES, AND LITERATURE:
Education Department General Administrative Regulations (EDGAR), Parts 74, 75, 77, 79, 80, 81, 82, 85, 86, 97, 98, and 99. For further guidance and other information, contact the program office.

INFORMATION CONTACTS:

Regional or Local Office:
Not applicable.

Headquarters Office:

SMALL *CFDA* ENTRY *(continued)*

EXHIBIT 11.7

U.S. Department of Education, OESE Academic Improvement and Teacher Quality Programs, 400 Maryland, Ave. S.W., Washington, DC 20202-6100. Contact: Irene B. Harwarth. E-mail Address irene.harwarth@ed.gov Telephone: (202)401-3751.

Web Site Address:
http://www.ed.gov/programs/lsl/index.html.

RELATED PROGRAMS:
None.

EXAMPLES OF FUNDED PROJECTS:
Approximately 50 percent of the funds are being used to improve collections. The projects are operating in approximately 580 schools serving 236,000 students. Two-thirds of the schools served are at the elementary level, the remaining third are split between middle and high schools. Projects funded in 2002 range from supporting a districtwide library revitalization project in elementary schools in Baltimore, Md.; developing a full-service school library in rural Minnewaukan, N.D.; and implementing a technology-based reading program in Madill, Okla.

CRITERIA FOR SELECTING PROPOSALS:
Selection criteria are contained in the program guidelines. Contact the program office for more information.

General Services Administration
Office of Chief Acquisition Officer
Regulatory and Federal Assistance Division (VIR)

Sample *CFDA* Entry *(continued)*

EXHIBIT 11.7

99

Uses and Use Restrictions: Compare your project to this description of eligible projects.

Eligibility Requirements: Be sure your organization is designated as a legal recipient. If it is not, find an organization of the type designated and apply as a consortium or under a cooperative arrangement. Determine whether your project can benefit those that the program is intended to benefit.

Application and Award Process: Review this information and record it on your federal grants research form. Do not let the deadline data bother you. If the award cycle has passed, you should still contact the agency and position yourself for the following year by asking for copies of old applications and a list of current grantees and by requesting to be a reviewer.

Assistance Considerations: Record any information on any match you are required to provide. This will be useful in evaluating funding sources. Matching requirements may eliminate some funding sources from your consideration. In addition, assistance considerations will help you develop your project planner (see chapter 13). When you know about matching requirements in advance, you can identify what resources your organization will be required to provide. Watch for confusing comments such as, "a match is not required, but is advised."

Post Assistance Requirements: This section provides you with report, audit, and record requirements.

Financial Information: This section gives you an idea of what funds the agency program may have received, but do not take the information here as the last word. One entry I reviewed said the funding agency had $3 million for research. When contacted, the agency had over $30 million to disseminate under the program described and similar ones in the CFDA. Refer to the entry, but investigate it further.

Program Accomplishments: This section provides you with information on how many and what types of projects were funded in the previous fiscal year.

Regulations, Guidelines, and Literature: Record and send for any information you can get on the funder.

Information Contacts: Record and use to begin contacting funders as outlined in this book. If provided, note the name, phone number, and email address of the contact person. While the contact person, phone number, or email address may have changed, you will at least have a place to start.

Related Programs: Some *CFDA* entries include suggestions of other programs that are similar or related to your area of interest. This is like a free redefinition. While these suggestions are usually obvious, you may not have already uncovered the programs in your research. Therefore, review this section for leads.

Examples of Funded Projects: Compare your project with those listed and ask yourself how your project fits in.

Criteria for Selecting Proposals: Review and record the information here. Criteria are frequently listed with no regard to their order of importance and lack any reference to the point values they will be given in the review. Therefore, you should also obtain the rules from the *Federal Register*, the agency publication, or a past reviewer.

After reviewing the *CFDA* entries, select the best government funding program for your project. Contact the federal agency by using the information listed under "Information Contacts." Once you have found an assistance program you wish to apply for, follow the directions contained within that program. Each program is unique and has its own requirements and procedures. Unlike Grants.gov, you cannot apply for an assistance program on the *CFDA* web site.

When researching federal grant opportunities it is necessary to search via both Grants.gov and the *CFDA*. These valuable resources use different keywords (search terms). In addition, they sometimes categorize granting opportunities differently. For example, when searching under "children and obesity," Grants.gov provides you with one all encompassing grant, Grants.gov funding number PA-06-256, NIH Exploratory/Development Clinical Research Grants In Obesity (R21), and then refers you in the synopsis to specific grants within the larger funding opportunity—CFDA 93.393 Cancer Cause and Prevention Research, CFDA 93.837 Heart and Vascular Diseases Prevention, and CFDA 93.949 Digestive Diseases and Nutrition Research. When searching under the same terms in the *CFDA*, you are automatically directed to CFDA 93.937 Heart and Vascular Diseases Prevention.

It is also necessary to look at both Grants.gov and the *CFDA* when searching for funding in the scientific fields. Again, funding opportunities are often categorized under different search terms. For example, when looking for grants in geophysics, one tool may list opportunities under the search term "geophysics," while the other may list geophysics opportunities under the search term "physics" and show no results under "geophysics."

Federal Register

The *Federal Register* is the official daily publication for rules, proposed rules, and notices of federal agencies and organizations, as well as exclusive orders and other presidential documents. Frequently requested materials from the *Federal Register* include grant information. However, not all funding agencies use the *Federal Register* as their public information vehicle. For instance, the National Science Foundation (NSF) and the National Institutes of Health (NIH) use their own agency publications to announce grant opportunities, program rules, and notices.

The *Register* can be accessed for free though the Internet at http://www.gpoaccess.gov/fr/index.html. A hard copy of this government publication is provided for free public use in federal depository libraries throughout the United States. Locate your nearest library by visiting http://www.gpoaccess.gov/libraries.html.

After you have used Grants.gov and/or the *CFDA* to select the best government funding program for your project, phone, fax, or email the contact listed in the synopsis and/or entry to find out what vehicle the funding agency uses to post legal notices regarding its grant programs. If it is the *Federal Register*, find out the day(s) the *Federal Register* published notices, proposed rules, and/or final rules and regulations regarding the program you are interested in. Ask for the volume(s), the number(s), the issue date(s), and the page(s). The more information you have, the easier it will be for you to locate the information for which you are looking.

When accessing the *Federal Register* through the Internet, you can search online for the information you need. In the sample search shown in exhibit 11.8, the grantseeker asked to search the February 16, 2007 *Federal Register* for notices on page 7630. Search results are shown in exhibit 11.9. By clicking on the first hit listed on the search results, the grantseeker retrieved the notice inviting applications for new awards for fiscal year 2007 under the Improving Literacy Through School Libraries Program CFDA No. 84.364A (see exhibit 11.10). The sample provided in exhibit 11.10 shows only pages 1 through 3 of this ten-page notice. The notice in its entirety provides a full text of the announcement, including a funding opportunity description, award information, eligibility information, application and submission information, application review information, award administration information, agency contact information, and other miscellaneous information. However, contents of notices do vary.

As you can see in exhibit 11.8, Notices is not the only section of the *Federal Register* that can be searched. Grantseekers can also look at Contents and Preliminary Pages, Final Rules and Regulations, Proposed Rules, Presidential Documents, Sunshine Act Meetings, Reader Aids, and Corrections.

FedBizOpps

Issued by the U.S. Government Printing Office and published on the web by Community of Science, FedBizOpps (FBO) lists notices of proposed government procurement actions, contract awards, sales of government property, and other procurement information over $25,000—all updated daily. Thousands of separate contracting offices and countless grant programs advertise billions in

GPO Access

Resources by Topic [Go]   Site Search advanced [Go]

LEGISLATIVE / EXECUTIVE / JUDICIAL / HELP / ABOUT

A-Z RESOURCE LIST | FIND A FEDERAL DEPOSITORY LIBRARY | BUY PUBLICATIONS

Home Page > Executive Branch > Federal Register > Advanced Search

Federal Register: Advanced Search

DATABASE FEATURES
- FR Main Page
- Browse
- Simple Search
- Advanced Search
- Retrieve an FR Page
- Search Tips
- About the FR

RELATED RESOURCES
- Regulations.gov
- Unified Agenda
- Code of Federal Regulations
- e-CFR
- List of CFR Sections Affected
- Search all Regulatory Applications
- All NARA Publications

ABOUT GOVERNMENT
Ben's Guide to U.S. Government

Get Acrobat Reader

Select a Volume(s):

☑ 2007 FR, Vol. 72	☐ 2002 FR, Vol. 67	☐ 1997 FR, Vol. 62
☐ 2006 FR, Vol. 71	☐ 2001 FR, Vol. 66	☐ 1996 FR, Vol. 61
☐ 2005 FR, Vol. 70	☐ 2000 FR, Vol. 65	☐ 1995 FR, Vol. 60
☐ 2004 FR, Vol. 69	☐ 1999 FR, Vol. 64	
☐ 2003 FR, Vol. 68	☐ 1998 FR, Vol. 63	

Select a Section(s): (if desired)

☐ Contents and Preliminary Pages	☑ Notices	☐ Reader Aids
☐ Final Rules and Regulations	☐ Presidential Documents	☐ Corrections
☐ Proposed Rules	☐ Sunshine Act Meetings (before 3/1/1996)	

Search by Issue Date: (if desired)

- Date Range (mm/dd/yyyy): From _____ to _____
- Specific Date (mm/dd/yyyy): ● ON ○ BEFORE ○ AFTER 02/16/2007

Search: "page 7630"   [Search Tips]

Maximum Records Returned: 50

- The FR citation 60 FR 12345 refers to page 12345. To search by page, enter "page 12345" (in quotes) in the search terms box. FR pages start with page 1 with the first issue and continue sequentially until the end of the calendar year.
- To search by CFR citation, enter (in quotes) the title, the words *CFR* and *part*, and the part number. For example: "40 CFR part 55".
- To narrow a search, use the Boolean operators ADJ (adjacent), AND, OR and NOT. For example: "environmental protection agency" AND superfund.
- To find variations on words, truncation can be used. For example: legislat* will retrieve both legislation and legislative.

SEARCHING THE *FEDERAL REGISTER* ONLINE

EXHIBIT 11.8

government contracts each year through FBO. These contracts may total hundreds of billions and are in addition to the $400 billion cited in Grants.gov.

Many successful nonprofit organizations have used the list of successful bidders to develop subcontracts and form consortia that work with the successful bidder to perform some aspect of the contract cost effectively. In the process they develop a track record of successful performance that will provide the basis for their own successful bid in the future. Through subcontracts and consortia, these organizations are able to build a track record and gain familiarity with both the contracts process and federal contract offices. The FBO also advertises notices of meetings that assist bidders in developing insight into upcoming contracts. FedBizOpps is available online, free of charge, at http://www.fedbizopps.gov/.

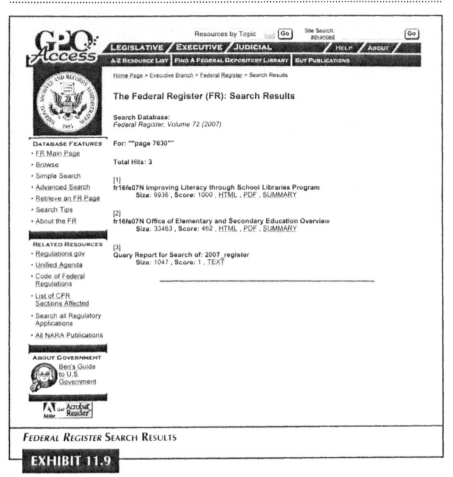

FEDERAL REGISTER SEARCH RESULTS

EXHIBIT 11.9

GRANTS DATABASES
GrantSelect

GrantSelect is an online grants database that provides information on more than 10,000 funding opportunities available from state and federal governments, corporations, foundations, and associations. Grantseekers can subscribe to the entire research grants database or to any one of the ten customized segments offered: arts and humanities, biomedical and health care, children and youth, community development, pre-K–12th grade and adult education, international programs, operating grants, faith-based grants, scholarships and fellowships, and special populations. For an additional fee, GrantSelect offers an email alerts service that will notify you immediately of new or changed records in its

---

[Federal Register: February 16, 2007 (Volume 72, Number 32)]
[Notices]
[Page 7630-7634]
From the Federal Register Online via GPO Access [wais.access.gpo.gov]
[DOCID:fr16fe07-65]

DEPARTMENT OF EDUCATION

Office of Elementary and Secondary Education Overview
Information; Improving Literacy Through School Libraries Program;
Notice Inviting Applications for New Awards for Fiscal Year (FY) 2007

Catalog of Federal Domestic Assistance (CFDA) Number: 84.364A.

DATES: Applications Available: February 16, 2007.
    Deadline for Transmittal of Applications: April 2, 2007.
    Deadline for Intergovernmental Review: June 1, 2007.
    Eligible Applicants: Local educational agencies (LEAs) in which at
least 20 percent of the students served by the LEA are from families
with incomes below the poverty line based on the most recent
satisfactory data available from the U.S. Census Bureau at the time
this notice is published. These data are Small Area Income and Poverty
Estimates for school districts for income year 2004. A list of LEAs
with their family poverty rates (based on these Census Bureau data) is
posted on our Web site at: http://www.ed.gov/programs/lsl/eligibility.html
.

    Estimated Available Funds: The Administration has requested
$19,486,000 for this program for FY 2007. The actual level of funding,
if any, depends on final congressional action. However, we are inviting
applications to allow enough time to complete the grant process if
Congress appropriates funds for this program. Contingent upon the
availability of funds and quality of applications, the Secretary may
make additional awards in FY 2008 from the list of unfunded applicants
from this competition.
    Estimated Range of Awards: $30,000--$300,000.

    Note: Actual award amounts will be based on the number of
schools and students served by the project.

    Estimated Average Size of Awards: $190,000.
    Estimated Number of Awards: 100.

    Note: The Department is not bound by any estimates in this
notice.

    Project Period: Up to 12 months.

Full Text of Announcement

I. Funding Opportunity Description

    Purpose of Program: The purpose of this program is to improve
student reading skills and academic achievement by providing students
with increased access to up-to-date school library materials; well-
equipped, technologically advanced school library media centers; and
well-trained, professionally certified school library media
specialists.

SAMPLE *FEDERAL REGISTER* NOTICE

EXHIBIT 11.10

database. For further information you may call GrantSelect at (812) 988-6400. Pricing information is also available on its web site at http://grantselect.com/. For questions on registration, pricing, and information for consortia, use sales@grantselect.com. For questions about the content of GrantSelect, use louschafer@grantselect.com.

Priority: This priority is from the notice of final priority for
this program, published elsewhere in this issue of the Federal
Register.
Competitive Preference Priority: For FY 2007, and any subsequent
year in which we make awards based on the lists of unfunded
applications from this competition, this priority is a competitive
preference priority. Under 34 CFR 75.105(c)(2)(i) we award up to an
additional 5 points to an application, depending on how well the
application meets this priority.
Under this priority, we give priority to projects that demonstrate
in their grant applications that the proposed literacy project services
are comprehensive and aligned with a school or district improvement
plan. A school improvement plan may include the required two-year plan
(under section 1116(b)(3) of the Elementary and Secondary Education Act
of 1965, as amended by the No Child Left Behind Act of 2001) that
addresses the academic issues that caused a school to be identified as
in need of improvement. The plan could also include a voluntary plan
developed by the school or district to improve academic achievement.
The applicant must clearly describe the improvement plan that is in
place, whether it is for the school or the entire district, the reasons
why the plan was put in place, and how the proposed project and the
operation of the school library media center will directly support the
academic goals established in the improvement plan.

Program Authority: 20 U.S.C. 6383.

Applicable Regulations: (a) The Education Department General
Administrative Regulations (EDGAR) in 34 CFR parts 75, 77, 79, 80, 81,
82, 84, 85, 97, 98, and 99. (b) The notice of final clarification of
eligible local activities, published in the Federal Register on April
5, 2004 (69 FR 17894). (c) The notice of final priority, published
elsewhere in this issue of the Federal Register.

II. Award Information

Type of Award: Discretionary grants.
Estimated Available Funds: The Administration has requested
$19,486,000 for this program for FY 2007. The actual level of funding,
if any, depends on final congressional action. However, we are inviting
applications now to allow enough time to complete the grant process if
Congress appropriates funds for this program. Contingent upon the
availability of

[[Page 7631]]

funds and quality of applications, the Secretary may make additional
awards in FY 2008 from the list of unfunded applicants from this
competition.
Estimated Range of Awards: $30,000-$300,000.

Note: Actual award amounts will be based on the number of
schools and students served by the project.

Estimated Average Size of Awards: $190,000.
Estimated Number of Awards: 100.

Note: The Department is not bound by any estimates in this
notice.

Project Period: Up to 12 months.

III. Eligibility Information

SAMPLE FEDERAL REGISTER NOTICE *(continued)*

EXHIBIT 11.10

BIG Online

BIG Online is the flagship product of Metasoft Systems Inc., a private corporation headquartered in Vancouver, British Columbia. It is a membership-based keyword and field searchable database with detailed information and profiles

1. Eligible Applicants: LEAs in which at least 20 percent of the
students served by the LEA are from families with incomes below the
poverty line based on the most recent satisfactory data available from
the U.S. Census Bureau at the time this notice is published. These data
are Small Area Income and Poverty Estimates for school districts for
income year 2004. A list of LEAs with their family poverty rates (based
on these Census Bureau data) is posted on our Web site at: http://www.ed.gov/programs/ls
.

2. Cost Sharing or Matching: This program does not involve cost
sharing or matching but does involve supplement-not-supplant funding
provisions. Funds made available under this program must be used to
supplement, and not supplant, other Federal, State, and local funds
expended to carry out activities relating to library, technology, or
professional development activities (20 U.S.C. 6383(i)).

IV. Application and Submission Information

1. Address To Request Application Package: You may obtain an
application package via the Internet or from the Education Publications
Center (ED Pubs). To obtain a copy via the Internet use the following
addresses: http://www.grants.gov or http://www.ed.gov/programs/lsl/applicant.html.
To obtain a copy from ED Pubs, write or call the
he
(toll free): 1-877-433-7827. FAX: (301) 470-1244. If you use a
telecommunications device for the deaf (TDD), you may call (toll free):
1-877-576-7734.
You may also contact ED Pubs at its Web site: http://www.ed.gov/pubs/edpubs.html
or you may contact ED Pubs at its e-mail address: edpubs@inet.ed.gov.

If you request an application from ED Pubs, be sure to identify
this competition as follows: CFDA number 84.364A.
Individuals with disabilities may obtain a copy of the application
package in an alternative format (e.g., Braille, large print,
audiotape, or computer diskette) by contacting the program contact
person listed under section VII of this notice.
2. Content and Form of Application Submission: Requirements
concerning the content of an application, together with the forms you
must submit, are in the application package for this program. An
Eligibility Form is included in the application package. You must fill
out the Eligibility Form, following the instructions provided in the
application package.
Page Limit: The application narrative (Part III of the application)
is where you, the applicant, address the selection criteria that
reviewers use to evaluate your application. You must limit Part III to
the equivalent of no more than 15 pages, using the following standards:
A ``**page**'' is 8.5'' x 11''; on one side only, with 1''
margins at the top, bottom, and both sides.
Double space (no more than three lines per vertical inch)
all text in the application narrative, including titles, headings,
footnotes, quotations, references, and captions, as well as all text in
charts, tables, figures, and graphs.
Use a font that is either 12 point or larger or no smaller
than 10 pitch (characters per inch).
The **page** limit does not apply to Part I, the cover sheet; Part II,
budget section, including the narrative budget justification; Part VI,
the assurances and certifications; or the one-**page** abstract, the
resumes, the bibliography, or the letters of support. However, you must
include all of the application narrative in Part III. Charter schools
and State administered schools must include some form of documentation
from their State educational agency (SEA) confirming eligibility for

SAMPLE FEDERAL REGISTER NOTICE *(continued)*

EXHIBIT 11.10

on 25,000 American and Canadian foundations, corporate donors, matching gift
programs, in-kind donations, and government grant makers. For membership
information or to take a free online tour of BIG Online, call (888) 638-2763
or email info@bigdatabase.com.

Sponsored Programs Information Network (SPIN)

SPIN is a computerized database produced by Infoed International, Inc. Originally developed by the Research Foundation of the State University of New York (SUNY), the database contains profiles on national and international government and private funding sources, including fellowships, research grants, publication support, sabbatical support, curriculum development, and more. Funding programs are summarized in abstracts and links are provided to the detail. The database is searchable using SPIN keywords, sponsor name(s), award type(s), applicant type(s), geographic region, and/or deadline date/date ranges. SPINPlus is also available. It is a web-based subscription package that bundles SPIN, the funding opportunities database with GENIUS, a CV/bio-sketch database, and SMARTS, an automated alerts system that matches investigators with grant and contract announcements based on their user profiles. More than 600 institutions worldwide subscribe to SPINPlus. You can reach InfoEd International by calling (800) 727-6427 or find out more about its products by visiting http://www.infoed.org/.

Illinois Researcher Information Service (IRIS)

IRIS, a unit of the University of Illinois Library at Urbana-Champaign, offers colleges and universities three fee-based online funding and research services:

- the IRIS Database, which is updated daily, contains over 9,000 federal and private funding opportunities in the sciences, social sciences, arts, and humanities. In addition to funding opportunities for faculty, the database also contains fellowships and scholarships for graduate students and undergraduates. Users can search IRIS by sponsor, deadline date, keyword, and other criteria.

- the IRIS Alert Service, which allows subscribers to create their own IRIS search profiles and select their preferred search frequency, delivery method (email or web), and keywords. The program runs the user's profile against the IRIS database and delivers the search results automatically.

- the IRIS Expertise Service, which enables researchers at subscribing institutions to create detailed electronic CVs ("biosketches") and post them to a web-accessible database for viewing by colleagues at other institutions, program officers at federal and private funding agencies, and private companies. The biosketches can also be used in the electronic submission of grant proposals.

The IRIS office does not sell subscriptions to individual researchers. Subscriptions are available to colleges and universities for an annual subscription fee. You can try IRIS for one month free by having a representative from your institution, such as your librarian, research officer, grants administrator, and so forth contact the IRIS office at (217) 333-9893. For more information about IRIS and IRIS subscriptions, visit http://www.library.uiuc.edu/iris/.

Community of Science (COS)

Community of Science (COS) is a global registry of information about scientists and the funding of science and is designed to meet the needs of the research and development community. The COS system includes the following:

- COS *Funding Opportunities*—a database of announcements for grants, fellowships, awards, and more, comprising more than 22,000 records worth over $33 billion.

- COS *Funding Alert*—a weekly email notification with a customized listing of funding opportunities based on specified criteria provided by the user.

- COS *Expertise*—a database containing more than 480,000 first-person profiles of researchers from over 1,600 institutions worldwide. (COS users, including researchers, scholars, and other professionals with expertise in their fields, have the opportunity to create COS profiles to showcase and share their research and expertise among researchers and scholars from universities, corporations, and nonprofits in more than 170 countries.)

COS *Funding Opportunities* is included as part of a full COS membership, but may also be purchased as a stand-alone information resource. There are two types of subscription plans—small business and institutional. Subscription plans are not available for individuals. For more information and subscription rates, visit http://www.cos.com/.

For smaller nonprofits and individuals, I suggest you involve university faculty and staff on your advisory committee, and ask them to access COS and other grants-related resources for you.

FEDERAL AGENCY INTERNET MAILING LISTS

Several federal agencies have established Internet mailing lists to electronically disseminate news about their activities and services. You can subscribe to these LISTSERVS to help keep up-to-date on federal funding opportunities. Following is a list of some of the federal agencies that provide this type of service:

- National Science Foundation—MyNSF, formerly the Custom News Service, allows you to receive email notifications about new content posted on the NSF web site. You can subscribe for MyNSF on NSF's home page at http://www.nsf.gov/.

- National Institutes of Health—National Institutes of Health will automatically email subscribers the Table of Contents (TOC) information for each week's issue of the NIH Guide for Grants and Contracts. Associated with each TOC entry is the web address (URL) for each Guide article. To subscribe to the Guide TOC Notification LISTSERV, send an email to listserv@list.nih.gov and, in the first line of the email message, not the subject line, provide the following information: subscribe NIHTOC-L *your name*. Your email address will be automatically obtained from the email message you send to the LISTSERV.

- Centers for Disease Control and Prevention (CDC)—At the Centers for Disease Control and Prevention, you can subscribe to several mailing lists. For a list of available mailing lists, and to subscribe, go to http://www.cdc.gov/subscribe.html.

- U.S. Department of Justice—JustInfo, sponsored by the U.S. Department of Justice National Criminal Justice Reference Service (NCJRS), is an electronic newsletter sent to subscribers on the first and fifteenth of each month highlighting agency initiatives, new publications, funding and training opportunities, conferences, and other news from NCJRS sponsoring agencies. View previous issues and subscribe at http://www.ncjrs.org/justinfo/dates.html/.

- U.S. Department of Education (DOE)—The Department of Education offers subscriptions to electronic mailing lists for several of its newsletters, including the following:

  - The Achiever—a community newsletter highlighting model schools and resources for improving learning. By subscribing to this newsletter you will also be put on the No Child Left Behind Mailing List and receive up-to-date information, events, and announcements concerning this program.

  - EDInfo—provides one to two email messages a week describing federal teaching and learning resources and ED funding opportunities.

  - ED Review—a biweekly update on DOE's activities relevant to the intergovernmental and corporate community and other stakeholders.

  - Education Innovator—promising innovations in education.

  - ED RSS—daily feed of ED news, funding, and teaching resources.

  - IESNEWS—offered by the Institute of Education Services for those interested in education research, evaluation, and statistics. Provides the latest information on funding and training opportunities, IES-sponsored research, news publications, and education facts and figures from the National Center for Education Statistics.

  - Education Statistics Quarterly—overview of products released each quarter by the National Center for Education Statistics.

- Teacher Updates—information and opportunities for teachers.
- PreventionEd—updates on substance abuse and violence prevention education issues, legislation, and funding opportunities.

For links to these newsletters and instructions on how to subscribe to their electronic mailing lists, visit http://www.ed.gov/news/newsletters/index.html.

- National Institute for Standards and Technology (NIST) provides NIST news releases and the NIST Tech Beat newsletter in an electronic format. NIST Tech Beat is a newsletter containing recent research results and other NIST news and is published biweekly. To subscribe to electronic news releases and/or the newsletter, go to http://www.nist.gov/public_affairs/mailform.htm.

Accessing the information you need to locate available government funding is not difficult or expensive. Whether you use the Internet, a commercial database, or hard copies of government publications, the key to locating federal grant funds and to commanding the respect of the bureaucrats you will interact with in your quest for grants is to do your homework and learn all you can about each program you are thinking about approaching.

CHAPTER 12

How to Contact Government Grant Sources

A t this point, you have researched a potential federal grant opportunity, but you may not be convinced of the importance of preproposal contact with a federal program officer, especially if you have bookmarked the program's web site, registered, and already have its application form and guidelines. Like many other prospective grantseekers, you probably do not want or see the need to talk to government bureaucrats. You just want to get your proposal submitted. However, you should remember that your goal is not to *apply* for a grant; it is to be *awarded* a grant. Therein lies the reason for making preproposal contact. In fact, after 30 years in the grants field, I can assure you that principal investigators and project directors who are consistently funded across the board, from health research to humanities, actually contact government grantors several times a year, and not just during the preproposal period.

Several years before the first edition of this book was created, a study of 10,000 federal grant applicants documented that those grantseekers who had made contact with federal program staff before submitting their applications experienced a threefold increase in success over those who simply submitted the application. The key to their success was the opportunity to ask questions that may not have been covered in *Catalog of Federal Domestic Assistance* (CFDA) program descriptions or agency publications.

When asked what the successful grantees discussed with the federal program officers, many said they asked questions that helped them to more closely meet the program guidelines. While this was the most frequent response, I believe they really asked questions aimed at uncovering what the program was actually interested in funding.

You can meet with program officers at conferences and professional meetings, as well as in their offices. Ask them what conferences are on their calendars and if they are speaking on any panels. Go to their presentations and ask if you could have a few minutes alone with them to ask questions. Some agencies have regional meetings that may be less expensive for you to attend. No harm can come from asking, only good!

When contacting a program officer make no mistake about your intention. It is to confirm your research and provide a more complete picture of what the grant program seeks to create and fund in your field. Your contact is professional, not personal. Even if you have very limited resources and no money for travel, do not be frustrated. While the study of 10,000 federal grantees was done years before email was possible, it revealed no differences between telephone and face-to-face contact. The crucial point is that while you have done your homework, you need to make preproposal contact to confirm what you do know and to find out more about the projects funded, how the submitted proposals will be evaluated, and by whom in order to prepare a winning proposal.

WHEN TO MAKE PREPROPOSAL CONTACT

The timing of contact is critical. Each of the 1,000-plus federal programs has a unique sequence of events related to its granting cycle. Review the diagram of the federal grants clock to help you determine where a particular federal agency program is in the grants process (see figure 12.1, the Federal Grants Clock).

The federal grants clock can be thought of as a five-step cycle or process.

1. The first step involves the dissemination of and comment on the rules and regulations governing each program to be reviewed, and comments are encouraged from any interested party. The comments are published, the final rules are printed, and the announcements of deadlines are made in such publications as the *Federal Register, NIH Guide,* and *National Science Foundation E-Bulletin.*
2. The federal program officer then develops the actual application package and places it on the agency's web site for public access. This package is referred to as the Request for Proposal or the Request for Application.
3. The deadline for submissions is published.
4. Once proposals have been submitted through Grants.gov they are forwarded to selected peer reviewers for evaluation. In some cases, the reviewers are required to go to a specified site to receive and review the proposals. In other cases, they can review them at home. The reviewers must follow the agency's evaluation system and score each proposal according to the published guidelines. There is usually a staff review that

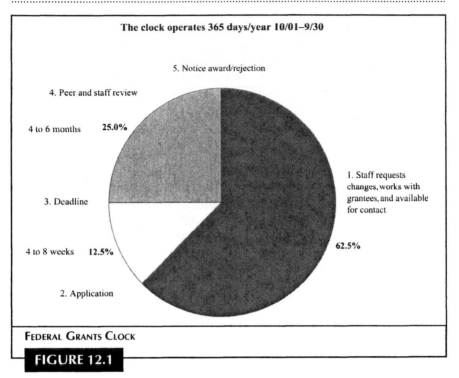

FEDERAL GRANTS CLOCK

FIGURE 12.1

follows the peer review. In all cases, the staff reviewers provide the head of the agency with a list of proposals recommended for funding.

5. The notices of award and rejection are made and the cycle starts again. Some federal programs with multiple deadlines repeat the process in four- and six-month cycles.

Establishing preproposal contact for the next funding cycle is most productive when initiated after the notices of award or rejection have been given (step 5) for the previous cycle and before the application packages are made available (step 2) in the new cycle. Use the techniques outlined in this chapter to maximize the benefits of preproposal contact and gain the insight you will need to prepare a grant-winning proposal.

GETTING THE MOST FROM PAST GRANTEES

You will find it beneficial to discover who has previously received funding by the program that interests you. In many cases you can locate a list of past grantees on the agency's web site, or you can use the sample email in exhibit 12.1 to request a list. Email the contact person identified in your research or the program

---

From:	<grantseeker@proactive.edu>
To:	<contact person@feds.gov>
Cc:	
Sent:	date, time
Subject:	RE: Information Request

Dear [Contact Person]:

I am interested in receiving information on [*CFDA #*, Program Title]. Please email relevant web site information and Internet addresses for application forms, guidelines, etc.

In order to increase my understanding of your program, I would also appreciate a list of last year's grant recipients. If this list is available on the Internet please provide the address. If it is not, please email the list to me as an attachment.

Thank you for your assistance.

Name
Title
Organization/Institution
Address
Telephone Number

SAMPLE EMAIL TO A FEDERAL AGENCY REQUESTING INFORMATION AND GUIDELINES

EXHIBIT 12.1

announcement. You may have to request the list of past grantees again by phoning the contact person. If you get his or her phone mail, leave a message on what you want and leave your phone number and your email address. Access to this list and the valuable information it provides is your right. If you do not receive a response to your initial request, request the list again, making sure to let the funding source know why you want it and also that you are aware that you are entitled to this list under the Freedom of Information Act. If all else fails, you may be able to get this information from the pubic information office of the agency, or you can ask your congressperson to get the list for you. By law, federal bureaucrats have to respond to a congressperson's request. He or she *will* get the list. Be aware, though, that bureaucrats may react negatively to the intervention of elected officials. Therefore, you should ask the elected official not to reveal for whom he or she is getting the list.

Several databases provide grantee information. For example, the *COS (Community of Science)* provides abstracts of grantees' proposals.

With your past grantee list in hand, you are now ready to begin the analysis of your chances for success. Complete the past grantee analysis worksheet (exhibit 12.2) and analyze the information contained in the list of grantees. When this worksheet is completed, you will be able to approach the grantor with knowledge and insight into its granting program.

1. Applications
   - How many applications were received? _____
   - How many applications were funded? _____

2. Award Size
   - What was the largest award granted? _____
     For what type of project? _____
     For how many years? _____
   - What was the smallest award granted? _____
     For what type of project? _____
     For how many years? _____

3. Grantor Type
   - What characteristics or similarities can be drawn from last year's list of grant recipients?

   - What is the size and type of grantee organization (i.e., public, private, college)?

   - What are the geographic preferences or concentrations?

4. Project Director/Principal Investigator
   - What title or degrees appear most frequently on the list of last year's recipients?

   - Does there seem to be a relationship between award size and project director degree?

5. From the list of last year's grantees, select two to contact for more information. Select grantees that you may have a link with and/or organizations that you are familiar with.

6. Based on the information gathered in questions 1–4, rate how well your Proposal idea matches the prospective grantor's profile.

   __ very well   __ good   __ fair   __ not well

7. What programs can you now ask the program officer/contact person about as a result of your analysis?

PAST GRANTEE ANALYSIS WORKSHEET

EXHIBIT 12.2

Contacting a Past Grantee

Successful grant recipients can be approached and will generally share helpful information with you. Grantees will generally feel flattered that you called. They are usually not competing with you for funds because you will be seeking first-year funding and they will be seeking a continuation grant. Select a past grantee to call. Choose one outside of your geographic area and one who is less likely to view you as a competitor. If you have a colleague at that grantee institution, contact him or her to help you connect with the principal investigator/project director. Tell the grantee how you got his or her name, congratulate him or her on the award, and then ask to speak to the person who worked on the proposal.

Select questions from the following list to ask the person who worked on the proposal, or ask any other questions that will help you learn more about the funding source:

- Did you call or go to see the funding source before writing the proposal?
- Whom did you find most helpful on the funding source's staff?
- Did you use your advocates or congressperson?
- Did the funding source review your idea or proposal before submission?
- Did you use consultants to help you on the proposal?
- Was there a hidden agenda to the program's guidelines?
- When did you begin the process of developing your application?
- When did you first contact the funding source?
- What materials did you find most helpful in developing your proposal?
- Did the funding source come to see you (site visit) before or after the proposal was awarded? Who came? What did they wear? How old were they? Would you characterize them as conservative, moderate, or liberal? Did anything surprise you during their visit?
- How close was your initial budget to the awarded amount?
- Who on the funding source's staff negotiated the budget?
- How did you handle matching or in-kind contributions?
- What would you do differently next time?

UNDERSTANDING THE PROPOSAL REVIEW PROCESS

To prepare the best possible proposal, you must know the background of who will be reviewing it and how it will be reviewed. Request information on the review process from the federal program officer. This can be done in writing, by phone, by email, or in person. I suggest sending an email and then following up with the other methods if necessary. Exhibit 12.3 provides a sample email you may use.

You want a profile of last year's reviewers or criteria related to what the grantor looks for in a reviewer so you can write a proposal based on the reviewers' expertise, reading level, background, and so forth. Once you have this information, ask the program officer if you can contact a reviewer to discuss the review process. Inform the program officer that the information you gather from this contact will help you perform a mock review of your proposal before submitting

From: \<grantseeker@proactive.edu\>
To: \<contactperson@feds.gov\>
Cc:
Sent: date, time
Subject: RE: Request for List of Reviewers

Dear [Contact Person]:

I am presently developing a proposal under your _____ program. I would find it very
helpful if you could email or send me a list of last year's reviewers, or the name and the e mail
address or phone number of a reviewer I could contact to more fully understand the process
from the reviewer's point of view.

I would also like information on the composition of your program's peer reviewers and the
areas of expertise represented on the review committee. This information will help me
prepare a quality proposal based upon the level, expertise, and diversity of the reviewers.

Information on the scoring rubric and process would also be helpful in that it would help me
perform a mock review of my proposal before submittal.

The information you provide will be appreciated and will help me produce a quality proposal.

Name
Title
Organization/Institution
Address
Phone Number
Fax Number

SAMPLE EMAIL TO A FEDERAL AGENCY FOR A LIST OF REVIEWERS

EXHIBIT 12.3

it. Remember, they like receiving quality proposals and working with grantseekers who are proactive.

Preferably you can get the program official to identify whom he or she
believes to be one of the program's best reviewers. Then you can contact them
for more specific information on the scoring system, how much time they spend
reading each proposal, how many proposals they have to read, and so on.

Some federal programs use the same reviewers each year and may be reluctant
to give you any names. If this is the case, tell the federal bureaucrat that you
would like to know at least the general background and credentials of the
reviewers so that you can prepare the best possible proposal by writing toward
their level. You would ultimately like to know the types of organizations the
reviewers come from, their titles and degrees, and, if possible, the selection criteria for choosing them. This is a good opportunity to make your interest in
becoming a reviewer known to the program officer. Whether the reviewers meet

in Washington, D.C., or review proposals at home or work, you would learn a great deal about the evaluation process and the grantor by being a member of a peer-review committee. Many programs will accept a reviewer as a learning experience. So, ask!

You may also ask colleagues or your grants office for the name, email address, and/or phone number of a past reviewer. If you know any of the awarded grantees, contact them since programs frequently use past grantees as reviewers.

If the system that the reviewers must adhere to has been published in the *Federal Register* or an agency publication, request a copy or the date of publication. Again, let the funding source know that you will be using a quality circle (see chapter 14) to perform a mock review of your proposal before submission and that you would like to mirror the actual review process as closely as possible. Request a copy of their reviewer training materials or the scoring system that was used.

Contacting a Past Reviewer

When calling a past reviewer, explain that you understand he or she was a reviewer for the program you are interested in and that you would like to ask a few questions about his or her experience as a reviewer for the program. Select a few questions to ask from the following list, or make up your own:

- How did you get to be a reviewer?
- Did you review proposals at a funding source location or at home?
- What training or instruction did the funding source give you?
- Did you follow a point system? What system? How did you follow it? What were you told to look for?
- How would you write a proposal differently now that you have been a reviewer?
- What were the most common mistakes you saw?
- Did you meet other reviewers?
- How many proposals were you given to read?
- How much time did you have to read them?
- How did the funding source handle discrepancies in point assignments?
- What did the staff members of the funding source wear, say, and do during the review process?
- Did a staff review follow your review?

TELEPHONING AND EMAILING FEDERAL AND STATE FUNDING SOURCES

Contacting public funding sources is an experience in itself. Your initial research should yield a contact name, email address, phone number, and fax number.

Because of personnel changes and reassignments the contact listed may not be the best person to assist you. However, he or she should be able to tell you who at the agency or program could best answer your questions. You can also check the agency's/program's web site to make sure your contact information is current. If your research does not yield the information you need, you could use the *United States Government Manual* (see list of resources) to track down the phone number and/or email address of the office likely to handle the funds you are seeking.

After you have identified the appropriate program officer, my first choice is to go to see him or her in person. However, if this is not possible, I recommend a combination of phone and email contact. The purpose of this contact is twofold.

1. You want to confirm the validity of the program information you have and ask intelligent questions that demonstrate your understanding of the program's grants system while eliciting information that will assist you in developing your proposal. You also want to gather any information you need to complete your past grantee analysis worksheet (exhibit 12.2).
2. You want to position yourself and your institution or organization as thorough and capable.

Demonstrate that you have done your homework (research) and know about the program, and then ask a question or make a request to further your knowledge of the grant opportunity. For example, if you are requesting information on matching funds, state what you know from your research, and then ask your question. Do not ask what the matching requirements are when you already uncovered this information in Grants.gov, the CFDA, or a program announcement. Instead, let the program officer know, for example, that you are aware that a match is not *required* (if this is the case), and then ask if past applicants that ultimately became grantees volunteered to provide one anyway and, if so, what was the average size or range.

What really bothers federal program officers is when they get calls or emails from grantseekers asking what kinds of projects they are funding this year or what they are looking for this year. These are what I call flavor of the month questions and are indicative of the types of questions asked by lazy, unsophisticated grantseekers.

In addition, several federal and state program officers have told me that they are overwhelmed with questions and requests from grantseekers for information that is readily available from other sources such as the CFDA, *Federal Register*, Grants.gov, program guidelines, and so on. One way they deal with these lazy grantseekers is to ignore their email and telephone requests. One federal program officer told me that his simple solution is to never respond to a first request for information unless it is an intelligent question that demonstrates that the grantseeker has done his or her homework (research). He then went on to say that 80 percent of the prospective grantseekers he does not respond to initially do not call or email a second time. His rationale for not responding initially is how critical could the information be if the grantseeker does not even call or email back. On the up side, he stated that he always responds to a second request. So the moral of the story is select intelligent questions to ask that demonstrate your knowledge of the program, be persistent, phone first, and then follow up with an email or vice versa.

Be careful not to ask too many questions or to make several requests at one time. Determine which of your possible questions will be the most critical in helping you determine your proposal approach, and ask one or two. If you do not get a response the first time, try again. In your follow-up contact, reformat the questions, note the date of your initial request, and ask again. Let the program officer know that you respect his or her time and understand how busy he or she is, but you need to know the answers to your questions and that you will recontact him or her another time if necessary.

Once contact is made with the program officer (whether it is by phone or email) you should gather the same information as you would face-to-face. Since it may be difficult for the funding official to discuss your idea and approaches without seeing a written description of your project, ask whether you could mail, fax, or email him or her a one-page concept paper and then recontact him or her for the purpose of discussion.

Although it may be difficult for you to "read" what the funding source is really saying through phone or email contact, you must at least try to uncover any hidden agenda so that you can meet the grantor's needs and increase your chances of success. Review the list of questions in the "Questions to Ask a Program Officer" section of this chapter.

Making an Appointment with a Public Funding Source Official

The objective of seeking an appointment is to get an interview with an administrator of the program. Start by sending or emailing a letter requesting an appointment. Exhibit 12.4 provides a sample email you may use. You may not get a response to this email/letter. Its intent is to show that you mean business. Then follow the next few steps.

1. Call and ask for the program officer or information contact.
2. Record the name of whomever you speak to and ask if he or she is the correct person to contact. If he or she is not, ask who is, and how and when that person can be reached.
3. Call back. Ask whether anyone else can answer technical questions about the program. You may get an appointment with an individual whose job is to screen you, but this is still better than talking to yourself. As an alternative, try to get an advocate to help you set up an appointment, or try going

From:	\<grantseeker@proactive.edu\>
To:	\<contactperson@feds.gov\>
Cc:	
Sent:	date, time
Subject:	RE: Request for an Appointment

Dear [Contact Person]:

My research on your funding program indicates that a project we are developing would be appropriate for consideration by your agency for funding under _____.

I would appreciate 5 to 10 minutes of your time to discuss the project and how it matches your program. The development of the project has created questions that I would like to discuss with you. Your insights and knowledge will help us in our focus.

My travel plans call for me to be in your area on _____. I will phone to confirm the possibility of a brief meeting during that time to discuss this important proposal.

Name
Title
Organization/Institution
Address
Telephone Number
Fax Number

SAMPLE EMAIL TO A FEDERAL AGENCY REQUESTING AN APPOINTMENT

EXHIBIT 12.4

in cold early in the week to set up an appointment for later in the week. Do not be surprised if this results in an immediate appointment. Staff members may decide they would prefer to deal with you on the spot rather than later. Be careful using elected officials to make appointments for you or to accompany you on an appointment. Bureaucrats and politicians often do not get along well.

4. When you get the program person on the phone, introduce yourself and give a brief (ten-word) description of your project. Explain that

   - the need to deal with the specific problem your project addresses is extreme,
   - your organization is uniquely suited to deal with this problem,
   - you understand that the grantor's program deals with this need, and
   - you would like to make an appointment to talk about program priorities and your approach.

When you get an appointment, stop and hang up. If an appointment is not possible, tell the program representative that you have some questions and ask about the possibility of asking them now or arranging a ten-minute phone call for the future. Fill in any information you get (names, phone numbers, and so on) on the federal grants research form (exhibit 11.1).

VISITING PUBLIC FUNDING SOURCES

A meeting is vital to getting the input you need to prepare a proposal that is tailored to the funding source. A visit also will provide you with the opportunity to update any information you have gathered on the funding source through your research.

The objective of this preproposal visit is to find out as much as possible about the funding source and how it perceives its role in the awarding of grants. Then you can use the newly acquired information to produce a proposal that reflects sensitivity to the funding source's needs and perception of its mission. According to the theory of cognitive dissonance, the more the funding source perceives a grantseeker as different from what the funding source expects, the greater the problems with communication, agreement, and acceptance. We want the funder to love us, so we need to produce as little dissonance as possible by looking and talking as the funder thinks we should. Just remember, Washington, D.C., is one of the most conservative areas in the country for dress. By dressing accordingly, you can avoid not getting heard because your attire creates dissonance.

Plan for Your Visit

When planning for a personal visit, remember that it is better to send two people than one and that an advocate, advisory committee member, or graduate of your program has more credibility than a paid staff member. In deciding whom to send, try to match the age, interests, and other characteristics of your people with any information you have on the funding official. Before the visit, role-play your presentation with your team members and decide who will take responsibility for various parts of the presentation and what questions each will ask.

What to Take

It may be helpful to bring the following items with you on the visit:

1. Materials that help demonstrate the need for your project.
2. Your proposal development workbook (Swiss cheese book).
3. A brief video, shown on your laptop, complete with sound, that documents the problem and the unique attributes that make you a logical choice as a

grantee. The video could also summarize your approach to solving the problem, but the entire presentation should be short (no longer than three minutes) and simple. You do not need a projection system and a PowerPoint presentation unless you will be meeting with five or more grantor staff members.

4. Information on your organization that you can leave with the funding official (but never leave a proposal).

Questions to Ask a Program Officer

Review the following list of possible questions to ask a program officer:

- I have located the program application on your web site and found references to (*rules, announcements, and so on*). Are there any other sources of information I should review?

- The (*CFDA, Grants.gov, or agency publication*) lists the program funding level at (*$$$$$$*). How many awards will be made out of this amount and what will the overall, average grant size be?

- Your average award in this area last year to an organization like ours was (*$$$$$*). Do you expect that to change?

- How will successful grantees from last year affect the chances for new or first applicants? Will last year's grantees compete with new grantees, or have their funds been set aside? If their funds have been set aside, how much is left for new awards?

- Are there any unannounced program or unsolicited proposal funds in your agency to support an important project like ours?

- The required matching portion is X percent. Would it improve our chances for funding if we provided a greater portion than this?

- The program announcement states that matching funds are suggested but not mandatory. I need to give my institution/organization an idea of how much match is needed to meet the "suggested" amount. Could you provide me with a figure, or select three past grantees at random, and tell how much match they (the grantees) provided?

- If no match is required, would it help our proposal if we volunteered to cost share?

- What is the most common mistake or flaw in the proposals you receive?

- Are there any areas you would like to see addressed in a proposal that may have been overlooked by other grantees or applicants?

- We have developed several approaches to this needs area. From your vantage point, you may know whether one of our approaches has been funded, but not yet published. Could you review our concept paper and give us any guidance?

- Would you review or critique our proposal if we get it to you early?

- Would you recommend a previously funded proposal for us to read for format and style? (Remember, you are entitled to see funded proposals, but be cool.)

- What changes do you expect in type or number of awards this year (for example, fewer new awards versus continuing awards)?

- Is there a relationship between the type of project or proposal and the amount awarded? Is there a sequence or progression in the type of grant awarded? For example, do you suggest getting a consultant grant before we apply for a demonstration grant or an evaluation grant?

- We will conduct a quality circle (mock review) to improve our proposal before we submit it. Could we get more information on the review process your office will conduct? Can we get a reviewers' package including instructions, scoring information, weighting of criteria, and so on? What is the background of the reviewers? How are the reviewers selected? Could one of our team members be a reviewer? How many

---

Before each visit to a funding source, review this sheet to be sure you are taking the correct materials, advocates, and staff.

Agency Director: _____ Email _____
Program Director: _____ Email _____
Contact Person: _____ Email _____

Profile: Birth date: _____ Birthplace: _____

Education: College: _____
             Postgraduate: _____

Work Experience: _____
Military Service: _____
Service Clubs: _____
Interests/Hobbies: _____
Publications: _____

Comments: _____
_____
_____

Note: Do not ask the staff person direct questions related to these areas. Instead, record information that has been volunteered or gathered from comments or observations made in the office.

FUNDING SOURCE STAFF PROFILE

EXHIBIT 12.5

Project Title: _____

Complete a public funding source contact summary sheet each time you contact a public funding source.

Agency Name: _____

Program Officer: _____

Contacted On (Date): _____

By Whom: _____

Contacted By: ___ Letter   ___ Phone   ___ Email   ___ Personal Visit

Staff or Advocate Present: _____

Discussed:

Results:

PUBLIC FUNDING SOURCE CONTACT SUMMARY SHEET

EXHIBIT 12.6

proposals do reviewers read? How much time do they take to read and score each proposal?

Immediately after your visit, record any information you have gathered about the funder on the funding source staff profile (exhibit 12.5). Record the results of your visit on the public funding source contact summary sheet (exhibit 12.6).

MAKING YOUR DECISION TO DEVELOP A PROPOSAL

So far you have not invested a tremendous amount of time in writing your proposal. You have taken time to gather data and contact potential grantors. Now you must decide which federal grant program you will apply to.

Your best prospect is the grant program that provides the closest match between the project you want to implement and the profile you have developed of the grantor. Seldom is there a perfect fit between your project and the grantor's program, and some tailoring and changes in your program will likely add to your chances of success. Use the tailoring worksheet (exhibit 12.7) to analyze each grant or program you are interested in and to select the closest match. After reviewing your answers on the tailoring worksheet, rate your prospect.

CFDA # _____   Prospect Rating   A. Excellent
Program Title _____   B. Good
Amount Requested _____   C. Fair
Percent Match/In-kind _____

                                 Estimated Success   A. 75% +
                                                      B. 50%
                                                      C. 25%

1.   How does your grant request match with the average award size to your
     type of organization? _____
     size of organization? _____
     location of organization? _____
     proposal focus? _____

2.   What was the number of applications received versus the number of grants
     awarded in your area of interest?
     applications received: _____
     grants awarded: _____

3.   How would you rate the funding staff's interest in your concept?

     ___ very interested
     ___ interested
     ___ not interested
     ___ unknown

4.   From the information you obtained on the reviewers and the review process, what
     should your writing strategy include?

5.   Based on the information you obtained on the review process, how will points be
     distributed in the funding source's evaluation process?

          Area   Point Value
     _____   _____
     _____   _____
     _____   _____
     _____   _____
     _____   _____

TAILORING WORKSHEET

EXHIBIT 12.7

Remember that the competition (alluded to in question 1) and the award rejection ratio (alluded to in question 2) are critical to calculating your chances of
success. After careful analysis, what chance do you think you have of attracting
a grant from this prospect? A 25-percent chance? A 50-percent chance? A 75-
percent chance?

Once you are fairly sure you are going to apply to a specific federal grant program, review its advertised procedures carefully. Many federal programs request

that prospective applicants submit a letter of intent to alert them of your plan to submit a full proposal. This letter has no legal implications. In other words, you could change your mind and not apply. Its purpose is to help the granting agency estimate how many proposals it will receive, and thus how many reviewers may be required for the peer-review process that will follow submittal.

The letter of intent is considered a courtesy, and I always side with being courteous with those who control money! Those who submit the letter of intent may also be those who perform quality circles/mock reviews and submit early. I do not know whether any agencies keep track of the grantors who try to make their jobs easier. But if some do, I want to be on the courteous list. The letter needs to state that you are considering developing a proposal for their competition and should include the exact title of the program as stated in the announcement, its *CFDA* number, and its deadline(s).

CHAPTER 13

Planning the Successful Federal Proposal

Each federal agency has its own proposal format to which applicants must adhere. If you have been successful in obtaining a copy of a previously funded proposal, you have a quality example of what the funding source expects. After reading exemplary proposals for 30 years, I have learned that really excellent proposals do stand out. One does not have to be an expert in a proposal's particular area of interest to determine whether the proposal is good. The required components or sections of each type of proposal—a research proposal or a good proposal for a demonstration or model project—are remarkably similar. In general, federal applications include sections on

- search of relevant literature/documentation of need: to demonstrate that you have a command of the relevant studies and knowledge in the field;
- what you propose to study, change, or test (for a research project, the hypothesis and specific aims; for a model project, the measurable objectives);
- proposed intervention: what you will do and why you have selected these methods or activities;
- budget: the cost of the project broken down by category of expenditure;
- evaluation: how you will establish the levels of change that constitute success and demonstrate that your intervention worked; and

- grantee credibility: unique qualities and capabilities that you possess and believe are relevant to support and complete the project.

Most federal grantors will also require a summary or abstract, a title, an agreement to comply with federal assurances, and attachment of pertinent materials that the reviewer may want to refer to while evaluating the proposal. Sections on future funding and dissemination of the research findings or model may also be included.

While the inclusion of these general components seems logical, the differences in terminology, space restrictions, and order or sequence from one federal application to another can be very perplexing. The novice grantseeker frequently asks why there is not a standard federal grant application form for all programs. It seems that this would make sense, but due to the variety of federal programs and the deep-seated conviction that each area of interest is distinct, this type of standardization will probably never happen. The point is that you must follow each agency's format exactly, make no changes and no omissions, and give each agency what it calls for, not just what you want to give.

Each federal agency has its own preferences concerning the components and the order. What is similar from agency to agency is that in one way or another, the grantseeker's proposal must establish that he or she has a project that needs to be carried out in order to advance the field of research, knowledge, or service. Chapter 14 on conducting a quality circle or proposal improvement exercise will deal in more detail with the federal agencies' systems for evaluating and scoring proposals, including how the different sections of the proposal compare in terms of importance in the final decision. When applying to a specific agency, it is expected that you will procure a copy of the desired proposal format and develop specific insights into the agency's scoring system and an idea of what an outstanding proposal looks like by obtaining a copy of a funded proposal.

Work through this chapter and collect the materials suggested. Then develop or rearrange your proposal in the format and order required by the grantor.

DOCUMENTATION OF NEED

Most grantseekers begin their proposal with *what* they propose or want to do. Government grantors want to know *why* there is a need to do anything at all. To gain the reviewer's respect, you must show that you are knowledgeable about the need in a particular area. Your goal in this section of the proposal is to use articles, studies, and statistics to demonstrate a compelling reason or motivation to deal with the problem now.

The grantor invariably must choose which proposals to fund this year and which to reject or put on hold; therefore, you must demonstrate the urgency to close the gap between what exists now and what ought to be in your special field (see figure 13.1). Your proposed project will seek to close or reduce this gap.

```
┌─────────────────────────────────────────────────────────────────────┐
│                              THE GAP                                  │
│                                                                       │
│                                                                       │
│   What exists now. What is real.          What could be. The goal.   │
│   What the present situation is. _____  The desired state of affairs,│
│                                            level of achievement.      │
│                                                                       │
├─────────────────────────────────────────────────────────────────────┤
│   THE GAP DIAGRAM                                                     │
└──┌──────────────┐─────────────────────────────────────────────────────┘
   │  FIGURE 13.1 │
   └──────────────┘
```

THE GAP DIAGRAM

FIGURE 13.1

In a research proposal, need documentation involves a search of relevant literature in the field. The point of the literature search is to document that there is a gap in knowledge in a particular area. Currently in the scientific community it is necessary to enhance the motivation of the reviewer to fund your research project by suggesting the value of closing the gap, in monetary terms or in terms of increased knowledge, and by proposing what this new knowledge can lead to.

In proposals for model projects and demonstration grants, this section is referred to as the needs statement or need documentation. To be successful in grantseeking, you must produce a clear, compelling picture of the current situation and the desired state. Grantors are buying a changed or better state of affairs.

Creating a sense of urgency depends on how well you document the need. Since not all proposals can be funded, you must make the funding source believe that movement toward the desired state cannot wait any longer. Those proposals that do not get funded did not do as good a job of

- documenting a real need (perceived as important),
- demonstrating what ought to be (for clients) or the field of interest, and/or
- creating the urgent need to close the gap by demonstrating that each day the need is not addressed the problem grows worse or that there is unnecessary suffering, confusion, and/or wasted efforts.

Documenting What Is

Use the following steps to document a need in a model or demonstration grant:

1. Review the section on performing a needs survey (chapter 2) to assess whether any of the methods described could help document the need.

2. Use statistics from articles and research (for example, "Approximately __ women in the United States were murdered by their husbands or boy-friends last year").
3. Use quotes from leaders or experts in the field (for example, "Dr. Flock-meister said children who are raised in a family with spouse abuse have a ____ percent chance of being abused or of abusing their partners").
4. Use case statements (for example, "John Quek, a typical client of the Fam-ily Outreach Center, was abused as a child and witnessed his mother and aunt being abused").
5. Describe a national need and reduce it to a local number that is more understandable (for example, "It is estimated that ____ percent of teen-agers are abused by their boyfriend or girlfriend by the time they reach age 17; this means that at West Side High School, ____ seniors in the graduating class may have already experienced abuse").
6. State the need in terms of one person (for example, "The abused spouse generally has...").
7. Use statements from community people such as police, politicians, and clergy.

When documenting what exists in a research grant, include the following:

1. The latest studies, research articles, and presentations to demonstrate your currency in the field.
2. Studies that demonstrate the scope and sequence of work in the field and its current state, and the necessity to answer your proposed research ques-tion before the field can move ahead.
3. A thorough literature search that does not focus only on a few researchers or data that reinforce your research position. Show how the diversity or conflict in the field reinforces the need to search for an answer to your question.
4. A logical flow of reference to the literature. The flow may consist of a chronological and conceptual documentation that builds to the decision to fund your work. Remember, the literature search should not be a com-prehensive treatise in the field that includes references to every contribu-tor but, rather, a convincing documentation of significant works.

Demonstrating What Ought to Be

To establish what ought to be, proven statistics may be difficult or impossible to find. Using experts' statements and quotes to document what ought to be is much more credible than using your opinion. Do not put your opinion in the needs statement. In this section you are demonstrating your knowledge of the field and showing that you have surveyed the literature.

Stay away from terms that point to a poorly documented needs statement. They include the words *many* and *most* and expressions like a *great number* and *everyone knows the need for*. Make sure your needs statement does not include any of these types of words or expressions.

It is relatively easy to say what ought to be in areas such as family violence or drug abuse, but more difficult when dealing with bench or pure research. However, it is still important to demonstrate the possible uses your research could be related to even if you are working in the hard sciences. Documenting the other side of the gap is a necessity if you want to close the gap of ignorance in your field.

Creating a Sense of Urgency

The needs section should motivate the prospective funding source. One way to do this is to use the funding source's own studies, surveys, or statistics. The same basic proposal can be tailored to two different funding sources by quoting different studies that appeal to each source's own view of the need. By appealing to the views of individual sources, you will appear to be the logical choice to close the gap and move toward reducing the problem.

If the proposal format required by the funding source does not have a section that deals with your capabilities, the end of the needs statement is the best place to put your credentials. To make a smooth transition from the need to your capabilities, do the following:

- State that it is the mission of your organization to deal with this problem.

- Summarize the unique qualities of your organization that make it best suited for the job. For example, your organization has the staff or facilities to make the project work.

- Capitalize on the similarities you share with other organizations. For instance, "Our project will serve as a model to the other agencies that face this dilemma each day." Such statements will help the prospective grantor realize that the results of your project could affect many.

- Emphasize that the needs are urgent and that each day they go unmet the problem grows. For example, "Each year that teacher education colleges do an inadequate job of integrating comprehensive computer education into their curriculum, a new group of teachers with limited computer skills enter our schools unable to utilize the Internet and the problem grows."

WHAT YOU PROPOSE TO STUDY OR CHANGE

Objectives outline the steps you propose to take to narrow or close the gap created in the needs statement. Objectives follow the needs statement because they cannot be written until the need has been documented.

Since the accomplishment or attainment of each objective will help to close the gap, you must write objectives that are measurable and can be evaluated. It is critical to be able to determine the degree to which the objectives have been attained and, thus, demonstrate the amount of the gap that has been closed. Grantseekers preparing research proposals should note that the objective of a research proposal is to close the gap of ignorance.

Government grantors have been putting increasing pressure on researchers to explain how their research can be used on a very practical level. Philosophical (and the author's) arguments aside, there are conservative elements that want a component of even basic research grants to deal with such issues as dissemination of results and how findings can be applied to benefit the general public.

Objectives versus Methods

Objectives tell the grantseeker and the funding source what will be accomplished by this expenditure of funds and how the change will be measured. *Methods* state the means to the end or change. They tell how you will accomplish the desired change. Naturally, the ability to accomplish an objective depends on the methods or activities chosen.

When in doubt as to whether you have written an objective or a method, ask yourself whether there is only one way to accomplish what you have written. If your answer is yes, you have probably written a method. For example, once a participant at one of my seminars told me that his objective was to build a visitors' center for his organization's museum. When asked why he wanted to build a visitors' center, he responded, "To help visitors understand the relationship between the museum buildings so that they can more effectively use the museum." Once he stated this out loud, he realized that his objective was really the effective utilization of the museums and that building a visitors' center was just one method for accomplishing this objective. In other words, building the visitors' center was a means to an end, just one way that my seminar participant could attempt to accomplish his objective. In fact, the reason a funding source might give money to support his project would be to help people use and appreciate the museum, not to build the visitors' center. The bricks and mortar that make up the visitors' center simply do not lend themselves to the kind of measurement that the issue of effective utilization does.

The following is a technique for writing objectives:

1. **Determine result areas.** Result areas are the key places you will look for improvement or change in the client population. Examples include the

BUTLER, HENRY D
84070
Unclaim : 8/24/2013

Held date : 8/14/2013
Pickup location : Garden Home Community Library

Title : The "how to" grants manual : s
uccessful grantseeking techniques for obtaining
public and private grants
Call number : 658.15224 BAUER
Item barcode : 33614044298767
Assigned branch : Hillsboro Main Library

Notes:

health of people over 65 years of age in St. Louis, better educated minority students, and more efficient use of a museum.

2. **Determine measurement indicators.** Measurement indicators are the quantifiable parts of your result areas. By measuring your performance with these indicators, you will be able to determine how well you are doing. Examples include the number of hospital readmissions of people over 65 years of age, scores on standardized tests, and the number of people who understand the relationship between museum buildings. Brainstorm a number of measurement indicators for each of your result areas, and then select the ones that reflect your intent and are the least difficult to use.

3. **Determine performance standards.** Performance standards answer the question "how much (or how little) of a change do we need to consider ourselves successful?" Using our above example, we might determine the following performance standards: a 10-percent drop in hospital readmissions, scores rising from the 80th to the 90th percentile for freshman on the Flockman reading scale, or a 50-percent reduction in direction giving by museum staff.

4. **Determine the time frame.** The time frame is the amount of time in which you want to reach your performance standards. It is your deadline. You might decide you want to see a 10-percent drop in hospital readmissions within 6 or 18 months. Usually, this time frame is determined for you by the funding source. Most grants are for 12 months. In setting your deadlines, use months 1 through 12 instead of January, February, and so on because you seldom will start the grant when you expect.

5. **Determine the cost frame.** This is the cost of the methods or activities you have selected to meet your objectives. (This cost estimate can be obtained retrospectively from the project planner, the document you will fill out next.)

6. **Write the objective.** This step combines the data you have generated in the previous five steps. The standard format for an objective is as follows: "To [action verb and statement reflecting your measurement indicator] by [performance standard] by [deadline] at a cost of no more than [cost frame]": for example, "To increase the reading scores of freshmen from the 80th to 90th percentile on Flockman's reading scale in 12 months at a cost of $50,000."

7. **Evaluate the objective.** Review your objective and answer the question "Does this objective reflect the amount of change we want in the result area?" If your answer is yes, you probably have a workable objective. If your answer is no, chances are that your measurement indicator is wrong or your performance standards are too low. Go back to steps 2 and 3 and repeat the process.

When writing program objectives, you should follow the same seven steps.

Again, remember to emphasize end results, not tasks or methods. Do not describe how you are going to do something; instead, emphasize what you will accomplish and the ultimate benefit of your program's work.

Hypothesis and Research Question

In a research proposal, the section on what the researcher proposes to study or change is referred to as the research question and hypothesis to be tested. The development of research proposals follows an analogous route to model and demonstration grants. There must be a clearly defined problem, question, or gap to be addressed.

Researchers are inoculated with the same virus that all grant seekers share—the "why virus." (Why does this happen? What can we do to change it?) The researcher asks a question and then must search the literature in the field to determine what is already known and who would care if the question was answered. (What is the value or benefit? Who would value the closing of the gap?) For example, the question of whether treatment X or Y influences the healing time of a pressure sore (bedsore) is subject to a search of the literature to see what work has already been done in this area and to determine the importance of the question. (What exists now? What is the incidence or extent of the problem, and what is the future impact of not addressing the question?) If there is no compelling or motivating reason to use grant moneys to answer the question, the researcher is not likely to be successful.

The research question must be specific and focused. Many researchers are overly optimistic and select too broad a question or too many questions to investigate. This sets them up for failure because they cannot control the situation. In other words, they have too many forces or variables to deal with that can influence the outcome.

Researchers must develop their questions into either a null hypothesis or an alternative hypothesis.

In a *null hypothesis*, the researcher

- predicts that there is no basic difference between the two selected areas. For example, "There is no difference between pressure sores treated with X or Y."

- sets up the study to measure the outcome, or the *dependent* variable (increased healing of pressure sores).

- manipulates or changes the intervention, or the *independent* variable (use of treatment X or Y), to observe the effect of the two treatments on the dependent variable.

- selects a statistical evaluation model before data are collected, which will be used to evaluate the differences in the intervention.

When there are significant differences between two treatments, the null hypothesis is disproved and the results are based on differences in treatment rather than on chance. A common level is .01 significance, which means the chances of this result occurring randomly is less than 1 in 1,000.

The *alternative hypothesis* predicts that there is indeed a difference between the two treatments and suggests the direction of that difference. For example, "Treatment X will result in a healing rate that is 50 percent faster than treatment Y." The research protocol then seeks to prove that there is a difference at the level that is substantiated by the evaluation design to be utilized.

PROPOSED INTERVENTION

The methods, activities, or protocol section is the detailed description of the steps you will take to meet the objectives. Methods identify

- what will be done,
- who will do it,
- how long it will take, and
- the materials and equipment needed.

The protocol of a research proposal details how each experiment or trial will be carried out.

The methods or protocols are all a function of what you set out to accomplish. The best order to follow is to write your objectives first and then develop your methods to meet them. In making up a realistic estimate of your project costs, avoid inflating your budget. Instead, consider adding several more methods to this section to ensure that your objectives are met. When you negotiate the final award, you will gain much more credibility with the funding source by eliminating methods instead of lowering the price for the same amount of work. The basic idea is that eliminating methods or steps impacts the ability to prove or create the desired change at the level of certainty wanted by both you and the grantor.

Historically, final awards for research proposals were arrived at in a manner much different from that for model project proposals. Notification of a research award was frequently followed by a letter that included a dollar amount significantly less than what was applied for, and there was little or no opportunity for negotiation. Criticism of this practice led many major grantors to announce that the methods for research and model/demonstration proposals should be cost analyzed and negotiated. Now both demonstration and research proposals must include an estimate of the cost of each method or activity and must show each activity's effect on the outcome.

Your methods section should

- describe your program activities in detail and demonstrate how they will fulfill your objectives or research study;
- describe the sequence, flow, and interrelationship of the activities;
- describe the planned staffing for your program and designate who is responsible for which activities;
- describe your client population and method for determining client selection;
- state a specific time frame;
- present a reasonable scope of activities that can be accomplished within the stated time frame with your organization's resources;
- refer to the cost-benefit ratio of your project;
- include a discussion of risk (why success is probable); and
- describe the uniqueness of your methods and overall project design.

The project planner (see exhibit 13.1) provides you with a format to ensure that your methods section reflects a well-conceived and well-designed plan for the accomplishment of your objectives. A copy of the project planner programmed to work with Microsoft Excel can be downloaded free of charge at http://www.dgbauer.com.

The Project Planner

An outcome of my 35 years of work in grant and contract preparation, the project planner is a spreadsheet-based planning tool designed to assist you in several important ways. It will help you

- create a budget narrative that describes expenditures;
- develop your budget by having you clearly define which project personnel will perform each activity for a given time frame, with the corresponding consultant services, supplies, materials, and equipment;
- defend your budget on an activity-by-activity basis so that you can successfully negotiate your final award;
- project a monthly and quarterly cash forecast for year 1, year 2, and year 3 of your proposed project; and
- identify matching or in-kind contributions.

The project planner will also help you develop job descriptions for each individual involved in the project and a budget narrative or written explanation documenting your planned expenses. Several federal granting agencies have been criticized for not negotiating final awards with grantees. Their practice has been to provide grantees with a statement of the final award with no reference or discussion of how the award differs from the amount budgeted in the

PROJECT PLANNER

PROJECT TITLE: _____

A. List Project objectives or outcomes A. B. B. List Methods to accomplish each objective as A-1, A-2, A-3 .... B-1, B-2 ...	MONTH		TIME	PROJECT PERSONNEL	PERSONNEL COSTS		
	BEGIN	END			SALARIES & WAGES	FRINGE BENEFITS	TOTAL
	C / D		E	F	G	H	I

© David G. Bauer Associates, Inc.
(800) 836-0732

TOTAL DIRECT COSTS OR COSTS REQUESTED FROM FUNDER ▶

MATCHING FUNDS, IN-KIND CONTRIBUTIONS, OR DONATED COSTS ▶

TOTAL COSTS ▶

THE PROJECT PLANNER

EXHIBIT 13.1

Sheet _____ of _____

Proposal Developed for _____

PROJECT DIRECTOR: _____ Proposed starting date _____ Proposal Year _____

CONSULTANTS • CONTRACT SERVICES			NON-PERSONNEL RESOURCES NEEDED SUPPLIES • EQUIPMENT • MATERIALS				SUB-TOTAL COST FOR ACTIVITY	MILESTONES PROGRESS INDICATORS	
TIME	COST/WEEK	TOTAL	ITEM	COST/ITEM	QUANTITY	TOT. COST	TOTAL I. L. P	ITEM	DATE
J	K	L	M	N	O	P	Q	R	S

T   ◄ % OF TOTAL
                         ◄
                100%   ◄

THE PROJECT PLANNER (continued)

EXHIBIT 13.1

application or how the reduction will affect the methods and outcome. As more importance is placed on budget negotiation and the planning of project years, the more valuable the project planner will become.

You will find the following explanations of each project planner column helpful as you review the blank project planner in exhibit 13.1 and the sample project planner in exhibit 13.2.

1. Project objectives or outcomes (column A/B): List your objectives or outcomes as A, B, C, and so on. Use the terms the prospective grantor wants. For example, grantors may refer to the objectives as major tasks, enabling objectives, or specific aims.
2. Methods (column A/B): Also in the first column, list the methods or protocol necessary to meet the objectives or outcomes as A-1, A-2, B-1, B-2, C-1, C-2, and so on. These are the tasks you have decided upon as your approach to meeting the need.
3. Month (column C/D): Record the dates you will begin and end each activity in this column.
4. Time (column E): Designate the number of person-weeks (you can use hours or months) needed to accomplish each task.
5. Project personnel (column F): List the key personnel who will spend measurable or significant amounts of time on this activity and the accomplishments of this objective or specific aim. The designation of key personnel is critical for developing a job description for each individual. If you list the activities for which the key personnel are responsible, and the minimum qualifications or background required, you will have a rough job description. Call a placement agency to get an estimate of the salary needed to fill the position. The number of weeks or months will determine full- or part-time classification.

   This column gives you the opportunity to look at how many hours of work you are providing in a given time span. If you have your key personnel working more than 160 hours per month, it may be necessary to adjust the number of weeks in Column E to fit a more reasonable time frame. For example, you may have to reschedule activities or shift responsibility to another staff member.
6. Personnel costs (columns G, H, I): List the salaries, wages, and fringe benefits for all personnel. Special care should be taken in analyzing staff donated from your organization. The donation of personnel may be a requirement for your grant or a gesture you make to show your good faith and appear as a better investment to the funding source. If you do make matching or in-kind contributions, place an asterisk by the name of each person you donate to the project. Be sure to include your donation of fringes as well as wages. As you complete the remaining columns, put an asterisk by anything else that will be donated to the project.

PROJECT PLANNER™

PROJECT TITLE: A Contract for Educational Cooperation - Parents Teachers & Students Charting A Course for Involvement

A. List Project objectives or outcomes A. B. B. List Methods to accomplish each objective as A-1, A-2, A-3 ... B-1, B-2 ...	MONTH		TIME	PROJECT PERSONNEL	PERSONNEL COSTS		
	BEGIN	END			SALARIES & WAGES	FRINGE BENEFITS	TOTAL
	C / D		E	F	G	H	I
Objective A: Increase Educational Cooperation of Teachers, Parents & Students 25% as Measured on the Educational Practices Survey in 12 Months at a Cost of $88,705							
A-1 Develop the Responsible Educational Practices Survey with the Advisory Committee	1/2		4	Proj. Dir PD Smith 2 Grad students (GS)	West State U.		
a. Write questions and develop a scale of responsibility for parents, teachers and students							
A-2 Administer the Survey to the Target Population	2/3		4	2 GS	''	''	''
a. Develop procedure			4	PD	''	''	''
b. Get human subjects approval thru West State University							
c. Graduate students to administer survey			4	2 GS	''	''	''
d. Input survey data			*4	Sec'y	800	160	*960
e. Develop results			1	PD	West State U.		
A-3 Develop Curriculm	3/6						
a. Review results of pre-test given to parents, students and teachers			1	PD	''	''	''
b. Develop a curriculum on			5	PD	''	''	''
responsibility concepts in			*8	Sec'y	1600	320	*1920
education for each group (includes workbook and video on each area of curriculum)			8	Senior Club - Corp.	High Video Using Jones Facility		
- responsible use of time							
- homework responsibility							
- communication skills							
- developing contract for change							
A-4 Promote & Carry Out Program	6/12		24	PD	West State U.		
a. Use advisory group to announce program			24	Sec'y	4800	960	*5760
b. Public service spots on radio & television							
c. Develop and send home a program							
d. Schedule meetings with parents							
e. Develop a student video							

© David G. Bauer Associates, Inc.
(800) 836-0732

TOTAL DIRECT COSTS OR COSTS REQUESTED FROM FUNDER ▶ 0
MATCHING FUNDS, IN-KIND CONTRIBUTIONS, OR DONATED COSTS ▶ 8640
TOTAL COSTS ▶ 8640

SAMPLE PROJECT PLANNER

EXHIBIT 13.2

Sheet __1__ of __1__

Proposal Developed for ___D. Smith_____

PROJECT DIRECTOR: _____ Proposed starting date _____ Proposal Year _____

CONSULTANTS • CONTRACT SERVICES			NON-PERSONNEL RESOURCES NEEDED SUPPLIES • EQUIPMENT • MATERIALS				SUB-TOTAL COST FOR ACTIVITY	MILESTONES PROGRESS INDICATORS	
TIME	COST/WEEK	TOTAL	ITEM	COST/ITEM	QUANTITY	TOT COST	TOTAL I. L. P	ITEM	DATE
J	K	L	M	N	O	P	Q	R	S
2	1000	2000	micro/word perfect			2500			
2	500	1000	printer/modem			175			
			phone expense			150			
4	500	2000							
4	1000	4000							
4	500	2000	travel allowance			800			
			modem/phone expense			150			
1	1000	1000	micro processor			---			
1	1000	1000							
5	1000	5000	layout & print			1250			
			workbooks	10	200	2000*			
			blank tapes	2	20	40			
			video studio	5000	5hrs	25000*			
			camera edit						
			character generation						
			video camera	1000	6	6000*			
		42000				5065	47065	53% ◄ % OF TOTAL	
		0				33000	41640	47% ◄	
		42000				38065	88705	100% ◄	

SAMPLE PROJECT PLANNER (continued)

EXHIBIT 13.2

7. Consultants and contract services (columns J, K, L): These three columns are for the services that are most cost-efficiently supplied by individuals who are not in your normal employ. They may be experts at a skill you need that does not warrant your training a staff member or hiring an additional staff person (evaluation, computers, commercial art, and so forth). There are no fringes paid to consultants or contract service providers.

8. Nonpersonnel resources needed (columns M, N, O, P): List the components that are necessary to complete each activity and achieve your objective, including supplies, equipment, and materials. Many a grantseeker has gone wrong by underestimating the nonpersonnel resources needed to successfully complete a project. Most grantseekers lose out on many donated or matching items because they do not ask themselves what they really need to complete each activity. Travel, supplies, and telephone communications are some of the more commonly donated items.

   Equipment requests can be handled in many ways. One approach is to place total equipment items as they are called for in your plan under Column M (item) and to complete the corresponding columns appropriately —cost per item (column N), quantity (column O), and total cost (Column P). However, this approach may cause problems in the negotiation of your final award. The grantor may suggest lowering the grant amount by the elimination of an equipment item that appears as though it is related to the accomplishment of only one activity, when in actuality you plan to utilize it in several subsequent activities. Therefore, I suggest that if you plan to list the total cost of equipment needed in your work plan next to one particular activity, designate a percentage of usage to that activity and reference the other activities that will require the equipment. This way you will show 100-percent usage and be able to defend the inclusion of the equipment in your budget request.

   In some cases, you may choose to allocate the percentage of the cost of the equipment with the percentage of use for each activity. If you allocate cost of equipment to each activity, remember that if you drop an activity in negotiation you may not have all the funds you need to purchase the equipment.

9. Subtotal cost for activity (column Q): This column can be completed in two ways. Each activity can be subtotaled, or you can subtotal several activities under each objective or specific aim.

10. Milestones, progress indicators (columns R, S): Column R should be used to record what the funding source will receive as indicators that you are working toward the accomplishment of your objectives. Use Column S to list the date on which the funding source will receive the milestone or progress indicator.

Please note that you might want to develop a computer-generated spread-sheet version of the project planner so that your objectives or other information could be easily added, deleted, or changed. (A downloadable Microsoft Excel version is available free of charge at http://www.dgbauer.com.) This would be especially useful when the grant amount awarded is less than the amount requested, because you could experiment with possible changes without too much trouble.

Indirect Costs

An aspect of federal grants that is critically important yet poorly understood by many grantseekers and other individuals connected with grants is the concept of indirect costs. Indirect costs involve repaying the recipient of a federal grant for costs that are difficult to break down individually but are indirectly attributable to performing the federal grant. These costs include such things as

- heat and lights,
- building maintenance,
- payroll personnel, and
- purchasing.

Indirect costs are calculated by using a formula that is provided by the Federal Regional Controller's Office and are expressed as a percentage of the total amount requested from the funding source (total from column Q of your project planner), or as a percentage of the personnel costs (total from column I of your project planner).

Recent developments in the area of indirect costs have led the federal government to strictly enforce the definition of costs eligible for reimbursement under a grant's direct expenditures versus those eligible under its indirect expenditures. Under the Office of Management and Budget's new guidelines, costs related to the handling of increased grant supported payroll or purchase orders are already covered under indirect costs. Therefore, any added personnel that fall under the category of secretarial support are not eligible to be added to your grant. All personnel in your grant should have a special designation, showing that their duties are not secretarial but rather extraordinary and thus eligible to be funded under the grant.

Budget

While preparing the budget may be traumatic for unorganized grantseekers, you can see that the project planner contains all the information you need to fore-cast your financial needs accurately. No matter what budget format you use, the information you need to construct your budget lies in your project planner.

The project planner, however, is not the budget; it is the analysis of what will have to be done and the estimated costs and time frame for each activity.

In most government proposal formats, the budget section is not located near the methods section. Government funders do not understand why you want to talk about your methods when you talk about money. As you know, the budget is a result of what you plan to do. If the money you request is reduced, you know you must cut your project's methods. Draw the public funding source back into your project planner so that they too can see what will be missing as a result of a budget cut. If you must cut so many methods that you can no longer be sure of accomplishing your objectives, consider refusing the funds or reducing the amount of change (reduction of the need) outlined in your objectives when negotiating the amount of your award. The sample budget in exhibit 13.3 is provided for your review. In a research proposal, show how limiting your intervention or protocol will affect the reliability and validity of your research.

If you are required to provide a quarterly cash forecast, use the grants office time line in exhibit 13.4. The project activities/methods (A-1, A-2, B-1, B-2) from your project planner should be listed in the first column. The numbered columns across the top of the timeline indicate the months of the duration of the project. Use a line bar to indicate when each activity/method begins and ends. Place the estimated cost per method in the far-right column. Use a triangle to indicate where milestones and progress indicators are to occur (taken from Columns R and S of your project planner). By totaling costs by quarter, you can develop a quarterly forecast of expenditures. Complete a separate grants office timeline and project planner for each year of a continuation grant or multiyear award.

One of the more common federal budget forms for nonconstruction projects is Standard Form (SF) 424A (see exhibit 13.5). The instructions for completing SF-424A are shown in exhibit 13.6. As with other budget forms, if you have completed a project planner, you already have all the information you need to complete SF-424A.

Many grantors also require that you submit a narrative statement of your budget, explaining the basis for your inclusion of personnel, consultants, supplies, and equipment. This is known as a budget narrative. Again, your completed project planner will help you construct the budget narrative and explain the sequence of steps. The budget narrative gives you the opportunity to present the rationale for each step, piece of equipment, and key person that your proposal calls for.

EVALUATION

Federal and state funding sources generally place a much heavier emphasis on evaluation than most private sources do. While there are many books written on evaluation, the best advice is to have an expert handle it. I suggest enlisting

PROJECT NAME: Nutrition Education for Disadvantaged Mothers through Teleconferencing	Expenditure Total	Donated/ In-Kind	Requested from This Source
	$148,551	$85,122	$63,429
1. PERSONNEL			
A. Salaries, Wages			
Project Director @ $2,200/mo.	13,200	13,200	
x 12 mos. x 50% time			
Administrative Assistant @	19,200		19,200
$1,600/mo. x 12 mos. x 100% time			
Data Input Specialist @ 1,300/mo.	15,600		15,600
x 12 mos. x 100% time			
Volunteer Time @ 9.00 x	36,000	36,000	
10 mos. x 400 hours			
B. Fringe Benefits			
Unemployment Insurance	1,440	450	990
(3% of first $18,600)			
FICA (6.2% of first $87,000	2,976	953	2,023
of each employee salary)			
Health Insurance ($150/mo. Per	5,400	1,800	3,600
employee x 12 mos.)			
Workmen's Compensation (1% of	480	144	336
salaries paid- $48,000)			
C. Consultants/Contracted Services			
Copy Editor ($200/day x 5)	1,000		1,000
PR Advisor ($200/day x 10)	2,000		2,000
Accounting Serv. ($250/day x 12)	3,000	3,000	
Legal Services ($500/day x 6)	3,000	3,000	
Personnel Subtotal	103,296	58,547	44,749
II. NONPERSONNEL			
A. Space Costs			
Rent ($1.50/sq. ft. x 400)	7,200	7,200	
sq. ft. x 12 mos.)			
Utilities ($75/mo. x 12 mos.)	900	900	
B. Equipment			
Desk ($275 x 1)	275		275
Computer, Printer, Copy	3,600		3,600
Machine, Rental ($300/mo x 12 mos.)			
Office Chairs ($50 x 3)	150		150
File Cabinets ($125 x 3)	375	375	

A SAMPLE PROJECT BUDGET

EXHIBIT 13.3

the services of a professional at a college or university who has experience in evaluation. Professors will generally enjoy the involvement and the extra pay and can lead you to a storehouse of inexpensive labor—undergraduate and graduate students. A graduate student in statistics can help you deal with the problem of quantifying your results inexpensively, while he or she gathers valuable insight, experience, and some much needed money.

Irrespective of who designs your evaluation, writing your objectives properly will make the process much simpler. Most grantseekers have little problem

PROJECT NAME:

Nutrition Education for Disadvantaged Mothers through Teleconferencing	Expenditure Total	Donated/ In-Kind	Requested from This Source
	$148,551	$85,122	$63,429
Electronic Blackboard & Misc. Equip. for Teleconferencing	7,200		7,200
C. Supplies (Consumables)			
(3 employees x 200/yr.)	600	600	
D. Travel			
Local			
Project Director ($.40/mile x	2,400		2,400
500 miles/mo. x 12 mos.)			
Administrative Assistant	3,600		3,600
($.40/mile x 750 miles/mo. x 12 mos.)			
Out-of-Town			
Project Director to Nutrition Conference			
in St. Louis, MO			
Airfare	450		450
Per Diem ($75/day x 3)	225		225
Hotel ($100/nt. x 3)	300		300
E. Telephone			
Installation ($100/line x 3)	300	300	
Monthly Charges ($25/line x 3	900	900	
lines x 12 mos.)			
Long Distance ($40/mo. x 12 mos.)	480		480
F. Other Nonpersonnel Costs			
Printing ($.30 x 25,000 brochures)	7,500	7,500	
Postage ($.34 x 25,000)	8,500	8,500	
Insurance ($25/mo. x 12 mos.)	300	300	
Nonpersonnel Subtotal	$45,255	$26,575	$18,680
Personnel Subtotal	$103,296	$58,547	$44,749
Project Total	$148,551	$85,122	$63,429
Percentage	100%	57%	43%

A Sample Project Budget *(continued)*

EXHIBIT 13.3

developing objectives that deal with cognitive areas or areas that provide for results that can be easily qualified. The problems start when they move into the affective domain, because values, feelings, and appreciation can be difficult to measure. Use consultants to assist you. You will gain credibility by using an independent third party to carry out your evaluation analysis.

If you use the techniques presented in this chapter for writing objectives and ask yourself what your client population will do differently after the grant, you should be able to keep yourself on track and develop an evaluation design that will pass even the most critical federal and state standards. For example, a grant to increase appreciation for opera could be measured by seeing how many of the

Activity Number	1	2	3	4	5	6	7	8	9	10	11	12	Total Cost of Activity

	1st Quarter	2nd Quarter	3rd Quarter	4th Quarter	Total

Quarterly Forecast of Expenditures

GRANTS OFFICE TIME LINE

EXHIBIT 13.4

subjects pay to attend an inexpensive performance after the free ones are completed.

THE SUMMARY OR ABSTRACT

The summary or abstract is written after the proposal is completed. After the title, the summary is the second most-often-read part of a proposal. The

BUDGET INFORMATION - Non-Construction Programs

OMB Approval No. 0348-0044

SECTION A - BUDGET SUMMARY

Grant Program Function or Activity (a)	Catalog of Federal Domestic Assistance Number (b)	Estimated Unobligated Funds		New or Revised Budget		
		Federal (c)	Non-Federal (d)	Federal (e)	Non-Federal (f)	Total (g)
1.		$	$	$	$	$ 0.00
2.						0.00
3.						0.00
4.						0.00
5. Totals		$ 0.00	$ 0.00	$ 0.00	$ 0.00	$ 0.00

SECTION B - BUDGET CATEGORIES

6. Object Class Categories	GRANT PROGRAM, FUNCTION OR ACTIVITY				Total (5)
	(1)	(2)	(3)	(4)	
a. Personnel	$	$	$	$	$ 0.00
b. Fringe Benefits					0.00
c. Travel					0.00
d. Equipment					0.00
e. Supplies					0.00
f. Contractual					0.00
g. Construction					0.00
h. Other					0.00
i. Total Direct Charges (sum of 6a-6h)		0.00	0.00	0.00	0.00
j. Indirect Charges					0.00
k. TOTALS (sum of 6i and 6j)	$ 0.00	$ 0.00	$ 0.00	$ 0.00	$ 0.00
7. Program Income	$	$	$	$	$ 0.00

Authorized for Local Reproduction

Previous Edition Usable

Standard Form 424A (Rev. 7-97)
Prescribed by OMB Circular A-102

STANDARD FORM (SF) 424A

EXHIBIT 13.5

150

SECTION C - NON-FEDERAL RESOURCES

(a) Grant Program	(b) Applicant	(c) State	(d) Other Sources	(e) TOTALS
8.	$	$	$	$ 0.00
9.				0.00
10.				0.00
11.				0.00
12. TOTAL *(sum of lines 8-11)*	$ 0.00	$ 0.00	$ 0.00	$ 0.00

SECTION D - FORECASTED CASH NEEDS

	Total for 1st Year	1st Quarter	2nd Quarter	3rd Quarter	4th Quarter
13. Federal	$ 0.00	$	$	$	$
14. Non-Federal	0.00				
15. TOTAL *(sum of lines 13 and 14)*	$ 0.00	$ 0.00	$ 0.00	$ 0.00	$ 0.00

SECTION E - BUDGET ESTIMATES OF FEDERAL FUNDS NEEDED FOR BALANCE OF THE PROJECT

(a) Grant Program	FUTURE FUNDING PERIODS (Years)			
	(b) First	(c) Second	(d) Third	(e) Fourth
16.	$	$	$	$
17.				
18.				
19.				
20. TOTAL *(sum of lines 16-19)*	$ 0.00	$ 0.00	$ 0.00	$ 0.00

SECTION F - OTHER BUDGET INFORMATION

21. Direct Charges	22. Indirect Charges.

23. Remarks:

Authorized for Local Reproduction

Standard Form 424A (Rev. 7-97) Page 2

STANDARD FORM (SF) 424A *(continued)*

EXHIBIT 13.5

INSTRUCTIONS FOR THE SF-424A

Public reporting burden for this collection of information is estimated to average 180 minutes per response, including time for reviewing instructions, searching existing data sources, gathering and maintaining the data needed, and completing and reviewing the collection of information. Send comments regarding the burden estimate or any other aspect of this collection of information, including suggestions for reducing this burden, to the Office of Management and Budget, Paperwork Reduction Project (0348-0044), Washington, DC 20503.

PLEASE DO NOT RETURN YOUR COMPLETED FORM TO THE OFFICE OF MANAGEMENT AND BUDGET. SEND IT TO THE ADDRESS PROVIDED BY THE SPONSORING AGENCY.

General Instructions

This form is designed so that application can be made for funds from one or more grant programs. In preparing the budget, adhere to any existing Federal grantor agency guidelines which prescribe how and whether budgeted amounts should be separately shown for different functions or activities within the program. For some programs, grantor agencies may require budgets to be separately shown by function or activity. For other programs, grantor agencies may require a breakdown by function or activity. Sections A, B, C, and D should include budget estimates for the whole project except when applying for assistance which requires Federal authorization in annual or other funding period increments. In the latter case, Sections A, B, C, and D should provide the budget for the first budget period (usually a year) and Section E should present the need for Federal assistance in the subsequent budget periods. All applications should contain a breakdown by the object class categories shown in Lines a-k of Section B.

Section A. Budget Summary Lines 1-4 Columns (a) and (b)

For applications pertaining to a *single* Federal grant program (Federal Domestic Assistance Catalog number) and *not requiring* a functional or activity breakdown, enter on Line 1 under Column (a) the Catalog program title and the Catalog number in Column (b).

For applications pertaining to a *single* program *requiring* budget amounts by multiple functions or activities, enter the name of each activity or function on each line in Column (a), and enter the Catalog number in Column (b). For applications pertaining to multiple programs where *none* of the programs require a breakdown by function or activity, enter the Catalog program title on each line in Column (a) and the respective Catalog number on each line in Column (b).

For applications pertaining to *multiple* programs where one or more programs *require* a breakdown by function or activity, prepare a separate sheet for each program requiring the breakdown. Additional sheets should be used when one form does not provide adequate space for all breakdown of data required. However, when more than one sheet is used, the first page should provide the summary totals by programs.

Lines 1-4, Columns (c) through (g)

For *new* applications, leave Column (c) and (d) blank. For each line entry in Columns (a) and (b), enter in Columns (e), (f), and (g) the appropriate amounts of funds needed to support the project for the first funding period (usually a year).

For *continuing* grant program applications, submit these forms before the end of each funding period as required by the grantor agency. Enter in Columns (c) and (d) the estimated amounts of funds which will remain unobligated at the end of the grant funding period only if the Federal grantor agency instructions provide for this. Otherwise, leave these columns blank. Enter in columns (e) and (f) the amounts of funds needed for the upcoming period. The amount(s) in Column (g) should be the sum of amounts in Columns (e) and (f).

For *supplemental* grants and changes to existing grants, do not use Columns (c) and (d). Enter in Column (e) the amount of the increase or decrease of Federal funds and enter in Column (f) the amount of the increase or decrease of non-Federal funds. In Column (g) enter the new total budgeted amount (Federal and non-Federal) which includes the total previous authorized budgeted amounts plus or minus, as appropriate, the amounts shown in Columns (e) and (f). The amount(s) in Column (g) should not equal the sum of amounts in Columns (e) and (f).

Line 5 - Show the totals for all columns used.

Section B Budget Categories

In the column headings (1) through (4), enter the titles of the same programs, functions, and activities shown on Lines 1-4, Column (a), Section A. When additional sheets are prepared for Section A, provide similar column headings on each sheet. For each program, function or activity, fill in the total requirements for funds (both Federal and non-Federal) by object class categories.

Line 6a-i - Show the totals of Lines 6a to 6h in each column.

Line 6j - Show the amount of indirect cost.

Line 6k - Enter the total of amounts on Lines 6i and 6j. For all applications for new grants and continuation grants the total amount in column (5), Line 6k, should be the same as the total amount shown in Section A, Column (g), Line 5. For supplemental grants and changes to grants, the total amount of the increase or decrease as shown in Columns (1)-(4), Line 6k should be the same as the sum of the amounts in Section A, Columns (e) and (f) on Line 5.

Line 7 - Enter the estimated amount of income, if any, expected to be generated from this project. Do not add or subtract this amount from the total project amount. Show under the program

SF-424A (Rev. 7-97) Page 3

INSTRUCTIONS FOR COMPLETING STANDARD FORM (SF) 424A

EXHIBIT 13.6

summary must be succinct, clear, and motivating so the reader (reviewer) does not lose interest. It is important to determine whether the grantor uses summaries or abstracts. These terms may not be interchangeable and, therefore, could require different consideration.

In a sense, the summary or abstract has a dual purpose. Its first purpose is to provide the peer reviewer with a clear idea of what the proposed research or

---

INSTRUCTIONS FOR THE SF-424A (continued)

narrative statement the nature and source of income. The estimated amount of program income may be considered by the Federal grantor agency in determining the total amount of the grant.

Section C. Non-Federal Resources

Lines 8-11 Enter amounts of non-Federal resources that will be used on the grant. If in-kind contributions are included, provide a brief explanation on a separate sheet.

> **Column (a)** - Enter the program titles identical to Column (a), Section A. A breakdown by function or activity is not necessary.
>
> **Column (b)** - Enter the contribution to be made by the applicant.
>
> **Column (c)** - Enter the amount of the State's cash and in-kind contribution if the applicant is not a State or State agency. Applicants which are a State or State agencies should leave this column blank.
>
> **Column (d)** - Enter the amount of cash and in-kind contributions to be made from all other sources.
>
> **Column (e)** - Enter totals of Columns (b), (c), and (d).

Line 12 - Enter the total for each of Columns (b)-(e). The amount in Column (e) should be equal to the amount on Line 5, Column (f), Section A.

Section D. Forecasted Cash Needs

Line 13 - Enter the amount of cash needed by quarter from the grantor agency during the first year.

Line 14 - Enter the amount of cash from all other sources needed by quarter during the first year.

Line 15 - Enter the totals of amounts on Lines 13 and 14.

Section E. Budget Estimates of Federal Funds Needed for Balance of the Project

Lines 16-19 - Enter in Column (a) the same grant program titles shown in Column (a), Section A. A breakdown by function or activity is not necessary. For new applications and continuation grant applications, enter in the proper columns amounts of Federal funds which will be needed to complete the program or project over the succeeding funding periods (usually in years). This section need not be completed for revisions (amendments, changes, or supplements) to funds for the current year of existing grants.

If more than four lines are needed to list the program titles, submit additional schedules as necessary.

Line 20 - Enter the total for each of the Columns (b)-(e). When additional schedules are prepared for this Section, annotate accordingly and show the overall totals on this line.

Section F. Other Budget Information

Line 21 - Use this space to explain amounts for individual direct object class cost categories that may appear to be out of the ordinary or to explain the details as required by the Federal grantor agency.

Line 22 - Enter the type of indirect rate (provisional, predetermined, final or fixed) that will be in effect during the funding period, the estimated amount of the base to which the rate is applied, and the total indirect expense.

Line 23 - Provide any other explanations or comments deemed necessary.

SF-424A (Rev. 7-97) Page 4

INSTRUCTIONS FOR COMPLETING STANDARD FORM (SF) 424A *(continued)*

EXHIBIT 13.6

---

project entails. Its second purpose is to provide prospective grantseekers with an example of the type of research or project the federal agency funds. This second purpose occurs after the proposal is accepted, when the summary or abstract becomes public information and is placed on the funding source's web site and in databases that are Internet accessible.

Unfortunately, some applicants do not devote enough time to preparing their summary or abstract and the description that is made public does not do the funding agency or the grantee's project/research justice. In order to get grantseekers to pay more attention to this section of their proposals, some federal agencies have begun to score the summary or abstract in the overall proposal evaluation. Whether this area is scored or not, it plays a critical role in setting up the expectations of the reviewer before he or she gets into the body of your proposal.

In general terms, the summary/abstract is a much abbreviated version of your proposal and should contain a concise description of the need for your project, your project's goals or hypothesis, objectives or specific aims, approach or protocol, and evaluation design. Use your summary or abstract to show readers that they will find what they want in your proposal (since you have the scoring system), and try to follow the same order in the summary or abstract as you do in your proposal. You can determine which components to emphasize in your summary or abstract by reviewing the point or evaluation system the funding source will apply. Place more emphasis by devoting more space in the abstract or summary to the components that will be weighted more heavily in the scoring/ review process. Make sure your abstract or summary is arranged so that it is easy to read. Do not crowd the contents by using every inch of space designated for this area. Instead, highlight important parts with bullets, bold print, or underlining as long as these visual aids are allowed.

Many funding sources have explicit requirements concerning the summary or abstract. Some designate the space and number of words or characters that can be used, while others require potential grantees to underline a certain number of key words or phrases. Exhibit 13.7 defines what the National Science Foundation (NSF) expects to be found in a project summary and provides very specific instructions in terms of what person the summary should be written in and what it should include. The NSF's guidelines even go so far as to state that the project summary should *not* be an abstract of the proposal. Be sure to verify your funding source's rules before constructing this critical part of your proposal.

TITLE PAGE

Federal granting programs have a required face sheet or title page that must be included in your federal grant applications or proposals. The most common is Standard Form (SF) 424 (exhibit 13.8; instructions for completing the form are included in exhibit 13.9). Remember, you are dealing with a bureaucracy and, therefore, should double-check all requirements and make sure all necessary forms are completed per instructions.

The title of a proposal is very important. It is the first part of your proposal to be read by reviewers, and, if it is unclear or misleading, it may be the only part read! Take the time to develop a title that ensures your proposal will get attention.

The title of your proposal should

- describe your project,

**From the National Science Foundation Grant Proposal Guide
NSF 04-23**

2.   Sections of the Proposal

b.   Project Summary

The proposal must contain a summary of the proposed activity suitable for publication,
not more than one page in length. It should not be an abstract of the proposal, but rather
a contained description of the activity that would result if the proposal were funded. The
summary should be written in the third person and include a statement of the objectives and
methods to be employed. It must clearly address in separate statements (within the one-page
summary): (1) the intellectual merit of the proposed activity; and (2) the broader impacts
resulting from the proposed activity. (See Chapter III for further descriptive information on the
NSF merit review criteria.) It should be informative to other persons working in the same or
related fields and, insofar as possible, understandable to a scientifically or technically literate lay
reader. **Proposals that do not separately address both merit review criteria within the one
page Project Summary will be returned without review.**

(To obtain information about NSF program deadlines, to download copies of NSF publications,
and/or to access abstracts of awards, visit the NSF web site at: http://www.nsf.gov)

NATIONAL SCIENCE FOUNDATION PROFILE SUMMARY

EXHIBIT 13.7

- express your project's end results, not methods,
- describe your project's benefits to clients, and
- be short and easy to remember.

The best titles are like newspaper headlines, descriptive and to the point.
Titles that try to entice the reader by giving only part of the story or creating a
mystery seldom work.

Do not use jargon, buzzwords, biblical characters, or Greek gods in your proposal title since you cannot be sure that the funding source will be familiar with
your reference. For example, calling your solar energy project "Apollo's Flame"
could work to your disadvantage if the reviewer does not know who Apollo is
or fails to make the connection.

Acronyms should be used only if the funding source has a preference for
them. Trying to develop a title that describes the benefits of your project is
difficult enough without trying to use specific words that will result in a catchy
acronym.

Since you have written the proposal, it is easy for you to develop tunnel vision
and attribute more meaning to the words in the title than a person reading it for
the first time would. To make sure this does not happen, read your title to other
people who know little or nothing about your proposal, and then ask them what

APPLICATION FOR FEDERAL ASSISTANCE				Version 7/03
1. TYPE OF SUBMISSION:		**2. DATE SUBMITTED**		Applicant Identifier
Application	Pre-application	**3. DATE RECEIVED BY STATE**		State Application Identifier
☐ Construction	☐ Construction	**4. DATE RECEIVED BY FEDERAL AGENCY**		Federal Identifier
☐ Non-Construction	☐ Non-Construction			

5. APPLICANT INFORMATION

Legal Name:	Organizational Unit: Department:
	Division:
Organizational DUNS:	
Address: Street:	Name and telephone number of person to be contacted on matters involving this application (give area code)
	Prefix:	First Name:
City:	Middle Name
County:	Last Name
State:	Zip Code	Suffix:
Country:	Email:

6. EMPLOYER IDENTIFICATION NUMBER (EIN):	Phone Number (give area code)	Fax Number (give area code)
☐☐-☐☐☐☐☐☐☐		

8. TYPE OF APPLICATION:	**7. TYPE OF APPLICANT:** (See back of form for Application Types)
☐ New ☐ Continuation ☐ Revision If Revision, enter appropriate letter(s) in box(es) (See back of form for description of letters.) ☐ ☐	Other (specify)
Other (specify)	**9. NAME OF FEDERAL AGENCY:**

10. CATALOG OF FEDERAL DOMESTIC ASSISTANCE NUMBER: ☐☐-☐☐☐ TITLE (Name of Program):	**11. DESCRIPTIVE TITLE OF APPLICANT'S PROJECT:**

12. AREAS AFFECTED BY PROJECT (Cities, Counties, States, etc.):

13. PROPOSED PROJECT		**14. CONGRESSIONAL DISTRICTS OF:**	
Start Date:	Ending Date:	a. Applicant	b. Project

15. ESTIMATED FUNDING:		**16. IS APPLICATION SUBJECT TO REVIEW BY STATE EXECUTIVE ORDER 12372 PROCESS?**
a. Federal	$	a. Yes. ☐ THIS PREAPPLICATION/APPLICATION WAS MADE AVAILABLE TO THE STATE EXECUTIVE ORDER 12372 PROCESS FOR REVIEW ON
b. Applicant	$	
c. State	$	DATE:
d. Local	$	b. No. ☐ PROGRAM IS NOT COVERED BY E. O. 12372
e. Other	$	☐ OR PROGRAM HAS NOT BEEN SELECTED BY STATE FOR REVIEW
f. Program Income	$	**17. IS THE APPLICANT DELINQUENT ON ANY FEDERAL DEBT?**
g. TOTAL	$	☐ Yes If "Yes" attach an explanation ☐ No

18. TO THE BEST OF MY KNOWLEDGE AND BELIEF, ALL DATA IN THIS APPLICATION/PREAPPLICATION ARE TRUE AND CORRECT. THE DOCUMENT HAS BEEN DULY AUTHORIZED BY THE GOVERNING BODY OF THE APPLICANT AND THE APPLICANT WILL COMPLY WITH THE ATTACHED ASSURANCES IF THE ASSISTANCE IS AWARDED.

a. Authorized Representative Prefix	First Name	Middle Name
Last Name		Suffix
b. Title		c. Telephone Number (give area code)
d. Signature of Authorized Representative		e. Date Signed

Previous Edition Usable Authorized for Local Reproduction	Standard Form 424 (Rev 9-2003) Prescribed by OMB Circular A-102

STANDARD FORM (SF) 424

EXHIBIT 13.8

they think the proposal is about based on the title. You may find that you are not the best person to write the title. Have friends read the proposal and ask them for title suggestions.

Titles can vary in length and can be up to 10 to 13 words. Some federal programs have rules on the number of characters or spaces used in a title. Check the rules.

INSTRUCTIONS FOR THE SF-424

Public reporting burden for this collection of information is estimated to average 45 minutes per response, including time for reviewing instructions, searching existing data sources, gathering and maintaining the data needed, and completing and reviewing the collection of information. Send comments regarding the burden estimate or any other aspect of this collection of information, including suggestions for reducing this burden, to the Office of Management and Budget, Paperwork Reduction Project (0348-0043), Washington, DC 20503.

PLEASE DO NOT RETURN YOUR COMPLETED FORM TO THE OFFICE OF MANAGEMENT AND BUDGET. SEND IT TO THE ADDRESS PROVIDED BY THE SPONSORING AGENCY.

This is a standard form used by applicants as a required face sheet for pre-applications and applications submitted for Federal assistance. It will be used by Federal agencies to obtain applicant certification that States which have established a review and comment procedure in response to Executive Order 12372 and have selected the program to be included in their process, have been given an opportunity to review the applicant's submission.

Item:	Entry:	Item:	Entry:
1.	Select Type of Submission.	11.	Enter a brief descriptive title of the project. If more than one program is involved, you should append an explanation on a separate sheet. If appropriate (e.g., construction or real property projects), attach a map showing project location. For preapplications, use a separate sheet to provide a summary description of this project.
2.	Date application submitted to Federal agency (or State if applicable) and applicant's control number (if applicable).	12.	List only the largest political entities affected (e.g., State, counties, cities).
3.	State use only (if applicable).	13.	Enter the proposed start date and end date of the project.
4.	Enter Date Received by Federal Agency. Federal identifier number: If this application is a continuation or revision to an existing award, enter the present Federal identifier number. If for a new project, leave blank.	14.	List the applicant's Congressional District and any District(s) affected by the program or project.
5.	Enter legal name of applicant, name of primary organizational unit (including division, if applicable), which will undertake the assistance activity, enter the organization's DUNS number (received from Dun and Bradstreet), enter the complete address of the applicant (including country), and name, telephone number, e-mail and fax of the person to contact on matters related to this application.	15.	Amount requested or to be contributed during the first funding/budget period by each contributor. Value of in kind contributions should be included on appropriate lines as applicable. If the action will result in a dollar change to an existing award, indicate only the amount of the change. For decreases, enclose the amounts in parentheses. If both basic and supplemental amounts are included, show breakdown on an attached sheet. For multiple program funding, use totals and show breakdown using same categories as item 15.
6.	Enter Employer Identification Number (EIN) as assigned by the Internal Revenue Service.	16.	Applicants should contact the State Single Point of Contact (SPOC) for Federal Executive Order 12372 to determine whether the application is subject to the State intergovernmental review process.
7.	Select the appropriate letter in this space provided. A. State B. County C. Municipal D. Township E. Interstate F. Intermunicipal G. Special District H. Independent School District I. State Controlled Institution of Higher Learning J. Private University K. Indian Tribe L. Individual M. Profit Organization N. Other (Specify) O. Not for Profit Organization	17.	This question applies to the applicant organization, not the person who signs as the authorized representative. Categories of debt include delinquent audit disallowances, loans and taxes.
8.	Select the type from the following list: • "New" means a new assistance award. • "Continuation" means an extension for an additional funding/budget period for a project with a projected completion date. • "Revision" means any change in the Federal Government's financial obligation or contingent liability from an existing obligation. If a revision enter the appropriate letter: A. Increase Award B. Decrease Award C. Increase Duration D. Decrease Duration	18.	To be signed by the authorized representative of the applicant. A copy of the governing body's authorization for you to sign this application as official representative must be on file in the applicant's office. (Certain Federal agencies may require that this authorization be submitted as part of the application.)
9.	Name of Federal agency from which assistance is being requested with this application.		
10.	Use the Catalog of Federal Domestic Assistance number and title of the program under which assistance is requested.		

SF-424 (Rev. 7-97) Back

INSTRUCTIONS FOR COMPLETING STANDARD FORM (SF) 424

EXHIBIT 13.9

The key to writing a good title is to ask funding officials what they prefer and to examine a list of titles used by past grantees. This will give you a more accurate idea of what the funding source really likes.

FUTURE FUNDING

Most funding sources are buying a piece of the future. It is in their best interest to see any project they fund continue even though their guidelines may prohibit them from supporting continuation. If the project continues they are able to take credit for it and its benefits over a greater length of time. Unfortunately, many grantseekers ignore the funding source's interest in keeping its investment alive and neglect to mention a future financing plan in their proposals. If you cannot think of ways to finance your project after your federal grant funds run out, try brainstorming with your advisory committee. Perhaps you could continue your project through

- service fees,
- membership fees,
- support from agencies like the United Way,
- big gift campaigns aimed at wealthy individuals,
- an endowment program,
- foundation and corporate grants,
- a direct-mail campaign, or
- other fund-raising mechanisms.

Include the cost of one or more of these activities in your expenses, and budget them in the grant. You are not automatically considered an ingrate for doing this; rather, you may come across as a good executor of the funding source's estate. You are planning for continuation.

DISSEMINATION

In addition to the good that will come from meeting the objectives and closing the gap established in your needs statement, much good can come from letting others know what you and the funding source have accomplished. Others in your field will come to know your name and ask you to enter into consortia with them. In addition, other funding sources will have knowledge of your application and possibly look at ways to extrapolate it to their program. The idea is to get more PR and mileage out of your work in addition to that which you will derive from having an article published in a journal in your field.

Explore how you could disseminate the results of your grant by

- mailing a final report, quarterly journal, or a newsletter to others in your field;
- sponsoring a seminar or conference on the topic;
- attending a national or international conference to deliver the results of the project (many government funding officials cannot travel to conferences, but they can fund you to go and disseminate the results);
- providing a satellite downlink to others in your field;

- producing a CD or video of the project; and/or
- creating a web site and allowing others to download parts of your work.

Activities aimed at disseminating project results are viewed positively by most funding sources. In general, they want their agency and program name up in lights and are willing to pay for it. So, build the costs related to dissemination into your budget. Remember, you can always negotiate down the cost for dissemination in your budget, but you may be surprised at how much the grantor will want to keep in.

ATTACHMENTS (APPENDIX)

The attachments can provide the winning edge when your proposal is compared to a competitor's. Throughout the proposal development process, you should be gathering materials that could be used in the attachment section of your proposal. Your final task is to select which materials to include. Naturally, you want to choose those that will best support your proposal and build credibility. Whether the funding source skims over them or examines them in detail, attachments may include

- studies or research, tables, charts, and graphs;
- vitae of key personnel;
- minutes of advisory committee meetings;
- a list of board members;
- an auditor's report or statement;
- letters of recommendation or endorsement;
- a copy of your IRS tax-exempt designation;
- pictures or architect's drawings;
- copies of your agency's publications; and
- a list of other funding sources you will approach for support.

Check funding source rules to determine what is required and the regulations regarding how long your attachments section can be. Guidelines usually state the maximum number of pages it can have. Many funding sources will not want you to include the full vitae of key staff and will specify that you attach abbreviated resumes or biosketches instead.

Also check funding source rules for the appropriate appendix format. Provide a separate table of contents for your appendix, and number the pages for easy reference.

WRITING YOUR FEDERAL OR STATE PROPOSAL

Your proposal must reflect what the funding source wants and what the reviewers will be looking for. To create a winning proposal

- follow the guidelines exactly (even when they seem senseless, or when you think you are repeating yourself),
- fill in all the blanks,
- double-check all computations, and
- include anything the funding source asks for, even if you think you already provided the information under another section of your proposal.

When writing your proposal, keep in mind that it must be readable and easy to skim. Place special emphasis on vocabulary, style, and visual attractiveness and, above all, consider the intended audience (the reviewer).

Vocabulary

Your contact with a past reviewer will have given you an idea of the reviewers' level of expertise and their depth of knowledge in your subject area. Be sure your proposal uses language appropriate to the reviewers. Shorter words are generally better than long, complex words, and avoid buzzwords unless you are sure the reviewer expects them. Define all acronyms, or avoid them completely. You want to avoid using language that is under or over their level.

Writing Style

By now you should know the background of the typical reviewer selected by the grantor agency and how much time the reviewers spend reading each proposal. These peer reviewers are under pressure to use their time efficiently, so you must produce a proposal that is poignant, yet organized and easy to read. Your best aid here is to review two or three successful proposals. After all, they followed the golden rule—they got the gold! When you analyze them, I bet you will find that they adhere to the following grant winner techniques:

- Use simple sentences (no more than two commas) and short paragraphs (five to seven lines).
- Begin each section with a strong motivating lead sentence.
- Make sure your writing style cannot be construed as cute or offensive to the reader.
- Avoid stating the obvious and talking down to the reviewer.
- Develop a user-friendly proposal. One of the peer reviewers may be chosen to defend your proposal to the rest of the review panel. In this

case, you want to be certain to make the reviewer your friend by organizing and referencing attachments in such a way that they can be used
to mount a good defense and to answer the other panelists' questions.

Visual Attractiveness

Even scientific research need not look boring to the reviewer. To enhance the
"readability" of your proposal and make your points stand out, use

- <u>underlining,</u>
- bullets,
- **different fonts,**
- various margins and s p a c i n g,
- **bold headings,**
- pictures and graphics,
- charts and tables, and/or
- *handwriting.*

While you must follow the grantor's rules regarding type font, number of
characters per inch, line spacing, and so on, your computer and laser printer
can provide you with a wealth of creative ways to make your proposal more
readable.

You will understand how important readability, writing style, and visual
attractiveness are after your read several samples of funded proposals followed
by your own. Tired reviewers need all the help you can give them to locate
and score the important sections of your proposal. Avoid creativity for its own
sake, but think of the reviewer and your goal to hit those review criteria as you
write your proposal.

Keep foremost in your mind that these federal funds are the result of taxes
paid by individuals like you, as well as corporations. It is your responsibility to
make the plan for how you propose to spend these moneys as precise and as
clearly related to the project outcome as possible. The tendency to "round up"
numbers and pad budgets is a threat to your credibility and could affect your ability to gain the peer reviewers' and federal staff's confidence.

Remember, do not leave anything to chance. All required forms must be
completed precisely.

Online Proposal Preparation

All federal agencies are moving toward meeting Congress's paperless environment mandate, and how it impacts proposal creation and submission is different
in each agency. Most agencies have replaced paper grant applications with electronic applications, and many are requiring electronic submission of grant

applications via the online portal of Grants.gov. Through your research you will learn where and how to apply for your specific grant. In many cases, you will need to check the *Federal Register* notice for your competition to determine whether electronic submissions will be accepted via Grants.gov or the funding agency's own electronic system and whether electronic submission is optional or required.

For example, the Department of Education is transitioning to Grants.gov and is encouraging all applicants to register with Grants.gov at http://www.grants.gov. However, some of their competitors are still allowing paper applications, and some are still requiring submittal through the Department's e-Application system. As with all grant-making agencies, the application notice for each competition is the final authority for that competition and specifies whether electronic applications are mandatory or voluntary and whether applicants are to submit them through Grants.gov or the agency's electronic submittal system. To determine if your program is accepting electronic applications and through which portal, visit the Department of Education's link to *Federal Register* notices at http://www.ed.gov/legislation/FedRegister/announcements/.

If the program is accepting electronic applications through the Department's electronic submittal system and you are a new user, you will need to register to use e-Application at http://e-grants.ed.gov/. You will then be given a user name and a password and be able to access your unique application. You can complete the application and all necessary forms online. However, only authorized individuals from your organization can submit the application. Check with your certifying official or sponsored research office before submission.

In furtherance of the President's Management Agenda, the National Science Foundation has also begun to require the use of Grants.gov for the electronic preparation and submission of proposals for *some* of its funding opportunities rather than NSF FastLane, its own electronic submittal system. In determining whether to use Grants.gov or the NSF FastLane system for the electronic preparation and submission of a proposal, applicants should note that neither collaborative proposals nor any other proposals that contain subawards may be submitted to NSF using Grants.gov. All collaborative proposals must be submitted via the NSF FastLane system. Since NSF does not use the Grants.gov system for all of its grant competitions, it is imperative that you check NSF's official program solicitation to determine the correct application procedures.

The National Institutes of Health (NIH) is also replacing paper grant applications with electronic applications and transitioning to the electronic submission of grant applications via the online portal of Grant.gov. Funding Opportunity Announcements with application packages attached can be found at both Grants.gov and in the NIH Guide for Grants and Contracts (often referred to as the NIH Guide) at http://grants.nih.gov/grants/guide/index.html.

While electronic systems are seeking to make proposal creation and submittal simple and accurate, there still are some shortcomings. For example, most of the existing systems do not allow for spell or grammar check. In some cases, you are instructed to download to perform those functions, and then upload the corrected proposal sections. In addition, electronic submission, especially through Grants.gov, can be very time-consuming—so much so that the Department of Education advises applicants to register early, submit early, and verify that their submissions were received timely and validated successfully.

Obviously, there are many new and interesting challenges we must face as we move closer toward a total electronic grant application system and away from print copy. However, we can take solace in knowing that electronic application and submission reduces paperwork, postal costs, and storage expenses, and even saves a forest or two!

CHAPTER 14

Improving Your Federal Proposal
The Grants Quality Circle

C onsistently funded grantees usually take advantage of a presubmission review of their proposals by a colleague or two. While this technique is positive, its value depends on how knowledgeable those reviewing your proposal are of the field and how much they know about the actual peer-review system that will be used by the actual reviewers. For example, while a four-hour review of your proposal by one of your colleagues will be quite detailed, it may actually be counterproductive in its suggestions if the real reviewer is going to spend just one hour reviewing it. The secret to improving your federal proposal is to conduct a mock review that emulates the actual review system as closely as possible. Of course, the *first* step is to be proactive and to make sure you have enough time to take advantage of this most valuable technique. The *second* step is to get the relevant information on the reviewers and the scoring process.

Proactive grantseekers initiate proposal development early in the federal grant cycle and therefore have sufficient time to have their proposals reviewed by their peers before submission. You will improve your proposal and significantly increase your chances for success by asking several colleagues or members of your grants advisory committee to voluntarily role-play being the review team that will ultimately pass judgment on your proposal. This presubmission review process is really a test run or mock review, and the group conducting it is your quality circle, as described in William Edwards Deming's work in total quality management (TQM).[1] If you follow the TQM model, you will not pay your mock reviewers to take part in the activity. They should be motivated by their desire to help you improve your proposal, increase its probability of acceptance, and, thus, enhance the image of your organization. It is to everyone's advantage to position your institution in the most favorable manner. In many institutions, the grants office will assist you in setting up this improvement exercise and, when necessary, may even pay the mock reviewers a small stipend. In some instances, course release time is also offered as an incentive for leading mock reviews.

As previously mentioned, the most significant factor in the success of this improvement exercise is how closely each aspect of the mock review resembles the actual federal or state review. The benefits you can derive from this technique are directly related to your ability to create the scenario in which the actual reviewers will find themselves.

To arrange a mock review that is similar to what the actual review will be like, secure pertinent information on the background of last year's reviewers, a copy of the scoring system that will be used, and an outline of the actual process. Through preproposal contact (see chapter 12), you should already have information about the setting in which your proposal will be reviewed.

To make this exercise as valuable as possible, provide your mock review group or grants quality circle with data on the following:

- the training each reviewer receives.
- the setting in which proposals are reviewed (the federal agency, the reviewer's home, both sites, and so on).
- the review process: Does one reviewer defend the proposal while others try to locate flaws or weaknesses?
- the scoring system: Are scores averaged? Are the highest and lowest scores eliminated and the remainder averaged?
- the amount of time spent reviewing each proposal.

It is essential that you instruct the members of your grants quality circle to spend only the same amount of time reviewing your proposal as the actual reviewers will. Some of your mock reviewers may mistakenly think they will be helping you by taking an inordinate amount of time to read your proposal carefully. However, if actual reviewers will skim parts of the proposal, then your mock reviewers should do the same. Remind your quality circle participants that they should be trying to *mirror* the actual reviewers, not do a better job than them! If the actual reviewers will invest over 60 minutes reviewing and scoring each proposal, consider distributing your draft proposal to the members of your grants quality circle before they come together.

The sample letter inviting an individual to participate in a grants quality circle (exhibit 14.1) and the federal/state grants quality circle worksheet (exhibit 14.2) will help you carry out this valuable exercise. After the

Date

Name
Address

Dear _____:

I would like to take this opportunity to request your input in helping our [organization, group, team] submit the very best grant proposal possible. We are asking that you review the enclosed proposal from the point of view of the federal reviewer. The attached materials will help you role-play the actual manner in which the proposal will be evaluated.

Please read the information on the reviewers' backgrounds and the scoring system and limit the time you spend reading the proposal to the time constraints that the real reviewers will observe. A grants quality circle worksheet has been provided to assist you in recording your scores and comments.

A meeting of all mock reviewers comprising our quality circle has been scheduled for [date]. Please bring your grants quality circle worksheet with you to this meeting. The meeting will last less than one hour. Its purpose is to analyze the scores and brainstorm suggestions to improve this proposal.

Sincerely,

Name
Phone Number

SAMPLE LETTER INVITING AN INDIVIDUAL TO PARTICIPATE IN A GRANTS QUALITY CIRCLE

EXHIBIT 14.1

suggestions from your mock review have been incorporated into your final proposal, you are ready to move on to submission.

In some cases it is not feasible to assemble a group of volunteers for a quality circle. There may be too few colleagues in your organization to conduct a role-playing activity such as this, confidentiality may be an issue, personality problems may exist, or competition in the field could rule out the possibility of such an activity occurring. One option in these instances would be to ask one or two individuals whom you trust from outside your organization or off campus to review your proposal. Provide them with the same data and worksheets discussed above, and, if necessary, offer them an honorarium for their efforts ($200 is common). You could request that they sign a nondisclosure agreement. Most university grant offices have these agreement forms and will be happy to share a copy with you. This way you can tailor the agreement to your project with

The following information is designed to help you develop the proper focus for the review of the attached proposal.

1. The Review Panelists
    Proposals are read by review panelists with the following degrees and backgrounds:
    Degrees: _____
    Backgrounds (Age, Viewpoints, Biases, and So On): _____
    _____
    _____

2. The Time Element and Setting
    Number of proposals read by each reviewer: _____
    Average length of time spent reading each proposal: _____
    Proposals are read at the: _____reviewer's home
                                      _____reviewer's work
                                      _____funder's location
                                      _____other site

3. The Scoring System
    a. The scoring system that will be employed is based on a scale of: _____
    _____

    b. The areas to be scored are (list or include attachment):

Area	Total Possible Points	Your Score

    c. According to the total points per area, how many points represent an outstanding, superior, adequate, weak, or poor score? For example, if the total points possible for one area are 25, 0-8 = poor, 9-12 = weak, 13-19 = adequate, 20-23 = superior, and 24-25 = outstanding.
    _____
    _____

    d. After recording your scores, list the positive points of the proposal that may appeal to the actual reviewer. Also list those areas that seem weak and may cost valuable points. List suggestions for improvement.
    _____
    _____
    _____

FEDERAL/STATE GRANTS QUALITY CIRCLE WORKSHEET

EXHIBIT 14.2

minimal effort. Seldom are these extraordinary security measures necessary with colleagues, but this is an option you may want to consider to ensure that no one steals your idea.

A look at a few selected scoring systems reveals the importance of knowing how your proposal will be reviewed and how important it is to share this information with your mock reviewers. The first example from the Office of

Educational Research and Improvement is characterized by a specific point system, heavily weighed toward national significance and project design.

Example 1

National significance	30 points
Quality of project design	30 points
Quality of potential contribution of personnel	15 points
Adequacy of resources	15 points
Quality of management plan	10 points
Total	100 points

In examples 2 and 3 the National Institute on Aging (example 2) and the National Science Foundation (example 3) do not use evaluation systems based on points. In situations like these, the grantseeker must ask more questions of the grantor so that he or she can ascertain what looks "good" under each criterion. After all, to play the game you need to know *all* the rules!

Example 2

- Scientific, technical, or medical significance
- Appropriateness and adequacy of approach
- Qualifications of principal investigator/staff
- Availability of resource
- Appropriateness of budget
- Adequacy of plans to include both genders and minorities
- Protection of human subjects

Example 3

- Criterion 1: What is the intellectual merit of the proposed activity?
- Criterion 2: What are the broader impacts of the proposed activity?

Few techniques suggested in this book will have a more dramatic effect on the quality of your proposals than the grants quality circle. Support for this activity will be rewarded through the promotion of a better image with reviewers and federal staff, as well as an increase in quality proposals from staff members participating in the activity.

NOTE

1. Gary Fellers, *The Deming Vision: SPC/TQM for Administrators* (Milwaukee: ASQC Quality Press, 1992).

CHAPTER 15

Submission

What to Do and What Not to Do

Although this chapter addresses the federal grants area, much of the information it contains can also be applied to other government funding sources such as state, county, and city. Irrespective of which type of public funding source you are submitting your proposal to, you do not want to do anything at this late stage that may have a negative impact on your submitted proposal's outcome.

WHAT TO DO

Submit your proposal a day or two before the deadline. Do not position yourself as a last-minute applicant who beats the deadline by a few minutes. After all your hard work you do not want to position yourself as a loser. Grantors have told me that they worry about funding last minute Herculean proposal developers because they are likely to experience problems with their expenditure rates (that is, having leftover money that ends up as a grant continuation or extension), late or missing reports and evaluations, and a host of other maladies that could make the grantor's program look bad to Congress.

Follow all instructions and every rule. Do not wait until your proposal has been written, has undergone a mock review, and is ready to be sent out before you read the submission rules. Review the submittal requirements early to make sure you have enough time to comply with them. Do not jeopardize your chances for success by failing to show funders that you have read and complied with their rules for submission.

Unfortunately, many grantseekers read the requirements too late and find that they cannot meet the grantor's deadlines. They then include a note with their proposal saying that they will forward the necessary documents at a later date. This is a red flag to grantors and alerts them that this applicant may be a problem. This may even get your proposal automatically rejected.

Even with extensive instructions, grantseekers make mistakes in obtaining appropriate or authorized signatures, page length, number of pages, assurances, and so on. In fact, it would be too time-consuming to list all of the problems federal grantors have in gaining compliance with their rules. Review and follow the submittal procedures contained in your application package carefully.

Grants.gov is the primary means for applying for federal grants, and its submittal procedures must be followed precisely. The process can be timely, and problems are bound to occur if you attempt it at the last minute. In fact, it can take longer to submit your proposal electronically than it did with the old hard copy system that Grants.gov has replaced. If you want to apply for a grant through Grants.gov you and your organization must complete the Grants.gov registration process. To register, your organization will need to provide its Dun & Bradstreet D-U-N-S Number. If your organization does not have one, you will need to go to the Dun & Bradstreet web site at http://fedgov.dnb.com/webform to obtain a number. Your organization must also be registered with the Central Contractor Registry (CCR). To ensure that it is, go to http://www.ccr.gov. You will also have to register yourself as an Authorized Organization Representative (AOR), or find out who is authorized as your AOR by your organization. These registrations are not done overnight. Some require four to six weeks. Therefore, start early so you do not miss any deadlines due to nonregistration.

WHAT NOT TO DO

It is recommended that you limit the use of elected representatives in the grants process, especially at submittal time. Your institution may have rules governing who can contact elected officials. Between the time it takes to get permission and the controversy over the earmarking of federal grant funds, I recommend you avoid congresspeople and senators. Federal bureaucrats view the use of congresspeople and their aides as potentially unethical and possibly illegal. Elected officials want to be viewed by you, the voter and grant applicant, as ready to help in any way, but their assistance should be enlisted only when your own efforts have failed in preproposal contact and information gathering about past grantees and reviewers.

Do not ask program officers for extra time or a later submittal date, and do not ask to send in any parts of the proposal after the deadline. Do not contact federal bureaucrats after submission. This is viewed as an attempt to influence the grantor's review process and decision. On a rare occasion, advancement in the field could dramatically effect a proposal you have already submitted. In this instance, you should alert the program officer of the ramifications of the advancement and how they will affect your proposal's protocol or budget. Send the program officer an email explaining the situation and let him or her decide whether to send the new information to the reviewers, and so on.

OTHER SUBMISSION TECHNIQUES

Several optional techniques may be helpful:

- Most federal agencies require electronic submittal and have their application forms available online. Many agencies use Grants.gov, while others have their own electronic submittal systems. For example, the National Science Foundation (NSF) uses an Internet/web-based system known as FastLane that allows customers to conduct business electronically with the NSF. Individuals sign on to the system and send/receive their transactions directly to/from the NSF. These transactions represent a wide range of activities, including proposal submittal by institutional research administrators. (To obtain instructions on how to use FastLane, visit http://www.fastlane.nsf.gov/.) Internet transmittal is becoming so common that now it is even the preferred method for peer reviewers to submit their proposal critiques.

  While the use of the Internet is growing in this field, it is still a good idea to check to see what your proposal looks like when received by electronic submission. What happens to graphics and to the layout and design? A little care may pay off dramatically.

  Double-check with your institution's grants office to see when it needs your proposal by to do its job and who the authorized agent is to make the transmittal official.

- Check with your grants office to see if you (or it) could send a copy of your proposal abstract or summary to your congressperson's office. Advise the congressperson that you do not want or expect any intervention at this point, but let him or her know the approximate or anticipated date of the notice of award (usually several months away). Many times, federal granting officials will inform the congressperson of awards before they notify the grantee. Therefore, it is important to alert your congressperson that you have submitted a proposal and that you will contact him or her again closer to the notification date. Let your congressperson know that you would appreciate it if he or she would contact you immediately if he or she receives notice of your award first, so that you can prepare a joint public relationships release.

CHAPTER 16

Federal Grant Requirements

Many nonprofit agencies exhibit great fear and trepidation over the rules regarding federal grant moneys. These fears are basically unwarranted and should be of concern only to nonprofit organizations that do not have adequate fiscal rules and regulations. The restrictions governing usage of federal funds are understandable and in most cases reasonable. Yes, there are instances of disallowed expenditures two or three years after a grant has been completed, but they are avoidable. Most people remember the exception rather than the rule. Over $400 billion in federal grant funds are awarded each year, and only a small fraction of grantees have their expenditures disallowed or experience a problem with an audit. Most likely, your existing personnel, accounting, and purchasing procedures will be adequate. If you must make changes in your system to ensure the adequate handling of federal funds, however, do so. Such changes will increase the credibility of your system.

The federal grants requirement worksheet (see exhibit 16.1) will help you comply with most federal grant requirements. If your institution has a grants administration office, this worksheet may not be necessary, but you, the project director, still need to know the facts so that you can help in the overall administration of your grant.

Project Title: _____

Project Director: _____

Federal Account Identification Number: _____

Agency Staff: _____

Agency Phone Number: _____ Agency Fax Number: _____ Agency Email: _____

Notification of Award Received On (Date): _____

Start Date of Project: _____ End Date of Project: _____

Dates Reports Are Due: _____

Final Report Due On (Date): _____

Number of Years Funding Can Be Applied For: _____

Matching or In-Kind Requirements: _____ % $ _____

Where Matching or In-Kind Records Will Be Kept: _____

Who Will Be Responsible for Keeping Them: _____

Federal Rules Governing This Grant

OMB Circulars/Guidelines Governing Grant Expenditures

_____

_____

Location of OMB Circulars/Guidelines Governing Grant Expenditures:

_____

_____

Special Rules and Federal Management Circulars (List from Assurances Section of Proposal):

_____

_____

Location of Special Rules and Federal Management Circulars:

_____

_____

Federal Rules and Your Organization's Policy On

Copyrights: _____

_____

Patents: _____

_____

Drug Usage and Counseling: _____

_____

Fair and Equal Employment:_____

_____

Institutional Review Boards (Include Person Responsible for Compliance and Approval)

Human Subjects

_____

_____

FEDERAL GRANTS REQUIREMENT WORKSHEET

EXHIBIT 16.1

Animal Subjects
_____
_____

Recombinant DNA
_____
_____

Radioactive Material
_____
_____

Research Misconduct
_____
_____

Other
_____
_____

FEDERAL GRANTS REQUIREMENT WORKSHEET *(continued)*

EXHIBIT 16.1

FEDERAL GRANTS REQUIREMENT WORKSHEET

The federal grants requirement worksheet will help you familiarize yourself with and keep abreast of the basic obligations your nonprofit organization agrees to fulfill by accepting federal grant funds.

1. Complete the first section of the worksheet when you receive notice of funding. Include the federal account identification number and all other information you can supply. It is critical that you record the actual start date or date funded so that you do not change any grant expenditures before the grant's official award date. Review your project planner and record the dates on which you must supply progress indicators/milestones/progress reports.
2. List the Office of Management (OMB) circulars that will govern your grant expenditures and where the circulars are located.
3. Record any information about the number of years of funding that can be applied for.
4. Indicate the percentage and dollar total of the cost-sharing/matching fund requirements, where the records will be kept, and who will be responsible for keeping them.
5. Acceptance of federal funds requires that your organization have a policy regarding drug use and counseling of employees.

6. If your grant calls for the creation of unique materials, make note of the rules regarding copyrights, patents, ownership, and use. Noting these in advance reduces problems later.
7. The fair and equal employment rules are reasonable and should pose no problems for most nonprofit organizations.
8. List the office or person responsible for approval of projects that involve copyrights or patents, or the use of human and animal subjects, recombinant DNA, or radioactive material. If you work for an organization that already has institutional review boards, be sure to check with those groups. If your organization does not have institutional review boards or committees, do not initiate them. Instead, involve a university- or college-related individual on your grants advisory committee, and ask him or her to use his or her institution's review boards.

Even though your proposal may not call for the performance of hard-core research, the federal government is very broad in its interpretation of what activities pose a potential danger to humans. In fact, federal officials even require human subjects' approval for most needs assessment surveys, model projects, and demonstration grants.

RAISING AND DOCUMENTING MATCHING FUNDS

One of the more confusing areas of federal grants is the requirement of matching funds or in-kind contributions (also known as cost sharing). An organization can be asked to supply either cash, services, or facilities to match a percentage of the grant. This requirement may change over the years that federal funds support the project. For example, year 1 may require a 20-percent match, year 2 a 40-percent match, and year 3 a 50-percent match.

In some cases, the federal instructions state that a match is not required but encouraged. If you have inquired into this matter, discovered that a match will help you get funded, and have designated a specific amount in your budget for a match or in-kind contribution, be aware that this match must be documented and will be subject to an audit to verify the amount. It is always wise to document and list the efforts and costs that will be provided by your organization and partners. Review your project planner for any personnel, consultants, contract services, supplies, equipment, or materials that will be contributed to your project. Remember not to list anything that is being supplied to this grant that was provided under any other federal program.

The worksheet on sources of matching funds (see exhibit 16.2) can help you plan a successful matching funds campaign before you approach federal agencies. The worksheet contains several standard methods for cost sharing and provides an evaluation system for each method. (This worksheet can also be useful when working with foundations and corporations that request matching support.)

Project Title: _____

Total Project Cost: $ _____

Match Required: _____ % $ _____

Review each of the following sources of matching funds. Check with federal officials to ensure that your match is in compliance with their rules and will be accepted. Make sure that nothing listed under your match has been provided from federal funds.

1.   Personnel – List the percentage of time and effort of each individual who will be contributing to the match. Include salaries, wages, and fringe benefits.

      Options:
      Include the time and effort of volunteers, consultants, and/or corporate sponsors if allowable by the grantor.

      If the project calls for staff training or development, will your organization be required to increase salaries? If so, check with the grantor to see whether this can be listed as a match.

2.   Equipment – List any equipment that will be purchased primarily to carry out this project. Include the cost of each piece and the total equipment cost.

3.   Facilities – List the location, square footage, and cost per foot for each facility and the total facilities (space) cost.

4.   Foundation/Corporate Grantors – What other grantors could you approach for a grant to match this grant?

      Foundations:

      Corporations:

5.   Fund-raising Activities – In some cases you may have to resort to fund-raising activities to develop your matching portion. List the activities and the net return expected from each.

      Special Events (Dance, Raffle, etc.):
      Sales of Products:
      Other:

WORKSHEET ON SOURCES OF MATCHING FUNDS

EXHIBIT 16.2

FEDERAL GRANTS MANAGEMENT CIRCULARS

The highly regulated, detailed rules about grant management are probably the most imposing characteristic of federal grants. These rules may specify allowable costs, indirect cost rates, accounting requirements, and the like. Before getting involved in government grants, you and/or your accounting department should review the appropriate grants management circulars. Such a review usually diminishes fears about your organization's ability to comply with federal grant requirements. In most cases you will find that your organization has safeguards in effect that meet the requirements.

The Office of Management and Budget produces circulars outlining uniform standards for financial dealings with government granting agencies. These circulars can be accessed online at http://www.whitehouse.gov/omb/circulars/index.html. To obtain circulars that are not available online, call the Office of Management and Budgets' information line at (202) 395-3080.

The following section is a broad description of OMB Circular A-110.

OMB Circular A-110

OMB Circular A-110 is entitled "Uniform Administrative Requirements for Grants and Agreements with Institutions of Higher Education, Hospitals and Other Nonprofit Organizations." This circular is a guide to the rules regarding federal grants. The circular is divided into the following four subparts:

- Subpart A—General
- Subpart B—Pre-Award Requirements
- Subpart C—Post-Award Requirements

    Financial and Program Management

    Property Standards

    Procurement Standards

    Reports and Records

    Termination and Enforcement

- Subpart D—After-the-Award Requirements

OMB Circular A-110 also includes an appendix that addresses contract provisions.

Colleges and universities will also be interested in OMB Circular A-21, which defines cost principles for federal research and development grants to educational institutions. All nonprofit organizations should familiarize themselves with OMB Circular A-122, "Cost Principles for Non-Profit Organizations," and state and local governments must also review OMB Circular A-87, "Cost Principles for State, Local and Indian Tribal Governments" and OMB Circular A-102, "Grants and Cooperative Agreements with State and Local Governments." Please be advised that you should always refer to the most current circular for the specific rules and regulations in your area.

Exhibit 16.3 lists all of the grants management OMB Circulars in numerical sequence. Fears concerning the expenditure of federal grant funds are reduced

Cost Principles
    A-21,   Educational Institutions
    A-87,   State and Local Governments
    A-122, Nonprofit Organizations

Administrative Requirements
    A-102, State and Local Governments
    A-110, Institutions of Higher Education, Hospitals, and Other Organizations

Audit Requirements
    A-133, States, Local Governments, and Nonprofit Organizations

GRANTS MANAGEMENT OMB CIRCULARS

EXHIBIT 16.3

when you request the appropriate OMB circulars for your type of organization and review the rules with your fiscal staff. From purchasing to personnel, your organization will most likely already have the necessary safeguards in place. Those areas that look as if they will pose a problem can be addressed in a general manner, for all federal grants, or handled separately, case by case, to avoid any difficulties.

CHAPTER 17

Dealing with the Decision of Public Funding Sources

The federal government is attempting to streamline the grants process. This includes making award determinations that are understandable and the same across all granting programs. Instead of making determinations that left grantseekers confused (such as "supportable but not fundable"), the federal government is now using the following determinations:

- accepted (as written);
- accepted with modifications (usually budget modifications, which will affect some activities);
- rejected with reviewers' comments (the proposal did not reach the level or score required for funding, but comments have been included, possibly to encourage resubmittal);
- rejected without reviewers' comments (the proposal did not reach the level or score required for funding, no comments were included, and thus, the grantseeker has no idea whether to resubmit).

ACCEPTED

If your proposal is accepted, consider taking the following steps:

1. Thank the grantor. Whether you are notified by phone, letter, or email, send the program or project officer a thank-you letter expressing your

appreciation for the time and effort staff and reviewers expended on your proposal.

2. Request the reviewers' comments, and include a self-addressed label for the funding source's convenience or your email address.

3. Ask the federal official for insight into what you could have done better. Yes, you can even improve a funded proposal. Learn how.

4. Invite the program or project officer for a site visit.

5. Ask the official what mistakes other grantees often make in carrying out their funded grant so you can be sure to avoid these errors.

6. Review the reporting structure. What does the grantor require (milestones, progress indicators, and so on) and when?

ACCEPTED WITH BUDGET MODIFICATIONS

Should your proposal receive this response, do the following:

1. Send the funding source a thank-you letter.

2. Call the funding source and suggest that the program officer refer to your project planner to negotiate the budget terms.

3. Discuss the option of eliminating some of the project's methods or activities.

4. If several activities must be eliminated, consider dropping the accomplishment of an objective or reducing the expected degree of change.

5. If you are forced to negotiate away the supporting structure necessary to achieve your objectives, be prepared to turn down the funds. After all, you do not want to enter into an agreement that will cause you to lose credibility later.

REJECTED WITH COMMENTS

If your proposal is rejected but reviewer suggestions and comments are provided, review them. Are there comments and/or suggestions common to several of the reviewers? Do the comments point to a basic problem with the approach or protocol or with the importance of dealing with the problem in general? Do the reviewers suggest changes that you could entertain in a resubmittal without dramatically altering your grants approach? Do the comments suggest resubmittal?

If you get the sense from the reviewers' comments that resubmittal with the suggested changes is a good idea, consider the following:

1. Sending the funding official a thank-you letter or email in appreciation for his or her time and effort as well as that of the reviewers and staff. Let the funding official know that although you were aware of the risk of failure

before you invested your time in applying, you would appreciate assistance in reapplying.
2. Asking the funding official for more suggestions.
3. Finding out whether your proposal could possibly be funded as a pilot project, as a needs assessment, or in some other way.
4. Asking whether there are any ways the funding source could assist you in getting ready for the next submission cycle, such as conducting a preliminary review.
5. Asking whether it would be wise for you to reapply. What are your chances and what would you have to change? (Reapply if the program officer is even the slightest bit optimistic.)
6. Asking whether you could become a reviewer to learn more about the review process.

By examining the reviewers' comments, you may find that some reviewers scored a section of your proposal as outstanding, while others gave the same section a low score. This situation can create a dilemma. Changing your proposal to reflect one reviewer's comments may negate another reviewer's comments, and your changes could result in resubmission scores that are just average. Ask the grantor what you can do about this situation. Also, ask an outside expert to review your proposal; even if you must pay someone to review the proposal, you need insight into what is causing this discrepancy.

Your resubmittal application should take the reviewers' comments to heart and be significantly changed. You may even mention that the changes made in your resubmittal were suggested by the original reviewers. Sending the same proposal in hopes of different reviewers and a better outcome is not viewed positively.

REJECTED WITHOUT COMMENTS

New agency reviewing procedures call for a process that eliminates proposals with a low likelihood of funding from a thorough review. Some grantors even require that 25 to 50 percent of the applications they receive are given this brief and expedited review and then returned to the applicants without detailed reviewer comments. Many of the rejected applications that are not read thoroughly or evaluated and scored are cited for errors in the application itself or for nonallowable costs and/or inappropriate ideas.

If your proposal is rejected outright and you do not receive comments, or if you receive a notice stating that there were many more credible proposals than funding available, develop a different approach and do not even consider resubmitting the same proposal. It does no good to defend your proposal or to write a nasty response. When rejected, I like to think that I may be ahead of my time and more visionary than the reviewers. Discuss options with your advisory group and brainstorm a different approach to solving the problem.

In addition, write or email the program officer to thank him or her for the opportunity and ask if you could

- be a reviewer to learn how to prepare a better proposal and
- meet with him or her to discuss a new approach.

No matter what the determination (accepted, accepted with modifications, rejected with comments, or rejected without comments), or the degree to which your proposal was reviewed, your response to your grant application's outcome must be positive. Whether you are jubilant or depressed, thank the grantor and demonstrate your willingness to learn from the experience and, if possible, the funding source's feedback.

CHAPTER 18

Follow-Up with Government Funding Sources

The objective of follow-up is to position yourself as an asset to funding sources and not as a pest. You want to develop professional relationships and maintain contact with funding sources throughout the grants process, not just at submittal and award time. In addition to advising funders of your willingness to serve as a reviewer, consider

- forwarding notes on special articles or books in your area to them,
- inviting them to visit your organization,
- asking whether they would like to speak at your professional group or association's conference, or at a special grants conference,
- asking them what meetings or conferences they will be attending so that you can look them up, and/or
- requesting information about what you can do to have an impact on legislation affecting their funding levels or allocations.

By remaining on grantors' mailing lists and reviewing their agency publications (that is, NSF Guide, NIH Bulletin) and/or the *Federal Register*, you will gain advance knowledge of the next funding opportunity. Do not wait until next year's deadline to begin thinking about your ensuing application. Start to plan for next year right after funding decisions are made for the current year.

The best way to learn what is going on is to visit the funding source personally. Keep in touch. Watch for meeting announcements in the *Federal Register*.

Testify at committee hearings that will affect the agency and its funding level. Send the agency blind copies of your efforts to have an impact on legislation for it (and yourself). Use your association memberships and legislative committees to push for changes that benefit the particular agency, and write to Senate and House appropriations committees to increase funding. Attend professional meetings and sessions that program officers are speaking at, and ask questions.

DEVELOPING CONTINUED GRANT SUPPORT

The key to continued success is to repeat the steps that have brought you to this point. If you have used the concepts presented in this manual to develop a proactive grants process, you have a system that alerts you to changes in program rules, deadlines, and the like through the *Federal Register*, mailing lists, personal contacts, and established links.

Although federal officials may change jobs and positions, they seem to reappear again and again. A systematic approach to recording research on funding sources and officials will prove useful as you come across old friends and make new ones. By maintaining your relationships, whether you have received funding or not, you demonstrate to funding sources that you plan to be around for awhile and that you will not forget them as soon as you receive their checks. Unfortunately, changes in staffing at government agencies make maintaining contacts more difficult. Just when things are going great, the program officers you have been working with will move on. But take heart; they may appear again somewhere down the grants road, so keep on their good side!

PART THREE

....

Private/Foundation Funding Opportunities

CHAPTER 19

Understanding the Private
Foundation Marketplace

The foundation grants marketplace is dynamic, fascinating, and very lucrative for the astute grants person. Foundations grant funds to many of the projects and research that government grantors will not. In addition to greater funding flexibility and variety, 99 percent of foundations require an abbreviated proposal that is typically less than two to three pages in length, and some may require only a one-page letter of intent. While this may sound great, the brevity of the process can encourage grantseekers to simply locate the name and address of 20 or 30 foundations and send the same letter proposal to each of them. This "dear occupant, please send foundation grant" approach is a fatal mistake, resulting in rejection and negative positioning. In addition, the foundations receiving these massive amounts of inappropriate proposals are totally overwhelmed. As Martin Teitel, a foundation director, writes in his book *"Thank You for Submitting Your Proposal,"* "People find or buy lists of funders, plug them into their database, and send out what must be immense numbers of generic proposals. These misplaced proposals waste the effort of busy grant-seekers, and clog up the funder screening system."[1]

In order to develop an appreciation of the dilemma caused by hundreds of thousands of misplaced proposals, you must look at the facts. In 2006 foundation grant making represented 12.4 percent of the $295 billion in philanthropic giving in the United States. This equates to roughly $36 billion for which approximately 900,000 nonprofit organizations competed. This $36 billion was granted by approximately 80,000 independent, community, and operating foundations.

A study of the 10,000 largest independent foundations conducted by the Foundation Center and the Urban Institute in collaboration with Philanthropic Research reported that nearly three-quarters of the independent foundations surveyed did not have *any* paid staff. A Foundation Center survey of 20,891 foundations with at least $1 million in assets, or making grants of $100,000 or more, substantiated this dismal statistic—only 16.8 percent or 3,532 of the 20,981 foundations surveyed reported having staff. The contrast to federal grantors could not be greater. *Every* federal granting agency has staff.

Because of the lack of staff, foundation board members are generally the ones who review all submitted proposals and make the granting decisions. Few foundations utilize professional reviewers or experts in the field to review proposals. If there is a support person, he or she is normally responsible for just logging in proposals and perhaps for an initial screening of them to see if they contain anything close to what the foundation values. Many foundations even share directors and support staff.

You might think that of 80,000 foundations, most would have a web site. A survey conducted by the Foundation Center of 20,981 of the larger foundations indicated that only 12.4 percent or 2,599 maintained a web site. While the federal government has moved toward electronic submittal, only a few hundred of the foundations with web sites provide an interactive application form that allows for electronic preparation and submission of proposals. While the number of foundations with web sites and electronic application processes will certainly increase, change is slow and most foundations lack the motivation to make submittal easier—a move that would make their workload greater!

To fully understand private foundations you need to think like the wealthy individuals who create them and serve on their boards. Let us assume you have created a foundation to move vast sums of your wealth into a tax deductible entity that will allow you, your family, and your friends to fund projects and organizations that further your values, beliefs, and life's work. According to IRS rules, you must give away at least 5 percent of the market value of your foundation's assets each year to the groups your bylaws designate as recipients or pay a tax. However, the costs related to the administration of your foundation (that is, staffing, office space, equipment, travel, board salaries, and so forth) are included in this 5 percent. For instance, if the market value of your foundation's assets is $10 million, and you decide to disburse the minimum required amount of 5 percent or $500,000, you can subtract from this the cost of your director, support staff, office, and overhead, which could easily reach $250,000, leaving you only $250,000 to give away in the form of grants. So what can you do to reduce your administrative costs and increase the portion of the 5 percent you distribute through the grants process? You can decide not to hire a director or create an office, or have a staff. After all, you do not need a staff or reviewers. You know what you want to fund; thus, you want to make as much money as possible available for grants. Now you are thinking like the creator of a foundation.

To be a successful foundation grantseeker, you must discover what your prospective foundation funding source values, seek to understand how it looks at the world, and present your project in such a way that to reject it would conflict with the foundation's values, stated beliefs, and past giving pattern. To assist you in this research process, read the following brief descriptions of the basic types of foundations and then review the Grantseekers' Private Foundation Decision Matrix (table 19.1) to help you select which of the four basic types of private foundations is right for your project—national general purpose, special purpose, community, or family.

NATIONAL GENERAL PURPOSE FOUNDATIONS

To be designated as a national general purpose foundation, a foundation does not need to fit a hard-and-fast definition. *National general purpose* refers to the foundation's scope and type of granting pattern. Foundations in this group have a philanthropic interest in several subject areas and make grants for proposals that will have a broadscale impact across the United States and the world. They prefer model, creative, innovative projects that other groups can replicate to solve similar problems. Since national general purpose foundations like to promote change, they do not usually fund deficits, operating income, or the many necessary but not highly visible or creative functions of organizations.

National general purpose foundations have staff and, in some instances, use professional consultants as reviewers. Their applications are usually longer than those of the other types of foundations, and they often have more rules and regulations. They expect those they fund to have major players on staff and in consortia, and their grant size is larger than those of the other foundations.

Of the 80,000 foundations, there are probably less than 200 national general purpose foundations. Even though there are so few, most people have no trouble naming one, such as the Rockefeller or Ford Foundation. This is because they get a lot of attention for the size of the awards they make and the initiatives they launch. Unfortunately, the public image of these well-known foundations is what leads many grantseekers into thinking that the foundation marketplace in general makes more and bigger grants than it actually does.

SPECIAL PURPOSE FOUNDATIONS

Often confused with national general purpose foundations because some are very large and financed by unusually large asset bases, special purpose foundations are different in that they define their area of concern quite specifically. For example, the Robert Wood Johnson Foundation is a special purpose foundation synonymous with the health field, and the Exxon Education Foundation and The Carnegie Foundation for the Advancement of Teaching are special purpose foundations focusing on education. While grant sizes can be considerable,

TABLE 19.1

Grantseekers' Private Foundation Decision Matrix

TYPE OF FOUNDATION	GEOGRAPHIC NEED	TYPE OF PROJECT	GRANT AWARD SIZE FOR FIELD OF INTEREST	IMAGE	CREDENTIALS OF P.I./P.D.	PREPROPOSAL CONTACT	APPLICATION	REVIEW SYSTEM	GRANTS ADMIN. (RULES)
NATIONAL GENERAL PURPOSE	National need—local regional population	Model Innovative	Large Medium	National image +	National +	Write, phone	Short concept paper—longer form if interested	Staff and some peer review	Few audits and rules
SPECIAL PURPOSE	Need in area of interest	Model Innovative Research	Large to Small	Image not as critical as solution	Image in field of interest +	Write, phone	Short concept paper—longer form if interested	Board review (some staff)	Few audits and rules
COMMUNITY	Local need	Operation Replication Building/Equipment	Small	Local Image +	Respected locally	Write, phone, go see	Short letter proposal	Board review	Few audits and rules
FAMILY	Varies—but geographic concern for need	Innovative Replication Building/Equipment Some Research	Medium Small	Regional image +	Local/Regional	Write, phone	Short letter proposal	Board review	Very few audits and rules
NONPROFITS, SERVICE CLUBS, ETC.	Local	Replication Building/Equipment Scholarship	Small	Local image and member involvement	Local	Write, phone, present to committee or members	Short letter proposal	Committee review and/or member vote	Few audits and rules

special purpose foundations put the applicant's likelihood of making a contribution, or a breakthrough, in their area of concern foremost and *may* put less importance on staff prestige, publishing, and so forth.

There are probably only a few hundred of these dedicated special purpose foundations, and the key to success in this marketplace is to match your project with the foundation's specific area of interest and to demonstrate how your project will impact it.

COMMUNITY FOUNDATIONS

According to the Foundation Center, there were 700 community foundations in the United States in 2004. Although they use a variety of geographic parameters to define *community*, community foundations are easy to identify because their name denotes the area they serve (for example, San Diego Foundation, Cleveland Foundation, North Dakota Foundation, and Oregon Foundation).

Some think that community foundations are family foundations that restrict their granting to a particular state, city, or zip code. This is not the case. Community foundations fund projects and programs that no other type of foundation would consider supporting. From program deficits, to operating funds, to seed money for a needs assessment that might lead to a larger state or federal grant, community foundations exist to deal with local needs. They do not care if prospective grantees have national stature in their field. They just want to make sure that the funds they grant will be used to make a difference in the communities they serve. In general, community foundations are concerned with what works and are more interested in supporting the replication of successful projects than in taking chances with experimental approaches or research.

Many community foundations have special programs that help smaller, family foundations by administering their investments and assisting them in advertising, selecting grantees, and meeting their reporting requirements.

FAMILY FOUNDATIONS

There were approximately 31,347 family foundations that made grants in 2004. These foundations represented more than one-half of all independent foundations and accounted for $12.67 billion in grant making. Because their granting patterns represent the values of the family members whose interests have been memorialized by the creation of the foundations, granting patterns of family foundations vary widely from foundation to foundation and change frequently. Therefore, you must research them thoroughly to keep abreast of changes in interests and commitment.

Sixty-three percent of all family foundations have assets of less than $1 million, and most fund locally and in small amounts. In fact, 65 percent gave less than $100,000 in 2004. However, if they value what you propose, and you are in the right locale, you should consider them when developing your grants plan.

NONPROFIT ORGANIZATIONS, MEMBERSHIP GROUPS, PROFESSIONAL SOCIETIES, AND SERVICE CLUBS

In addition to the four basic types of private foundations, many nonprofit organizations, membership groups, professional societies, and service clubs award grants, and some even have foundations attached to them. The awards made through these groups are usually small and limited to a special field of interest. For example, a Kiwanis group may choose to provide support only for the purpose of improving business education in local schools.

The application forms used by these groups are typically short and easy to complete, and they will often provide funding for things that the four basic types of foundation would not consider supporting. While they have been known to provide matching funds for government grants, support for travel to conferences and meeting, and honorariums for experts and guest lecturers, they are particularly interested in funding things that will improve their image and the image of their members in their community.

TYPES OF GRANTS MADE BY PRIVATE FOUNDATIONS

The major vehicle of support by private foundations is a cash grant or award. The majority of foundations do not make grants to individuals except in the form of scholarships, and even those may be made through institutions. Most private foundations prefer that the third-party 501(c)3 tax-exempt organization affiliated with the grantee handle and disburse the award.

Program-related investments (PRIs) are a growing alternative to cash grants and awards, and foundations that make them, make them as a supplement to their existing grant programs. In the PRI vehicle your organization applies to a foundation for a loan, venture capital, or an investment in a charitable-use property. In 2004, independent, community, and operating foundations used PRIs for approximately $227.3 million. While this is only a small percentage of the $36 billion in total foundation giving in 2006, it is a growing interest and should be considered as a potential component of your grants plan.

PRIs are often made to organizations with an established relationship with the grant maker. A large portion of PRI dollars support affordable housing and community development. However, PRI support has also been provided for a variety of capital projects such as preserving historical buildings, repairing churches, emergency loans to social service agencies, and protecting and preserving open space and wildlife habitats.

Another type of foundation that is becoming a financial force in more and more local communities is the private grant making health foundation created from the conversion of nonprofit hospitals and health maintenance organizations to for-profit status. Federal law requires that proceeds from the sale of assets of tax-exempt entities go to charity. One way this requirement can be met is to establish a foundation to benefit the community previously served by the nonprofit. The Foundation Center identified 71 active private grant making new health foundations in 2004. Most of these foundations are dedicated to funding health-related projects, although some define health broadly and do provide funding for a variety of community purposes.

GRANTSEEKERS' PRIVATE FOUNDATION DECISION MATRIX

The Grantseekers' Private Foundation Decision Matrix (see table 19.1) summarizes the principal types of private foundation funding sources, their major funding characteristics and preferences, and their similarities and differences. Familiarizing yourself with this information will help you to create a prioritized list of the best foundations to approach and to determine the appropriate amount of funding to request from each.

Keep in mind that the majority of foundation grant award sizes are smaller than grantseekers think. Instead of making the mistake of asking for an inappropriate amount of funding from one foundation, consider breaking your proposal into fundable parts with each part appealing to the values of a different type of foundation funder.

Column 1 of the matrix lists the major foundation funding source types. Columns 2 through 10 provide information on variables such as geographic area/need, type of project, and award size. Please note that the matrix is meant to point you in the right direction only. Follow-up research will allow the proactive grantseeker to further estimate the funder's interest, the appropriateness of the project, and the proper grant size to request before proposal preparation and submission.

To achieve grants success you must be vigilant in attempting to consider all aspects of your proposal from the grantor's point of view. It should be increasingly evident that the "one proposal fits all" method of grantseeking will not meet with a positive response from such a diverse group of private grantors.

WHO AND WHAT PRIVATE FOUNDATIONS FUND

Most foundations award the majority of their funding in the states where they are located, and, unfortunately, there is great disparity in the number of foundations from state to state. In fact, almost one-half of the 50 largest foundations in the United States are located in just 3 of the 50 states (California, New York, and New Jersey).

If you are located in one of the other 47 states, remember that even nonprofit organizations in states with none of the 50 largest foundations still attract *some* grants from foundations located in other states. For example, Montana, a state with none of the largest foundations, was still able to draw 202 grants totaling $36,091,488 in 2004 from foundations in other states. In addition, you may be able to select a consortium partner located in a state with more foundations and win a foundation grant that you could share through a subcontract agreement. (To see where your state's foundation grants are coming from, visit http://foundationcenter.org/findfunders/statistics/states02_04.html.)

In 2005 approximately $15 billion was awarded in grants of *less* than $10,000 by approximately 63,968 foundations, and approximately $15 billion was awarded in grants for *more* than $10,000 by the remaining 1,172 foundations. The larger grants, those over $10,000, were tracked and analyzed by the Foundation Center. The data culminating from this analysis provide valuable insight into what foundations prefer to fund. Grantseekers willing to review this information and use it in a creative manner will be paid well for their efforts.

Instead of spending time rationalizing that your project fits into a grantor's funding priorities, spend your time considering the areas in which foundations concentrate their support and how you can redefine your project to fit into those areas with the greatest percent of foundation grants. Table 19.2 illustrates foundation grants by recipient category. A quick review of this table demonstrates clearly that education receives the greatest percentage of foundation grants. Table 19.3 breaks education into several subcategories and shows that of the grants given to education, higher education receives the greatest percentage, followed by elementary and secondary education. With this in mind, if elementary education is your project's original focus and you redefine it to include a higher education component by partnering with a college or university, you could

TABLE 19.2

FOUNDATION GRANTS BY RECIPIENT CATEGORY

RECIPIENT CATEGORY	PERCENT OF FOUNDATION GRANTS
Education	23.4%
Human Services	13.9%
Health	22.3%
Arts/Culture	12.8%
Public/Society Benefit	13.0%
Environment/Animals	5.3%
Science/Technology	2.9%
International	2.7%
Religion	2.3%
Social Science	1.4%

TABLE 19.3

PERCENT OF FOUNDATION GRANTS BY EDUCATION SUBCATEGORY

EDUCATION SUBCATEGORIES	PERCENT OF EDUCATION GRANTS BY SUBCATEGORY
Policy Management	0.2%
Elementary/Secondary	6.8%
Vocational/Technical	0.1%
Higher Education	9.3%
Graduate/Professional	3.0%
Adult/Continuing	0.1%
Library Science/Libraries	1.3%
Student Services	1.0%
Education Services	1.6%
Total Percent of Foundation Grants to Education	**23.4%**

substantially increase your chances of receiving a grant from a foundation. While I do not want you to become a sheep in wolf's clothing by making your project look like something it is not, review how you can redefine your project (chapter 5) and think of how a consortium or a different lead partner would provide a better match to foundation interests and granting patterns.

Also review the *type* of support you are searching for (that is, building and renovation, program development, research, and so on), and ask yourself if you could change your focus slightly (redefine it) to appeal to more grantors because of their preferences for certain types of support. Table 19.4 shows types of support awarded by dollar value of grants. Based on this table's data, if you were looking for computers or another type of equipment, it would be better to work the equipment into a program that integrated higher and elementary education. If it also could include research, you could make it even more fundable.

Many colleges and universities have rules about who can contact foundations. While I applaud the idea of coordination and control to protect the grantseeker's image, a review of Table 19.4 documents how absurd it is to keep tight control of foundation grants in order to keep the development officer's interest in capital campaigns as a priority, especially since capital campaigns represent only 2.1 percent of the dollar value of foundation grants!

Not only is the private foundation grants marketplace misunderstood by individual grantseekers, but also by entire institutions that have added to the confusion by arbitrarily deciding that government grant applications and contracts

TABLE 19.4

Types of Support Awarded by Dollar Value of Grants

TYPE OF SUPPORT	DOLLAR VALUE OF GRANTS
General Support	**21.0%**
Capital Support	**16.9%**
Capital Campaigns	2.1%
Building/Renovation	8.9%
Computer Systems/Technology	0.6%
Equipment	0.8%
Land Acquisition	0.5%
Endowments	2.4%
All Other	1.6%
Program Support	**46.8%**
Program Development	37.2%
Conferences/Seminar	1.1%
Faculty/Staff Development	2.2%
Curriculum Development	0.9%
Electronic Media/Online Services	1.3%
All Other	4.1%
Research	**8.8%**
Student Aid Funds	**3.9%**
Other	**2.1%**

should go through a university grants office, and that foundation grant proposals should be handled by an institution's development office. One reason in support of this decision is that the development office in most universities is tied to a university foundation—the 501(c)3 entity required to submit proposals. However, the problem lies in the fact that many development offices limit the access that faculty members have to private foundations so that they (the development offices) can use the foundation marketplace to attempt to fund administrative priorities, such as capital campaigns and endowments. This problem is compounded by the fact that only a small percentage of foundations dollars is actually awarded to fund these types of capital support projects. For example, a quick review of table 19.4 (types of support) demonstrates clearly that foundations *prefer* to fund the types of projects that emanate from faculty, such as program and research grants.

While some universities have dealt with this issue by developing two separate 501(c) tax-exempt entities, one for the university's overall grants effort and another for its development effort, one thing is critical for the grantseeker to understand. The quest for a private foundation grant needs to be coordinated within your institution or organization so that you can make sure you do not approach a foundation that is already being approached by several of your colleagues. Not only is this embarrassing, but it presents the prospective grantor with a negative image of you and your institution.

Many foundations allow only one proposal from one institution at one time and will immediately disallow all of the proposals submitted by the institution if they receive multiple applications. To avoid this type of problem, use one or more of the research tools presented in Chapter 20 to locate the foundation most suited to fund your project, and then develop a profile of what it funds. Take this profile to your grants office (or any other pertinent office) to gain approval to make preproposal contact. This will provide your institution with the heads up it needs to ensure its integrity with prospective funding sources and to move you one step closer to grants success.

NOTE

1. Martin Teitel, *"Thank You for Submitting Your Proposal"*: *A Foundation Director Reveals What Happens Next* (Medfield, MA: Emerson & Church Publishers, 2006), pp. 28–29.

CHAPTER 20

Researching Potential Private Foundation Grantors

How to Find the Foundation That Is Best Suited to Fund Your Project

A key to successful grantseeking with foundations is to gather the most complete and accurate information possible on funding sources before you approach them. The foundation research form (see exhibit 20.1) will help you do this. Review exhibit 20.1 carefully so you know what to look for and how to use this information. Complete one worksheet for each foundation you research. Seldom will you uncover all the data requested in exhibit 20.1, but try to complete as much information on the form as possible, and remember that even a partially completed worksheet will help you make a more intelligent decision on whether you should solicit grant support from a particular funding source.

For each foundation your research uncovers, look first at their areas of interest, activities funded, organizations funded, and geographic funding preferences. Do not even bother recording the foundation's name and address on the worksheet (exhibit 20.1) unless they fund what you want where you are. You should think of yourself as a broker that is seeking to match the interests of each partner. If there is a match, move right to the money. Although foundations can grant more than the minimum 5 percent of their assets required by the IRS, many follow the 5-percent guideline. Therefore, uncovering financial information such as the amount of their asset bases can be very insightful.

In addition to the research you conduct on grant-making foundations, you should also uncover and record as much information as possible on the decision

The following form outlines the data you need to collect in order to make a decision to seek funding from this grant source. Your attempts to collect as much of this information as possible will prove rewarding. (When feasible, record the source of the information and the date it was recorded.)

1. Name of Foundation: _____
Address: _____
Phone: _____ Fax: _____ Email: _____
Web site: _____

2. Contact Person: _____
Title: _____
Any Links from Our Organization to Contact Person: _____
_____

3. Foundation's Areas of Interests: _____
_____
_____

4. Eligibility Requirements/Restrictions:
a. Activities Funded/Restricted: _____
_____
_____

b. Organizations Funded/Restricted: _____
_____
_____

c. Geographic Funding Preferences/Restrictions: _____
_____
_____

d. Other Requirements/Restrictions: _____
_____
_____
_____
_____

5. Information Available   In Possession Of

   IRS 990-PF Tax Return (Year)   _____
   Guidelines   _____
   Newsletters   _____
   Annual Report   _____
   _____   _____
   _____   _____

FOUNDATION RESEARCH FORM

EXHIBIT 20.1

makers in those foundations. The funding executive research worksheet (see exhibit 20.2) is designed to help you do this.

Naturally, you do not have to have information on a foundation's executives (that is, directors, trustees, board members, contributions officers, and so forth) in order to consider submitting a proposal, but the more you know about the

6. a. Board Members:

_____

_____

_____

   b. Staff   Full Time   Part Time

_____   _____   _____

_____   _____   _____

_____   _____   _____

7. Deadline: _____

Application Process/Requirements:

_____

_____

_____

8. Financial Information
   Asset Base: $_____
   Are there current gifts to build the asset base?   Yes _____   No_____
   If yes, how much? $_____
   Total number of grants awarded in 200_: _____
   Total amount of grants awarded in 200_: $_____
    High Grant: $_____
    Low Grant: $_____
   Average Grant: $_____
   In our interest area there were _____ grants, totaling $_____
   High grant in our interest area: $_____
   Low grant in our interest area: $_____
   Average grant in our interest area: $_____

9. Grants Received Versus Grants Funded
   Number of proposals received in 200_: _____
   Number of proposals funded in 200_: _____

10. Sample Grants in Our Area of Interest:

             <u>Recipient Organization</u>   <u>Amount</u>

_____   _____

_____   _____

_____   _____

_____   _____

FOUNDATION RESEARCH FORM *(continued)*

EXHIBIT 20.1

decision makers, the greater your chances of success. The information you collect and record on your funding executive research worksheet will help you in three major ways:

- It will allow you to determine, in advance, likely preferences and biases you will encounter if you are lucky enough to arrange an in-person meeting.

1. Funding Source Name: _____
2. Name of Contact Person/Contributions Officer: _____
3. Title: _____ Birth Date: _____
4. Business Address: _____
   _____
5. Home Address: _____
   _____
6. Education
   Secondary: _____
   College: _____
   Post Graduate: _____
7. Military Service: _____
8. Clubs/Affiliations: _____
   _____
9. Corporate Board Memberships: _____
   _____
10. Business History (Promotions, Other Firms, etc.): _____
    _____
11. Other Philanthropic Activities: _____
    _____
12. Newspaper/Magazine Clipping(s) Attached: Yes _____   No _____
13. Contacts/Linkages in Our Organizations: _____
    _____
14. Recent Articles/Publications: _____
    _____
15. Awards/Honors: _____
    _____

FUNDING EXECUTIVE RESEARCH WORKSHEET

EXHIBIT 20.2

- It will make it easier to locate links between your organization and a funding source.
- It will assist you in structuring your proposal and in presenting the problem and the solution in a way that will attract the attention of the decision makers.

Recording accurate research on foundation decision makers will raise your chances of success. In addition, your ability to attract future funding will increase as you develop a history and file on each of the grantors in which you are interested. Enlist volunteers to ferret out the information you need. Let your research guide your solicitation strategy and proposal development process. Talk to your college or university librarian after you read this chapter to see what additional resources and techniques he or she suggests.

FOUNDATION FUNDING SOURCE RESEARCH TOOLS

Basic research tools for developing your list of potential foundation grantors can be accessed at little or no charge on the Internet and usually within a short distance from your workplace. The whole point of your research effort is to focus on the sources most likely to fund your proposal. Even if you are a novice grant-seeker, do not be tempted to send letter proposals to any and all foundations that are even remotely related to your project area. If preproposal contact is allowed or a proposal format is provided or suggested, take every opportunity to develop an individualized, tailored proposal for each of your best prospects.

THE FOUNDATION DIRECTORY

The Foundation Directory is the major source of information on the largest U.S. foundations. Available in hard copy, on CD-ROM, and through a variety of online subscription options, the 2007 edition provides information on approximately 10,000 independent, community, and company-sponsored foundations. The *Directory* contains key facts on fields of interest, contact information, financial data, names of decision makers, and 50,000 sample grants. In addition there are several indexes to help in your search for potential funding sources.

One technique that will add a whole new dimension to your foundation grants effort is to become adept at using the index to donors, officers, and trustees, which contains approximately 68,000 names. When your organization's friends provide you with their links, pay special attention to those people who list board memberships or friends on foundation boards. In most cases, your friends will be willing to discuss your project with fellow board members or with friends who serve on other boards.

If you are really intent on looking up affiliations of the people connected with U.S. foundations, you might also be interested in the *Guide to U.S. Foundations: Their Trustees, Officers, and Donors.* The publication covers nearly 70,000 foundations and features detailed information on more than 400,000 decision makers.

The Foundation Directory Part 2 is also available for your use. The 2007 edition of this directory includes the next 10,000 largest foundations by total giving and features 2,000 foundations covered for the first time and over 40,000 sample grants.

You may also access *The Foundation Directory Supplement*, which provides revised entries for hundreds of foundations in *The Foundation Directory* and the *The Foundation Directory Part 2*. Changes in financial data, contact information, and giving interests are highlighted in new entries.

The directories described above and the supplement are published by the Foundation Center, 79 Fifth Avenue, New York, NY 10003. To order one of these products or for more information on *Foundation Directory Online* subscriptions plans, call the Foundation's customer service line at (800) 424-9836 or visit the Foundation Center's web site at http://foundationcenter.org/marketplace.

Using *The Foundation Directory*

The most productive approach to using the *Directory* is to first review chapter 5 on redefining your project idea. After identifying key words and fields of interest (for example, environment, health education curriculum development, and folk arts for children), you can use the *Directory*'s subject index to determine which foundations have an active interest in the area for which you are seeking grant support. Another approach is to use the types of support index to identify foundations interested in your type of project (for example, conferences/seminars, building/renovation, equipment, program development, and matching or challenge grants).

Before you rush into reviewing the actual foundation entries, remember that a significant portion of foundations possess a geographic homing device. In other words, they give only where they live. The *Directory*'s geographic index will point you in the direction of those foundations that may be interested in your project because of its location.

The best match will be a foundation that funds your subject area, type of project, and geographic area. Do not despair if the use of the geographic index produces limited prospects. Many foundations have a national and even international interest in certain areas. While these foundations may not have granted funds in your state or community before, they may do so if approached properly.

As you do your research, be sure to record the name of the foundation, the state, and the directory entry number for each foundation you are interested in. Recording this information will help you refer to the foundation quickly.

The sample *Foundation Directory* entry provided in exhibit 20.3 shows the contents or data elements found in most of the directory's entries. For a complete listing of data elements, review the "How to Use the *Foundation Directory*" section in the publication's introduction. Please note that the sample shown in exhibit 20.3 was taken directly off of the Foundation Center's web site and that you would have to refer to the actual entry to view the information for The Community Foundation of Greater Birmingham in its entirety. However, for the purpose of explanation, assume that the grantseeker is interested in securing a grant for a project aimed at introducing low-income children in Birmingham to theater. The Community Foundation of Greater Birmingham may be a good choice for the prospective grantee to examine further because the grantseeker's project falls within one of the foundation's stated fields of interest—the arts—and will take place in one of the foundation's preferred geographic funding areas—Jefferson County, Alabama. The prospective grantee will have to conduct more in-depth research to discover how much money the Community Foundation of Greater Birmingham has actually awarded to similar projects and to determine the high, low, and average size grants awarded in the arts area.

Sample Entry

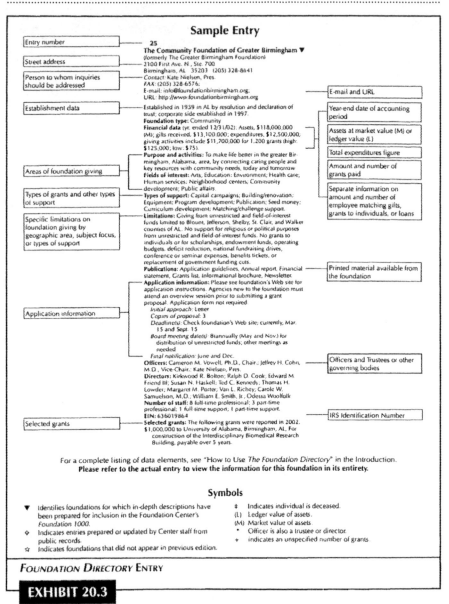

Entry number		**25**
		The Community Foundation of Greater Birmingham ▼
		(formerly The Greater Birmingham Foundation)
Street address		2100 First Ave. N., Ste. 700
		Birmingham, AL 35203 (205) 328-8641
Person to whom inquiries should be addressed		Contact: Kate Nielsen, Pres.
		FAX: (205) 328-6576.
		E-mail: info@foundationbirmingham.org.
		URL: http://www.foundationbirmingham.org

- Entry number → **25**
- Street address → 2100 First Ave. N., Ste. 700
- Person to whom inquiries should be addressed → Contact: Kate Nielsen, Pres.
- E-mail and URL

Establishment data → Established in 1959 in AL by resolution and declaration of trust; corporate side established in 1997.

- Year-end date of accounting period

Foundation type: Community

Financial data (yr. ended 12/31/02): Assets, $118,000,000 (M); gifts received, $13,100,000; expenditures, $12,500,000; giving activities include $11,700,000 for 1,200 grants (high: $125,000; low: $75).

- Assets at market value (M) or ledger value (L)
- Total expenditures figure
- Amount and number of grants paid

Purpose and activities: To make life better in the greater Birmingham, Alabama, area, by connecting caring people and key resources with community needs, today and tomorrow.

Areas of foundation giving →

Fields of interest: Arts; Education; Environment; Health care; Human services; Neighborhood centers; Community development; Public affairs.

Types of grants and other types of support →

Types of support: Capital campaigns; Building/renovation; Equipment; Program development; Publication; Seed money; Curriculum development; Matching/challenge support.

- Separate information on amount and number of employee matching gifts, grants to individuals, or loans

Specific limitations on foundation giving by geographic area, subject focus, or types of support →

Limitations: Giving from unrestricted and field-of-interest funds limited to Blount, Jefferson, Shelby, St. Clair, and Walker counties of AL. No support for religious or political purposes from unrestricted and field-of-interest funds. No grants to individuals or for scholarships, endowment funds, operating budgets, deficit reduction, national fundraising drives, conference or seminar expenses, benefits tickets, or replacement of government funding cuts.

Publications: Application guidelines, Annual report, Financial statement, Grants list, Informational brochure, Newsletter.

- Printed material available from the foundation

Application information →

Application information: Please see foundation's Web site for application instructions. Agencies new to the foundation must attend an overview session prior to submitting a grant proposal. Application form not required.

Initial approach: Letter

Copies of proposal: 3

Deadline(s): Check foundation's Web site; currently, Mar. 15 and Sept. 15

Board meeting date(s): Biannually (May and Nov.) for distribution of unrestricted funds; other meetings as needed

Final notification: June and Dec.

Officers: Cameron M. Vowell, Ph.D., Chair.; Jeffrey H. Cohn, M.D., Vice-Chair.; Kate Nielsen, Pres.

- Officers and Trustees or other governing bodies

Directors: Kirkwood R. Bolton; Ralph D. Cook; Edward M. Friend III; Susan N. Haskell; Ted C. Kennedy; Thomas H. Lowder; Margaret M. Porter; Van L. Richey; Carole W. Samuelson, M.D.; William E. Smith, Jr.; Odessa Woolfolk

Number of staff: 8 full-time professional; 3 part-time professional; 1 full time support; 1 part-time support.

EIN: 636019864

- IRS Identification Number

Selected grants →

Selected grants: The following grants were reported in 2002. $1,000,000 to University of Alabama, Birmingham, AL, For construction of the Interdisciplinary Biomedical Research Building, payable over 5 years.

For a complete listing of data elements, see "How to Use *The Foundation Directory*" in the Introduction.
Please refer to the actual entry to view the information for this foundation in its entirety.

Symbols

▼ Identifies foundations for which in-depth descriptions have been prepared for inclusion in the Foundation Center's *Foundation 1000*.

◆ Indicates entries prepared or updated by Center staff from public records.

☆ Indicates foundations that did not appear in previous edition.

‡ Indicates individual is deceased.

(L) Ledger value of assets.

(M) Market value of assets.

* Officer is also a trustee or director.

+ Indicates an unspecified number of grants.

FOUNDATION DIRECTORY ENTRY

EXHIBIT 20.3

INTERNAL REVENUE SERVICE TAX RETURNS

Form 990-PF is the annual tax return that U.S. private foundations must file with the IRS. Federal law requires that all foundations provide their tax returns for public information purposes. A foundation's 990-PF return gives fiscal details on receipts and expenditures, compensation of officers, capital gains or losses, and other financial matters and provides the foundation's application guidelines, the names of its board members/officers/trustees, and a complete list of the grants it has paid.

While *The Foundation Directories* are useful reference tools, they are basically compilations of information from many sources, and there is no guarantee as to the accuracy of the information provided. The Internal Revenue Service, however, deals in specifics. By reviewing the returns of the private foundations you believe to be your best funding prospects, you can find valuable information such as the actual amount of assets, new gifts received, total grants paid out, and so on. Most important, you can view a list of all the grants they have paid, including grants for less than $10,000.

Larger foundations often issue annual reports and/or have web sites that contain a listing of their grants. But the IRS form 990-PF may be the only source where you can find a complete grants list for smaller and mid-sized foundations.

Exhibit 20.4 is a sample of parts of form 990-PF. Taken off of the Foundation Center's web site, this sample demonstrates that finding the information you need on a 990-PF is relatively easy.

- Page 1, top section and line 25 provides date, name, address, assets, and grants paid.
- Page 6, Part VIII, line 1 provides the list of board members/officers/trustees.
- Page 9, Part XV, line 2, a, b, c, d, provides application information.
- Page 10, Part XV, line 3 provides grants paid during the year and those approved for future payments (which gives you some indication of how involved the funding source is in awarding multiple-year grants).

For more information on what Forms 990-PF are and where you can find them, visit http://foundationcenter.org/getstarted/faqs/html/990pf.html.

Copies of tax returns for the past three years for all 65,000 plus foundations can be viewed for free at the Foundation Center's reference collections in New York City and Washington, D.C. The Atlanta, Cleveland, and San Francisco offices of the Foundation Center contain IRS Form 990-PF returns for the Southeastern, Midwestern, and Western states, respectively.

You can also access foundation tax returns on the web in PDF format at the following sites:

- http://foundationcenter.org/findfunders/990finder,
- http://www.guidestar.org, and
- http://www.grantsmart.org.

Please note that the tax returns you will be able to access will typically be one to two years behind. In addition, if you cannot find a particular organization's

IRS FOUNDATION ANNUAL RETURN

PAGE 6

IRS FOUNDATION ANNUAL RETURN FORM 990-PF

EXHIBIT 20.4

PAGE 9

Form 990-PF (2002)

Part XIV Private Operating Foundations (see page 25 of the instructions and Part VII-A, question 9)

1a If the foundation has received a ruling or determination letter that it is a private operating foundation, and the ruling is effective for 2002, enter the date of the ruling . . .

b Check box to indicate whether the organization is a private operating foundation described in section ☐ 4942(j)(3) or ☐ 4942(j)(5)

2a	Enter the lesser of the adjusted net income from Part I or the minimum investment return from Part X for each year listed . . .	Tax year			Prior 3 years		(e) Total
		(a) 2002	(b) 2001	(c) 2000	(d) 1999		
b	85% of line 2a						
c	Qualifying distributions from Part XII, line 4 for each year listed . . .						
d	Amounts included in line 2c not used directly for active conduct of exempt activities . .						
e	Qualifying distributions made directly for active conduct of exempt activities. Subtract line 2d from line 2c . .						
3	Complete 3a, b, or c for the alternative test relied upon:						
a	"Assets" alternative test—enter:						
(1)	Value of all assets . . .						
(2)	Value of assets qualifying under section 4942(j)(3)(B)(i)						
b	"Endowment" alternative test— Enter ⅔ of minimum investment return shown in Part X, line 6 for each year listed . . .						
c	"Support" alternative test—enter:						
(1)	Total support other than gross investment income (interest, dividends, rents, payments on securities loans (section 512(a)(5), or royalties)						
(2)	Support from general public and 5 or more exempt organizations as provided in section 4942(j)(3)(B)(iii)						
(3)	Largest amount of support from an exempt organization						
(4)	Gross investment income						

Part XV Supplementary Information (Complete this part only if the organization had $5,000 or more in assets at any time during the year—see page 25 of the instructions.)

1 Information Regarding Foundation Managers:

a List any managers of the foundation who have contributed more than 2% of the total contributions received by the foundation before the close of any tax year (but only if they have contributed more than $5,000). (See section 507(d)(2).)

b List any managers of the foundation who own 10% or more of the stock of a corporation (or an equally large portion of the ownership of a partnership or other entity) of which the foundation has a 10% or greater interest.

2 Information Regarding Contribution, Grant, Gift, Loan, Scholarship, etc., Programs:

★ Check here ▶ ☐ if the organization only makes contributions to preselected charitable organizations and does not accept unsolicited requests for funds. If the organization makes gifts, grants, etc. (see page 26 of the instructions) to individuals or organizations under other conditions, complete items 2a, b, c, and d.

a The name, address, and telephone number of the person to whom applications should be addressed:

APPLICATION INFORMATION

b The form in which applications should be submitted and information and materials they should include:

c Any submission deadlines:

d Any restrictions or limitations on awards, such as by geographical areas, charitable fields, kinds of institutions, or other factors:

Form **990-PF** (2002)

*If checked, foundation does not accept unsolicited applications

PAGE 10

Form 990-PF (2002)

Part XV Supplementary Information (continued)

3 Grants and Contributions Paid During the Year or Approved for Future Payment

Recipient		If recipient is an individual, show any relationship to any foundation manager or substantial contributor	Foundation status of recipient	Purpose of grant or contribution	Amount
Name and address (home or business)					
a Paid during the year					

GRANTS PAID

| Total . . . . ▶ 3a | | | | | |

b Approved for future payment

FUTURE GRANTS

| Total . . . . ▶ 3b | | | | | |

Form **990-PF** (2002)

IRS FOUNDATION ANNUAL RETURN FORM 990-PF (continued)

EXHIBIT 20.4

990-PF, it may be because the organization you are looking for files a 990 instead. In general, churches, hospitals, schools, and publicly supported organizations file 990s.

THE FOUNDATION CENTER

Incorporated as a nonprofit organization in 1953, the Foundation Center was formed by a foundation as an independent national service center. Part of the Foundation Center's mission is to provide accurate information on philanthropy with special emphasis on foundation grant making. The center covers its operating expenses through grants from foundations and corporations, the sale of publications, and fee-based subscriber services. The center operates five reference collections, one in New York City, one in Washington, D.C., one in Cleveland, one in San Francisco, and one in Atlanta. Each of these is staffed by Foundation Center employees.

There are also many Foundation Center Cooperating Collections operated by libraries, community foundations, and other nonprofit agencies throughout the United States.

Locate the Collection nearest you by visiting http://foundationcenter.org/ collections. In addition to having a core collection of the Foundation Center's publications, many Cooperating Collections have IRS tax returns for their state and/or neighboring states. The Collections will also have several other valuable grants resource materials, including

- computer-generated printouts or guides that list grants by subject area,
- state foundation directories,
- other publications from the Foundation Center (see the list of resources for more detail), and
- searchable foundation grant-related databases.

ELECTRONIC RETRIEVAL AND DATABASE SEARCHES

Many public libraries, university libraries, and higher education grants offices are able to perform electronic searches of *The Foundation Directory* and other resources containing foundation grants information. Explore the possibility of computer search and retrieval by contacting an established grants office near you.

The Foundation Center offers *FC Search: The Foundation Center's Database on CD-ROM.* It provides detailed profiles on over 88,000 grant makers (foundations, corporate givers, and grant-making public charities) and describes over 350,000 grants. It also provides links to grant-maker and corporate web sites, as well as to thousands of current IRS Form 990-PF returns. (Internet access is required to access these links.) In addition, it provides 21 search criteria; indexes to help develop targeted prospects lists; trustee, officer, and donor names; and detailed application guidelines and program descriptions for the largest funders. The Foundation Center offers free sessions on the effective utilization of FC Search in all five Center libraries and at some Cooperating Collections.

There are several other electronic funding databases and CD-ROMs available that are accessible by subscription only, but offer current and in-depth information and vary in price.

- GrantSelect, the online version of the GRANTS Database, compiled and edited by Schoolhouse Partners, contains approximately 10,000 funding opportunities provided by more than 4,000 sponsoring organizations. See http://www.grantselect.com.

- *The Chronicle Guide to Grants* presents all corporate and foundation grants listed in *The Chronicle of Philanthropy* since 1995. See http://www.philanthropy.com/grants.

Foundation Web Sites and the Internet

The use of the Internet to research private grantors and to apply online is limited, but growing. In 1999, 70 percent of the 100 largest foundations and roughly 400 of the more than 50,000 independent foundations in the United States had a web site. At the beginning of 2003, approximately 81 percent of the largest foundations and more than 1,600 of the more than 59,000 independent foundations in the United States had a web site. There are a variety of reasons why more do not have web sites, including lack of staff and limited geographic giving interests. Many foundations give only locally and do not want the unsolicited worldwide proposals that having a web site may bring. Some private grantors, particularly those that are technology based, do allow Internet submittal of proposals, but that number is also surprisingly small.

Through portals such as the Foundation Center's foundation finder (http://lnp.foundationcenter.org/finder.html), grantseekers can find links to the web sites of a few thousand foundations, corporate grant makers, grant-making public charities, and community foundations. In addition, the Council on Foundations (http://www.cof.org) offers links to over 1,800 of its members' web sites, and Philanthropy News Network Online (http://www.pnnonline.org) provides links to many private foundations, corporations, and community foundations.

Exhibit 20.5 is a sample of a foundation's web site and the type of information you can sometimes gather online. In this example, you can obtain the Jean and Louis Dreyfus Foundation's guidelines, application procedure, grants list, and roster of trustees and staff from its web site. (Note that the Dreyfus Foundation was so overwhelmed with proposals that it did not accept new letters of inquiry for the entire fall 2006 grant cycle.) However, for the majority of grant makers you will still need to use alternative research methods for obtaining this information.

	THE
Grant Guidelines	**JEAN & LOUIS DREYFUS**
	FOUNDATION, INC.
Application Procedure	
	Suite 626
Grants List	**420 Lexington Avenue**
	New York, NY 10170
Trustees and Staff	**Tel: 212-599-1931**
	Fax: 212-599-2956
Web site design and hosting by: **THE FOUNDATION CENTER**	**E-mail: jldreyfusfdtn@hotmail.com**

SAMPLE FOUNDATION WEB SITE

EXHIBIT 20.5

Several nonprofit organizations have developed web sites with grantor information. There are also bulletin boards and chat boxes that focus on foundation and corporate grantors. Check with your membership groups and your peers to see what is available, or perform your own Internet search.

Research to locate your most likely foundation grantor need not be labor-intensive or costly. Using electronic databases and web sites in your search will save you time, but the actual information you will find is identical to that in the print form. The key is to locate the data that will enable you to estimate your chances for success before you invest any more time in seeking a foundation grant.

GRANT GUIDELINES

THE JEAN & LOUIS DREYFUS FOUNDATION, INC.

> *Grant seekers are advised that due to an overwhelming number of requests pending, the Foundation will not be accepting new letters of inquiry for the Fall 2006 grant cycle. The Foundation will again be accepting new letters of inquiry for the Spring 2007 cycle, and these should be sent in December/January, no later than February 1st.*

The Jean and Louis Dreyfus Foundation, Inc. was established in 1979 from the estate of Louis Dreyfus, a music publisher, and that of his wife, Jean. The mission of the Foundation is to enhance the quality of life of New Yorkers, particularly the aging and disadvantaged. Grants are disbursed mainly within the five boroughs of New York City, and primarily in fields supportive of aging, arts-in-education, education and literacy, and social services.

The Foundation is committed to funding direct service organizations and those projects which will produce systemic change. To this end the Foundation supports pilot programs which can eventually be replicated or which will be funded by independent or government sources in the future. Occasionally organizations will be awarded grants to strengthen their infrastructure or for general operating support. The Foundation encourages matching funds from other charitable organizations, public financial drives, individuals, and government bodies.

Grants are made only to organizations whose tax exempt status has been recognized by the IRS. Grants are never made to individuals.

SAMPLE FOUNDATION WEB SITE *(continued)*

EXHIBIT 20.5

APPLICATION PROCEDURE

THE JEAN & LOUIS DREYFUS FOUNDATION, INC.

HOME

Grant
Guidelines

Application
Procedure

Grants List

Trustees
and Staff

> *Grant seekers are advised that due to an overwhelming number of requests pending, the Foundation will not be accepting new letters of inquiry for the Fall 2006 grant cycle. The Foundation will again be accepting new letters of inquiry for the Spring 2007 cycle, and these should be sent in December/January, no later than February 1st.*

Initial inquiries should consist of a one to two page letter describing the grantee organization and outlining the project in question. Letters should be sent by mail to:

Ms. Edmée de M. Firth
Executive Director
Jean and Louis Dreyfus Foundation, Inc.
Suite 626
420 Lexington Avenue
New York, NY 10170
Tel: 212-599-1931 • Fax: 212-599-2956
E-mail: jldreyfusfdtn@hotmail.com

All such inquiries will be acknowledged indicating whether or not a general application is justified (the Foundation uses its own application form). Letters of inquiry are due no later than February 1st and August 1st for the Spring and Fall board meetings respectively. Letters received later than these deadlines will be held over until the next review cycle. Any discussion or indications of interest concerning a grant application should not be construed as a commitment by the Foundation. All requests will be approved or rejected in writing.

Any questions about the Foundation and its application procedure should be directed to Jessica Keuskamp, Program Assistant (please see contact information above).

SAMPLE FOUNDATION WEB SITE *(continued)*

EXHIBIT 20.5

HOME

Grant
Guidelines

Application
Procedure

Grants List

Trustees
and Staff

GRANTS LIST

THE
JEAN & LOUIS DREYFUS
FOUNDATION, INC.

2005 Grants for:
Aging | Arts | Education | Social Service

GRANTS FOR AGING

Bay Ridge Center General Support.	$10,000
Citizens Advice Bureau Senior Minor Repair Program.	$15,000
Friends and Relatives of the Institutionalized Aged (FRIA) General Support.	$10,000
Goddard Riverside Community Center Phelps House Aging in Place Project.	$15,000
International Longevity Center Emergency Preparedness and Vulnerable Older Persons in New York City.	$15,000
Jewish Community Council of Greater Coney Island, Inc. Sunday Senior Center.	$10,000
Lawyer's Alliance for New York Elder Services Initiative.	$10,000
New York-Presbyterian Hospital Columbia Cooperative Aging Program.	$10,000
North General Hospital House Call Program	$20,000
One Stop Senior Services One Stop Senior Support Project.	$10,000
Partnership for the Homeless Peter's Place.	$20,000
Presbyterian Senior Services GrandparentFamily Apartments.	$15,000
Queens Botanical Garden	$15,000

SAMPLE FOUNDATION WEB SITE *(continued)*

EXHIBIT 20.5

CHAPTER 21

Contacting a Private Foundation Before Submission

Contacting the private foundation before you write your proposal will help you validate your research and gather additional information about the grantor's priorities and interests. More importantly, preproposal contact will allow you to tailor your proposal according to the particular approach or method that each private foundation will find interesting and provide you with the information needed to determine the appropriate amount to request. You can also use this contact to explore the grantor's feelings about funding only a portion of the total amount your project requires. The purpose of this contact is not to convince the grantor to fund your proposal but to ensure that your approach will meet the grantor's needs. By contacting the foundation funding source before you submit, you increase your chances of success over five times. Do not miss out on this tremendous opportunity if you have a contact person or you have a linkage to help get you in the door.

HOW TO CONTACT PRIVATE FOUNDATION GRANTORS

Now that you realize how important preproposal contact is, here is the bad news. Most private foundations are understaffed, and as many as 70,000 have no staff. Therefore, making contact with them is very difficult. Many private foundation application instructions state "no contact except by letter," and your research will show that many addresses for private funding sources are actually addresses for trust departments of banks, accountants' offices, web sites, or post office boxes.

Naturally, you do not want to talk to a trust officer at a bank, but speaking with a foundation board member would be a big help. With less than 3,000 foundations occupying their own offices, the chances of talking to a foundation's director or staff are limited to the largest foundations. What is significant, however, is that each foundation usually has eight to ten board members. This means that there are approximately 800,000 board members serving the 80,000 foundations, and you may be surprised at how many your advocates know! These board members are the actual decision makers, and they can be contacted effectively through your webbing system.

One foundation director underscored the importance of using links to board members when she told me the following:

- one-third of her foundation's grants will be awarded to her board members' favorite nonprofit organizations,
- one-third will go to her board members' friends' favorite nonprofits, and
- one-third will be up for grabs to those who write creative, persuasive proposals that match the interests and values of her foundation.

At this point your research should already include the names of your best foundation prospects' decision makers and board members. Ask the leaders of your organization whether they know any of these people and, if so, whether they would help you by using this informal means of contact. Perhaps your link can set up lunch or a conference call. If you do not uncover a link, your plan should be to follow the grantor's guidelines as outlined in the various resource publications (see chapter 7 for more information on webbing and links).

If there is an office and contact is not ruled out or discouraged, you should

- write a letter of inquiry,
- telephone to set up a visit or phone interview, and/or
- make a personal visit to the grantor.

Contact by Letter

Be very selective when sending a letter requesting an appointment and information on a grantor's program. Since very few private foundations have the staff resources necessary to respond to written requests, do not be surprised if you receive a proposal rejection notice even though you asked only for application guidelines or an appointment.

Exhibit 21.1 provides a sample letter to a foundation requesting information. (This letter could be sent as an email, but not all foundations provide email addresses for correspondence purposes.) Please note that this is not a letter

---

Date

Name
Title
Address

Dear _____:

I am developing a project that deals with _____ and provides benefits to [or in]
_____. My research indicates that this area is an important concern of the
[name of foundation].

Please use the enclosed email address or label to send me information on your desired format
for proposals or other guidelines. I would also appreciate it if you could add us to your mailing
list so that we could receive your annual reports, newsletters, and any other materials you think
might be useful to us as we work on this and related projects.

Thank you for your cooperation.

                                                       Sincerely,

                                                       Name/Title
                                                       Organization
                                                       Address
                                                       Email Address

SAMPLE LETTER TO A PRIVATE FOUNDATION REQUESTING INFORMATION

EXHIBIT 21.1

---

proposal or a letter of inquiry. These types of proposals will be described in
chapter 22.

Contact by Telephone

Telephone contact with a private foundation may take the place of face-to-face
contact or may be used to set up a visit. When you are successful at telephoning a
private foundation, you can be sure you have contacted one that falls within the
2 percent that have an office and a paid staff. Even if you are telephoning the
grantor in hopes of setting up a visit, be ready to discuss your project. Many
grantors use the telephone very effectively for quickly assessing projects and
determining their interest in them before agreeing to discuss the project face-
to-face, or inviting you to make a written application. After all, it is much easier
to tell a grantseeker that they are not really interested in a project over the

telephone than it is in person, or to have to read about an idea that is not going to make it.

If the grantor wants to discuss your project before giving you an appointment, ask whether you could fax, email, or mail a one- or two-page letter of inquiry or a concept paper and call back when he or she has your outline in hand and has had time to review it.

If he or she agrees to a visit, set the date. Do not offer any more information at this time, but do ask what he or she recommends that you bring. Also ask about

- presenting a laptop-driven PowerPoint presentation or full motion video;
- the number of staff to be present so that you can bring the appropriate number of copies of information about your organization;
- the possibility of him or her making a visit to your location; and
- his or her travel plans, whether he or she will be near you, or whether he or she will be attending any conferences or meetings you will attend or where you will be presenting.

If a personal visit is not possible, you will be forced to discuss your project over the telephone. The questions you ask over the phone will actually be the same as those you would ask if you were to make a personal visit. Therefore, review the following section on the visit and designate the questions to ask a funding source.

The Visit

Visiting in person is the best way to get to know the foundation, but visits are difficult to arrange since foundations are not heavily staffed. If you are fortunate enough to get a visit, use your time wisely.

Who Should Go? Your credibility will be higher if you take a nonstaff representative with you. An articulate, impressive volunteer, advocate, advisory committee member, or board member is an excellent choice. Two people are the maximum. You do not want to overpower the grantor by sending three or more people. Use the information you collected from your webbing and linkages to choose a partner that provides a close match to the funding source. Use age, education, club affiliation, and other personal characteristics as the basis for your choice. Dress according to the information you have about the funding source. Dress in the foundation world is generally conservative, and usually it is better to be overdressed than underdressed. Dress codes differ in the East, the West, the South, and the Midwest, so be aware of geographic influences. The best person to ask about the appropriate dress for a particular funding source is a link who knows the grantor or a past grantee.

Materials to Bring. The materials you will need to bring are those you have already gathered and organized in your proposal development workbook (Swiss cheese book). You may also want to bring simple audiovisual aids that document the need in a more interesting or vivid manner and help show the funding source how important it is to meet the need *now*. If you do use audiovisual aids, make sure they are in balance with your request. A three- to five-minute video would be appropriate if you are making a large request ($250,000), but inappropriate for a smaller ($5,000) request. At this point it is still proper to have several possible approaches to meeting the need. Therefore, you should have the cost and benefits and pros and cons of each approach outlined and ready for presentation. You want to learn which approach the prospective funding source likes best; you are not trying to convince the grantor that you have "the one and only way to solve the problem." Your cost-benefit analysis worksheet from chapter 4 will usually elicit more than enough response to begin a conversation.

Be ready to use the various parts of your Swiss cheese book for answers to questions like "Why should we give the money to you instead of some other organization?" Refer to your section on the uniquenesses of your organization (personnel, mission, and so on).

Questions to Ask a Foundation Funding Source. Review these questions to determine which would be the most appropriate to ask based on your current knowledge of the funding source. You may want to assign specific questions to each of the two individuals going to the meeting and prepare for the visit by role-playing various answers.

1. We have developed several feasible approaches. Would you please look at them and comment on which one looks the most interesting to you (or would look the most interesting to the board)?
2. Last year, your foundation awarded $____ to our kind of project and the average size was $____. Will this remain consistent?
3. Our research indicates that your deadlines last year were ____ and ____. Will they be the same this year?
4. Does it help you if proposals are submitted early? Do proposals that are submitted early receive more favorable treatment?
5. How are proposals reviewed by your foundation? Who performs the review? Outside experts? Board members? Staff? Is there a scoring system or checklist they use that you could share with us?
6. Are there more current granting priorities? (Give them a copy of your research sheet to determine whether your research accurately reflects their priorities.)
7. What do you think of submitting more than one proposal in a funding cycle?
8. Is the amount we are requesting realistic in light of your current goals?
9. Have you ever provided grant support jointly with another funding source and, if so, is that approach appropriate here?

The following two questions should be asked only when the grantor seems very encouraging.

10. Would you look over our proposal before our formal submission if we finished it early?
11. May I see a proposal you have funded that you think is well written? This would provide us with a model for style and format.
    Ask question 12 only if the grantor is not very encouraging.
12. Can you suggest any other funders who may be appropriate for this project?

Private Foundation Report Form

Each time a member of your staff contacts a funder in person, over the phone, or through email, he or she should complete and file a private foundation report form (see exhibit 21.2). This simple procedure has a number of important benefits. It will keep you from damaging your credibility by repeating the same questions or having the funder say, "I gave that information to _____ from your organization. Don't you people ever talk to each other?" Also, it will allow another person from your organization to pick up where you leave off when you take that next promotion.

Complete one of these forms after each contact with a private foundation.

Funding Source: _____

Funding Source Address: _____

Funding Source Contact Person: _____

Telephone Number: _____ Fax:_____ Email: _____

Contacted On (Date): _____

Contacted By (Name): _____

Type of Contact: Phone _____ Visit _____ Other (Explain) _____

Objective of Contact: _____

_____

_____

Results of Contact: _____

_____

_____

_____

Follow-up: _____

_____

PRIVATE FOUNDATION REPORT FORM

EXHIBIT 21.2

Successful grantees recognize the importance of contacting the funding source before writing the proposal. The purpose of the contact is not to make small talk, but to validate research and gather data needed to address the grantor's hidden agenda. Using the techniques in this chapter to contact and record contact with private grantors will be an essential part of your grantseeking strategy.

CHAPTER 22

Applying for Private Foundation Funds

Letter of Inquiry—Letter Proposal

CREATING A WINNING LETTER OF INQUIRY

While this may sound like an exercise in semantics, a letter of inquiry (LOI) is really just a very short proposal. It is a one- to two-page mini proposal aimed at interesting the foundation enough to invite you to submit a full proposal. It is qualitatively different from a letter proposal in that it lacks the specifics and details. However, it still must include and indeed, highlight, the components of your project or program that will motivate the grantor to request more information. You do not have to explain how you will do everything, but you must establish that you have a plan and that you will provide more information in the full proposal.

The natural tendency when faced with the challenge of writing a one- or two-page letter of intent is to focus intently on what it is *you* want to accomplish and how you want to do it. In contrast, most prospective grantors are self-focused and intent on what *they and their* organization want to do.

If you look at this process from the grantors' point of view, they are responsible for skimming hundreds to thousands of proposals in search of those that reflect and reinforce their values. They are generally adverse to risks (unless your research shows otherwise). They are understaffed, and few have experts in the field to refer to for scientific or programmatic evaluation. Staff members who perform initial screening and logging of proposals may have little professional training and usually base their initial screenings on a general description of the areas in which the foundation board is interested. Therefore, it is imperative that your LOI immediately focuses on the grantor and provides a clear picture or summary within the first few sentences of what your project seeks to create. You will be able to do this if you have done a good job researching your foundation prospect and have reviewed its most recent 990-PF tax return (see chapter 20).

Letters of inquiry are more difficult to create than other types of proposals that allow more words. With a LOI you must weigh each word and spend hours, not minutes, on each paragraph. After all, you have only a few words to hook the reader. You must write from the foundation's vocabulary, values glasses, and point of view, and avoid terms, acronyms, and buzzwords that shift the focus to you.

Your LOI should be on your best stationary, preferably with a list of your board members' names in the left margin. Board members provide credibility. If you have formed a special advisory committee for your project, you might want to consider having their names in the margin, especially if some of them are nationally or even locally known.

Almost all proposals, whether they are letters of inquiry or letter proposals, start with a title. The title is a necessary handle on which the grantor will rely to log your proposal into his or her database and to refer to your proposal when, and if, it comes up for discussion by the board. Your title should not be too lengthy, but like the rest of your proposal it should focus on what will be changed, how it will be changed, and who will benefit. Foundation grantors see their funds as impacting a problem, changing a target population, or furthering a favorite solution or protocol. Your LOI, and its title, should focus on the problem to be solved and the difference that will be made.

Foundation board members make assumptions based on titles. They assume they understand what the project proposes to accomplish based on the words used in the title. Unfortunately, there may be a disjuncture here, and the proposal may not deal with their expectations at all. To make sure this does not happen to you, read your title to several individuals who know nothing about your project, and ask them what they think the proposal that follows is all about. You will probably be amazed at the misconceptions and find yourself creating a new, clearer title aimed at steering the reader in the right direction.

Follow the title with a short paragraph (two to three sentences) summarizing the project. Use positive action words and a few well-chosen facts.

The next paragraph should focus on the issue that the project will seek to reduce or solve. Your research should provide some insight into other projects and approaches the foundation has funded. Yours should not be identical, but you can pick up a theme or preference by looking at what they have invested in in the past. It is not, "We hope to change this situation." It is, "Together we *will* change this situation."

Follow this with a paragraph on how you will impact the problem or issue. Include a few sentences on how and why your organization or consortium is particularly well suited to bring about the change you suggest. Most foundations will require some idea of the budget and cost. Usually in an LOI the budget can be in paragraph form. But be sure to be clear on what the total cost will be and if there are any other funders (already committed or to be approached) and any in-kind or matching commitment from your organization or consortium.

The secret to a successful letter of inquiry is to follow the foundation's specifications and to create a mini proposal that is motivating and compelling. The goal is to have the funding source request a full proposal that meets its needs and interests.

If you have submitted a letter of inquiry that has won you the opportunity to submit a full proposal, or the grantor's guidelines request that you submit a full or longer proposal, the following format will assist you. Remember, even a full proposal is usually thought of as a letter, not as a lengthy treatise on the topic. Many grantseekers have reported that they like to prepare the slightly longer letter proposal described in this chapter and then edit it to a shorter letter of inquiry making sure that they are keenly aware of what they choose not to say.

THE LETTER PROPOSAL

Historically, private foundations have used the letter proposal format as the primary component of their application process. Now federal and state granting programs are showing a shift in this direction, and some have instituted a preapplication process that is similar to creating a letter proposal or concept paper. Public funding sources may call the letter proposal a white, preproposal, or concept paper. In some cases grantors will not send a prospective grantee an application package unless they like the approach outlined in this letter proposal or concept paper. Although this preproposal screening may sound negative at first, it really is not such a bad idea because it prevents grantseekers from completing a more lengthy application for a project that the prospective grantor has little interest in funding or reviewing.

Foundations use the letter proposal format simply because they do not have the time or staff to read long, tedious proposals. They *want* short, concise letters and grant billions of dollars each year based on two to three pages of content. Some larger foundations may send out a request for proposals. They will specify details such as length, but most are less than five pages and many request that they be double-spaced.

Letter proposals are often read by board members during relatively brief meetings. A survey of foundations revealed that most foundations meet one to three times a year for an average of one to three hours each time. Within this short time frame, they must read an overwhelming number of letter proposals; therefore, it is imperative that your proposal attract and retain their interest.

If your research provides you with an application format to follow, use it exactly as outlined. However, review the components presented here to be sure that the suggested areas are included in your prospective funding source's required format. Some of the foundations that have a web site provide an application form that can be printed off-line, but the majority still request a letter proposal.

When applying to the BellSouth Foundation, I was delighted to see that the specified proposal length was five pages or less. Further instructions clarified that the proposal also had to be double-spaced. Clearly BellSouth wanted submitted proposals to be written so that they could be easily and quickly read.

CONSTRUCTING A LETTER PROPOSAL

The main components of a letter proposal are as follows:

- an introductory paragraph stating the reason for writing,
- a section explaining why this grantor was selected,
- a needs section that presents the problem you will solve,
- a solution section that states what you will do and how,
- a uniqueness paragraph that shows why your organization is the best choice for implementing the solution,
- a request for funds section that asks for the money and summarizes your budget,
- a closing paragraph that provides a contact for more information if needed,
- signatures of your highest ranking officials and partners, and
- attachments, if allowed.

Introductory Paragraph

Begin by stating your reason for writing to the funding source, and mention your link to the grantor when possible. In some cases your link may prefer to remain anonymous and endorse your proposal at a board meeting. In other instances your link may actually instruct you to refer to him or her in your proposal. If so, you could say something such as the following:

Kate Macrae [your link, a past board member, trustee, or staff member of the foundation] and I have discussed the mutual concerns of the Kleineste Foundation [funding source] and my organization in meeting the nutritional needs of the elderly [subject area or problem].

If you cannot mention a link, begin your letter proposal with the next most important factor—why the grantor was selected for solicitation or how you knew the grantor would be interested in your proposal.

Why the Grantor Was Selected

Foremost in the reader's mind is why he or she should be reading your proposal. This is your opportunity to position yourself and your organization as winners that do their homework. You want the prospective funding source to know you are not blanketing the foundation world with a "one proposal fits all" approach. What you need to make clear in this paragraph is that, based on what you have discovered through your research, you believe the funding source is likely to find your proposal interesting. This means saying, for example, "Our research indicates that your foundation is committed to the support of health care for the indigent. In the last three years you have dedicated over $400,000 to this important area." In this example, you could also refer to the percentage of the funding source's total grant dollars that went to supporting health care for the indigent or mention a major or significant accomplishment made in this area through a previously awarded grant.

This paragraph need not be long. You want to demonstrate that you have taken the time to research the funding source's interests and that your proposal will address an issue that has been a concern of the grantor. By doing so, your proposal will command the respect of the reader and warrant the investment of time he or she will make to review it. At this point, it is obvious that this proposal is tailored to this foundation.

Again, you are following Festinger's theory of cognitive dissonance. To keep the reader interested in your proposal, you are going to have to present a proposal that reinforces his or her values and feelings of worth and importance. Seek to align your organization with the values of the grantor by adding something such as, "It is with our mutual concern for (or commitment to) the welfare of the indigent that we come to you with this proposal."

Needs Section

While this may be referred to as your vision or statement of purpose, there must be an underlying situation or problem that must be remedied or changed by your joint action. You do the work, and the grantor supplies the necessary ingredient —the money.

If you have constructed a proposal development workbook as suggested in chapter 3, you already have gathered statistics, case studies, quotes, and articles to document a compelling statement of need for action. The main difference between stating the need in a letter proposal to a foundation and stating it in a federal grant application is that you have the opportunity to incorporate the human element in your appeal to the private grantor. While your letter proposal must be based on fact, you can help the foundation motivate itself by presenting the more human side of the problem. The challenge is to portray compelling needs without overusing either the facts (by quoting too many research articles) or the human-interest aspects of the problem.

Select the components of the need that will most likely convince the grantor that the gap between what is and what ought to be must be closed *immediately*. To accomplish this you must have done research on the values and perspective of the grantor. Use what you have learned to describe the gap in a manner that is tailored to each particular funding source. With today's technology you could even scan a picture into your needs paragraph that may be worth a thousand words.

In a few paragraphs, your letter proposal must

- include a few well-chosen statistics,
- exhibit sensitivity to the geographic perspective of the grantor, and
- portray the human side of the problem.

Whether your proposal is for a model project, research, or a service model, your statement of need must be more compelling than your competitor's to keep the reader interested. Readers must want to read the rest of your proposal to discover what you are going to do about closing the gap you have so eloquently and succinctly documented. Many novice grantseekers overlook or underestimate the importance of the needs section of their letter proposal; they assume readers must already know about the need since they have granted funds to this area in the past. This assumption is a mistake. Grantors do know about the need, but they expect you to command their respect by proving *your* expertise in the field as in the following example:

> The need for cancer prevention and treatment in the United States continues to grow—but not equally for all races. If you were diagnosed with cancer in 1950, you would have a slightly higher survival rate if you were black. Today, however, the statistics are dramatically reversed. In a study by Stotts, Glynn, and Baquet, African Americans were ranked first among U.S. ethnic groups with the lowest cancer survival rate and first with the highest age-adjusted rates of cancer incidence and mortality. What happened to reverse this rate of survival?

The importance of documenting the gap between what exists now and what could be, should be, or will be with your foundation partner's investment is the basis for your accountability. If you can provide a visual and dramatic picture of the problem and document the incidence and severity of it and how it affects your target population, you can then tell the grantor how the situation will change and how the change will be measured in the solution section of your letter proposal. It is not a canceled check that the grantor wants; it is a changed situation, and the achievement of your project's objectives and goals.

Solution Section

What will you do to close the gap you have just documented? The solution section of your proposal calls for a brief description of the approach you propose to use to solve the problem. In most cases your approach will not totally eliminate the problem, but you must describe how much of the gap you will close (your objective). While describing how you will close the gap, include the measurement indicator you will use to evaluate the success of your approach. Foundations do not want elaborate evaluation designs here. However, you do need to give them an idea of how much will change as a result of your proposed solution. Review the section in chapter 13 on writing objectives.

Depending on the number of total pages allowed, one entire page of your proposal may be dedicated to this section, or you may have to limit this section to one or two paragraphs of five to seven lines each. While you need to have a legitimate plan, you must guard against making the methodology too elaborate. Since you are the content expert, you may have difficulty viewing your proposal from the reader's point of view. Ask yourself the following questions:

- How much does the reader really need to know?
- Will the reader understand my plan?
- Will the words used in the description of my solution be familiar to the reader?
- Is all the information included critical to convincing the funder that I have a sound, worthwhile plan, or am I including some of it just for myself?

Remember, while you are concerned with how you will solve the problem, grantors are concerned with what will be different after their money is spent. If possible, use this section to summarize your approach and objectives and refer the funder to your project planner for more information as in the following example:

> What can we do in Smithville to promote the sharing of responsibility for education among schools, parents, and children? At Smithville Elementary School we have developed a program aimed at increasing responsible behavior and encouraging parental involvement in the classroom and at home. Teachers will actually work with parents and students to develop tailored, individual contracts to produce increases in all levels of education and the quality of course work. The attached project planner outlines each objective and the activities that will foster the changes we desire. Through the education and involvement of parents in their children's responsible use of out-of-school time, our program will provide the catalyst for decreasing television viewing by students, increasing the completion of homework assignments, and improving test scores.

Uniqueness Section

This part of your letter proposal could also be called the "why we are capable and qualified" section. In the uniqueness section, you want to assure the grantor that your organization is the best choice for implementing the solution. Assuming you have held the reader's interest up to this point, he or she knows

- why you have selected the funding source,
- that there is a compelling need, and
- that you have a plan to address this need.

The key question in the grantor's mind at this critical moment is whether your organization is the right one to address the problem.

If you have completed the uniqueness exercise in chapter 6, you already have a list of your organization's strengths and positive qualities and, if appropriate, the unique advantages of your consortia members. Select items from the list to include in this section of your letter proposal. Choose credibility builders that will convince the grantor that you have the commitment, staff, skill, buildings, and equipment to do the job. For example, you could say something like,

Serving the elderly has been the sole mission of Rock of Ages Home for over 50 years. Since our inception we have continually received superior ratings from the state board. Our staff members represent over 300 years of experience, and their commitment to doing more than their call of duty is exhibited by their willingness to *volunteer* time to develop this model approach for serving Alzheimer patients.

Request for Funds Section

You must make a precise request for money. If you want to demonstrate that you have done your homework, refer to the fact that your request is (or is close to) the grantor's average-size award for your area of interest.

If your request from this grantor does not cover the entire cost of the project, mention those other sources that have already given support, list the others you will be approaching, or mention that such a list is available upon request.

You can summarize the budget categories that make up your total request, or you can provide prospective grantors with the portion of the budget that you would like them to fund. Since you are working under a severe space limitation, your budget summary should be arranged in paragraph form or in several short columns. If you submit your project planner with your proposal, you can refer to the column subtotals in your planner. For example, "The salary and wages, including fringe benefits, total $24,000. The work of the project director and other employees called for in this proposal is documented on page 3 in columns G, H, and I of the project planner."

To keep the focus on the value of the project and the results that you are seeking, you may want to divide the cost of the project by the number of people who will benefit from it. Consider the effect your project may have over several years, and calculate a cost per person served or affected by the project. For example, "In the next five years the equipment that you provide under this grant will touch the lives of approximately 5,000 students by helping them to read on grade level for the first time, and at a cost of only $5.63 per person served."

This section should also make reference to how you expect to sustain the project/program after its creation. Foundations do not want to look bad because a program they started ultimately left its recipients in the lurch.

Closing Paragraph

Many grantseekers close their letter proposals with a statement reflecting their willingness to meet with the prospective grantor to discuss their proposals. While a visit is highly unlikely unless the prospective grantor is a large foundation with a staff, I have had a foundation grantor make a visit before making the funding decision. However, references to such a meeting are usually futile. Instead, use the closing of your proposal to underscore your willingness to provide any further documentation or information the funding source may desire.

This brings up the question of who from your organization will be the best person to communicate with the prospective grantor. While you may have written the proposal, you probably will not be the individual to sign it. Therefore, in your closing paragraph request that the prospective grantor contact you (or the individual responsible for the project) for more information or to answer any questions. For example, "I encourage you to telephone me at my office or to call Ms. Connors directly at _____ to respond to technical questions or for additional information." Be sure to include a telephone number and extension, and test the line that will be used for this purpose to be certain that it is answered by a courteous and knowledgeable representative of your organization.

The closing paragraph is also the appropriate place to include your organization's designation as a 501(c)3 organization.

Signatures

Even though you are submitting what seems to be a letter, it is a grant application and constitutes an agreement between your organization and the grantor if it is accepted. Therefore, as is standard in agreements, the administrator or officer who holds rank and responsibility should sign it. If the link to the grantor is not your chief operating officer or chief executive officer, there is no reason why two individuals cannot sign the proposal—the link and the administrator or your consortia partner.

Because the board is legally responsible for the consequences of your organization's actions, including a board member's signature along with the chief

Abraham Donaldson, Executive Director
Foundation for the Terminally Ill
One East Third Avenue
Washington, DC 22222

Dear Mr. Donaldson:

    While working with your colleague David Ketchum, I learned of your foundation's efforts to support the hospice movement. Your underwriting of a book on AIDS and your concern for serving AIDS patients have prompted us to write this letter and request your foundation's support of the Central Aids Hospice Project. This is a unique project that will serve over 1,000 AIDS p atients in Georgia over the next five years.
    The Central Hospital is located in Smithville and adjoins Central Medical College. A leader in caring for medically underserved minorities, Central has been in the forefront of health promotion since 1904.
    The current AIDS epidemic has hit our minority population hard. The enclosed chart illustrates the cumulative number of AIDS patients diagnosed in Georgia and those who were in the active stage as of January 1, 2007. Central Hospital lies in Region I – Middle Georgia. In addition to serving the 987 known cumulative cases and the 842 active cases in our region, we also serve AIDS patients in the west and south districts, which pushes our totals to 1,129 known cumulative and 906 active cases. Naturally, these figures represent a conservative estimate of the true number of cases.
    Some of our AIDS patients have family members and friends to take care of them at home at the onset of their disease. Others are alone and destitute. Because our catchment population consists primarily of the medically underserved, we know many do not enter our treatment system until the later stages of their disease. No matter what the individual situation may be, it is at this final stage of life that our AIDS patients so desperately need an in-patient hospice facility to care for them.
    Central Hospital has agreed to provide 20 patient rooms for an AIDS hospice unit. We have the space, we have the patients, and we have the commitment and support of the hospital and the medical college. What we don't have are the funds for furniture (estimated at $16,000), renovations (estimated at $18,000), or special staff training (estimated at $5,000).
    Our plan of action is outlined on the project planner found on page 2. (A complete and itemized budget is available upon request.) We will start with a 6-bed unit, and then increase it to 8, then to 10, and so on. We forecast that the unit will be self-sufficient through third-party payments by the sixth month of operation.

SAMPLE LETTER PROPOSAL TO A PRIVATE FOUNDATION

EXHIBIT 22.1

executive officer's may impress the grantor. Just remember that the purpose of the signature is to provide the proposal with legal commitment and credibility.

Attachments, if Allowed

Most foundations do not encourage prospective grantees to submit any additional materials with their proposal. This includes attachments as well as videotapes, audiotapes, compact discs, and so on.

    Consider including your project planner as a page in your proposal rather than as an attachment, and be sure to always refer to it by page number. In

We feel confident that this project is a meaningful contribution to the Smithville community and Georgia for many years to come. First, look at our mission. Central Hospital and Central Medical College are unique in their extraordinary and admirable mission to provide medical training *and* patient care to minorities. Second, consider our graduates. Over 75 percent of Central's graduates go on to choose medically underserved urban and rural settings in which to practice medicine. And finally, look at our staff. The hospital staff members responsible for developing this project and for operating it, Dolores Levell and Mel Campo, have over 61 years of cumulative experience in nursing and long-term patient care!

It will take $39,000 to make our AIDS in-patient hospice facility a reality. However, a $15,000 grant from the Foundation for the Terminally Ill would give us the boost we need to solicit the rest of the funds locally. Your foundation's investment in our project will provide us with the motivation, positive image, and credibility we need to raise the remainder.

In recognition of your generous and truly caring gift, we would like to dedicate the entire 20-room facility to the Foundation for the Terminally Ill and have you and your board members attend our ribbon-cutting ceremony here in Smithville. You will also be proud to know that your foundation's name will be placed on 10 of the rooms and that you and your donors, through a grant of $15,000, made a needed, meaningful contribution to the disadvantaged minority population of Georgia.

Please call Dolores Levell at _____ to discuss this further and to arrange a visit to Central Hospital and Central Medical College.

Sincerely,

Thomas Watkins, Ph.D.
Chief Executive Officer
Central Hospital

Adele Trent, M.D.
President
Central Medical College

SAMPLE LETTER PROPOSAL TO A PRIVATE FOUNDATION (continued)

EXHIBIT 22.1

general, your proposal should give the impression that you have more information you are willing to give the prospective grantor if desired. Including too much with the proposal, however, may reduce the likelihood that it will be read.

In general, use more white space, bullets, and short inviting paragraphs. Never use small fonts. Use 12 to 13 characters per inch. Some grantors may require double spacing. Read and heed all application guidelines.

The letter proposal follows an orderly progression that focuses on the needs and interests of the funding source. As you gain insight into your prospective grantor, you will develop the ability to write grant-winning foundation proposals.

A sample letter proposal to a foundation (see exhibit 22.1) is included for your review.

CREATING YOUR PROPOSAL ON THE GRANTOR'S WEB SITE

Some foundations have web sites that offer their application guidelines and forms online. Often the application forms are not interactive. Therefore, you usually cannot change the amount of space allotted to each section. Whatever the case may be, follow all guidelines exactly, but look for opportunities where you can insert all or any of the main components of the letter proposal.

CHAPTER 23

Proposal Submission, the Decision, and Follow-Up
Private Foundation Funding Sources

FOUNDATION QUALITY CIRCLE/PROPOSAL REVIEW COMMITTEE

B efore submission, you want to ensure that your proposal is of the highest quality. Just as with government grant proposals, you should put your foundation proposal through a quality circle or proposal review committee critique. This process is much easier than it is with federal proposals since foundations seldom have a scoring system or peer review. But, the lack of information on what foundation board members are looking for and how they evaluate proposals is disconcerting to the serious foundation grantseeker. The best suggestion I can provide is to invite a group of four to six people whose backgrounds most closely resemble those of the foundation board's to come together for one hour to review your proposal. This exercise works well when you provide breakfast or lunch.

You can find a list of the foundation's board members on the foundation's tax return (990-PF), and then you could also look each of them up in *Who's Who in America*, which can be found in your public library. However, you will not go wrong if you assume the educated and wealthy want to carry out projects that reflect similar values as those of the past projects they have supported. Their values and interests change very slowly.

Provide your group with any background data that you can come up with, and ask the group members to read your proposal rapidly, in three minutes or less, and designate those areas they think the foundation's board would like with a plus symbol (+) and those areas they think could be improved with a minus symbol (−). Ask them for their suggestions and how they think you can incorporate them, and rewrite your proposal accordingly. Thank your mock review/quality circle participants and tell them you will let them know the outcome. Send them a thank-you note a week or two after the exercise.

SUBMITTAL

The submittal deadlines set by private foundation funding sources must be taken just as seriously as those of the government. If you cannot meet a deadline, you will appear to be a poor steward of funds, so try to be prompt, or, better yet, early. Private foundations, unlike the government, have been known to give a few extra days' "grace" period when the prospective grantee has a good explanation for the delay and the benefit of personal contact. However, it still does not look good when you need extra time, especially when the deadline has been published for a year or more.

When you are submitting your request to a large foundation, you can

- deliver it in person,
- have an advocate or board member deliver it for you,
- send it in by the United States Postal Service or private carrier, or
- submit it electronically via the Internet if allowed.

Although there is not as much advantage to hand delivery in the private sector as in the public sector, hand delivery makes an impression and helps avoid problems with delivery service. In other words, you can be sure the proposal is there! If you decide to mail your proposal, send it with a return receipt requested. You can also obtain delivery confirmation when using United Parcel Service (UPS), FedEx, or the United States Postal Service's priority and next-day services. This way you will have proof that your proposal arrived on time, and a signature that could prove useful in follow-up.

While still limited, a growing number of foundations that have web sites offer online proposal submittal. While very few offer this option, if your prospective funding source has a web site, be sure to check if this alternative method of submittal is available to you. Even if you submit your proposal electronically, print it off and make sure that electronic submittal did not some how affect its visual attractiveness. In several of my online submittals I have asked the grantors if I could supply a duplicate print copy, and they have agreed. Note on each copy that a duplicate has been provided, and be sure to get both copies (the electronic and the print version) in before the deadline.

Make note of the following:

- Send the contacts or people you discovered through the webbing and linkage process a copy of your letter proposal.

- Ask these friends to push for your proposal at the board meeting or to contact their friends or other board members to encourage a favorable decision.

- Minimize personal contact once you have submitted your proposal to avoid appearing pushy.

THE DECISION AND FOLLOW-UP

Private foundation grantors are generally more prompt than government funders at letting you know their decision about your proposal. They will give you a simple yes shortly after the board's scheduled meeting. If the answer is yes, you should do the following immediately:

- Send a thank-you letter to the funding source. One foundation trustee told me that one of the only records that foundation keeps on grantees is whether or not they thank the foundation. She said, "If an organization that receives a grant doesn't thank us, they do not receive another grant from us."

- Find out the payment procedures. Usually the acceptance letter comes with a check. If a check is not enclosed, the letter will at least inform you of when you will receive payment. Due to staff shortages, small foundations will usually grant the entire amount requested in one lump sum. Large foundations with staff may make partial or quarterly payments based on your cash forecast.

- Check on any reporting procedures that the funding source may have. Most small foundations consider the canceled check a completion report. However, I suggest you send the funding source a more formal completion report as a courtesy.

- Ask the funding source when you might visit to report on the grant, and invite funders to visit you when traveling in your area.

- Ask, or have your link ask, the funding source what was best about your proposal and what could have been better. Although most grantors will not comment on your proposal, it cannot hurt to ask.

Most funding sources feel neglected once they have given away their money. You can get on their list of good grantees by following up. Your follow-up checklist should include

- putting funding sources on your public relations mailing list so that they will receive news or press releases,

- keeping your funding source files updated and having a volunteer maintain current lists of grants funded by each of your grantors, and

- writing to funding sources two years after they have funded you to let them know how successful you are and to thank them again for their farsightedness in dealing with the problem.

Since you are now aware of the critical staff shortage in foundations, you should not be surprised that some do not even send out rejection notices. Hopefully, this will be less and less the case as more foundations use email. A woman in one of my seminars remarked that she was still waiting to hear about a foundation proposal she submitted two years prior. I told her it was rejected. With foundation grants, no news is bad news. In either case, rejection or no news, I suggest you

- Send a thank-you letter to the funding source. Express your appreciation for the time and effort spent on reviewing your proposal.

- Remind the funder of what an important source of funds it is.

- Ask for helpful comments on your proposal and whether the funding source would look favorably on resubmission with certain changes.

- Ask whether the funder could suggest any other funding sources that may be interested in your project.

If the foundation has no staff and you have no links, you may not find answers to your questions. Try again. Successful grantseekers are persistent! However, you should also be aware of the fact that you may not hear *anything* from the funding source.

The steps suggested in part three of this book follow the book's unifying principle; that is, look at everything you do from the perspective of the grantor. From preproposal contact, to writing your thank-you letter, to follow-up, consider how you would want to be appreciated and recognized for your contribution now and in the future.

PART FOUR

. . . .

Private/Corporate Funding Opportunities

CHAPTER 24

Understanding the Corporate Marketplace

To understand the present corporate marketplace and to make any predictions concerning its future, one must look at corporate grants and corporate philanthropy from a historical perspective.

The concept of self-interest as the guiding principle of corporate philanthropy actually has its basis in law. The Internal Revenue Act of 1935 made it legal for corporations to deduct up to 5 percent of their pretax revenues for charitable donations. The general consensus was that these gifts (which many still view as the purview of the stockholders and not the corporation) were to be used for purposes that directly benefited the corporation's business or interests.

However, in 1953 in *A.P. Smith Manufacturing Co. v. Barlow, et al.*, the New Jersey Supreme Court ruled that corporate contributions for purposes other than a direct benefit to the business are legal. The case involved a contested gift of $1,500 made by the A.P. Smith Manufacturing Company's board of directors to Princeton University for general maintenance. Until that time, the company's corporate practice had been only to sponsor educational research projects that related to the company's business. The stockholders charged that the gift was a misappropriation of corporate funds, but the Supreme Court ruled otherwise. This ruling has been referred to as the "Magna Carta" of corporate philanthropy, and it ultimately changed the ground rules for corporate contributions forever.

Even though 2003 marked the 50th anniversary since it has become truly legal for a corporation to award gifts and grants that do not directly benefit its business, corporate giving is still motivated by corporate self-interest. Corporate giving is usually a "this-for-that" exchange. Corporations are not in business to *give away* money; they invest it and expect a return. As a corporate grantseeker you must view their proposed investment in your organization (your grant) through their values glasses.

Toward that end, the fields of education and health and human services are the two biggest recipients of corporate contributions.

Historically, education has received the largest portion of the corporate philanthropic dollar. As you ponder your ability to attract corporate support for your college, university, school, or educationally related nonprofit group, you need to consider the following. Traditionally higher education has been industry's subcategory of choice. Corporations figured out long ago that, without the raw ingredient of a trained work force, they could not produce salable products or services. Today, they realize that they need higher education graduates to maintain a competitive place in an increasingly global marketplace. However, higher education cannot assume that it will always receive the largest share of the corporate education dollar. Recently, a considerable challenge has been successfully mounted by secondary education, elementary education, and even preschool education.

For example, while working at an institution of higher education in Alabama, I noticed that many grants were going directly to local elementary and secondary schools from automobile and technology-dependent companies new to the area, such as Mercedes-Benz. When I inquired why our institution's higher education proposals were not being funded, the corporation's hidden agenda became obvious. In order to recruit the highly technical personnel they needed, they had to ensure their prospective employees that the K–12 education their children would receive upon relocation would be of the highest quality. Of course another reason to support the schools was to provide a future work force. This type of situation calls for some project redefinition, the development of consortia with the best lead organization, and an emphasis on the role that higher education also plays in creating an educated work force.

The bottom line is that as you develop your corporate grants strategy, you must review your institution's or organization's ability to provide corporations with what they value.

While education has historically attracted the most cash share of corporate philanthropy, health and human services is now receiving a greater percent of total corporate contributions when you consider all forms of support (cash and noncash). One reason for this shift may be the escalating costs of health care and the fact that health and human services programs, projects, and research may provide direct benefits to employees, which decrease the need for services and, hence, lower the corporation's employee health costs.

While one could argue that support for education and health and human services makes a company look good and enhances the general community, how would you explain a corporation's interest in culture and arts or civic and community affairs? As a past board member and grantseeker for a museum, I once asked a corporate contributions' committee member how I could make my museum proposal more attractive to the committee. I was told I should document certain overriding factors, such as

- the use of the museum by current corporate employees, their families, and their friends;
- the number of corporate employees and/or their family members who volunteer at the museum;
- how the museum interfaces with the local chamber of commerce and how its presence promotes tourism and visitors to the area; and
- the existence of programs designed to provide family tours and so forth to those whom the corporation is seeking to recruit.

As a result of our conversation, we developed a community introduction program that matched our board members with prospective employees that the corporation was seeking to hire and move to our area. This moved us from a grant to support the museum to a contract to provide an introduction service, but it was undesignated cash that we could use as we saw fit.

Whether a corporation supports education, health and human services, culture and the arts, or civic and community affairs, you can be sure that its expenditures, be they philanthropic dollars or noncash gifts, are related to its enlightened corporate self-interests.

As the global marketplace expands and the multinationals merge and make hostile takeovers, corporate philanthropic activities become even more difficult to track and predict. U.S. companies purchased by foreign-based corporations have a very different sense of and experience with philanthropy. And international giving has become a growing category of corporate philanthropy as more and more companies have developed a worldwide presence.

Before you begin to refine your approach, consider the varied mechanisms that companies employ to make their corporate investments.

CORPORATE INVESTMENT MECHANISMS

Corporations use four basic mechanisms for investing in and making grants to nonprofit organizations.

Corporate Contributions Program Grants

Corporate contributions programs are the mechanism of choice in corporate philanthropy. Usually high-ranking corporate officials decide what portion of their corporation's net earnings before taxes (the bottom line of profits after manufacturing, sales, and marketing costs have been deducted) will be made available as gifts and grants. This money is then deducted from the corporate taxes due the government and directed to a corporate contributions committee to disperse to colleges, universities, and other nonprofit organizations that the corporation values. Interests vary from company to company, but generally fall within the categories listed above (education, health and human services, culture and arts, and civic and community affairs). Committee members may be corporate executives and/or representatives of employee groups or unions. Since many of the existing 5 million corporations are relatively small, with only a few employees, it can be surmised that the larger the company, the more likely it is to have a corporate contributions program and to engage in this mechanism of corporate philanthropy.

The latest IRS rule allows corporations to donate up to 10 percent of their pretax income (bottom line) in gifts and grants to nonprofit organizations as a tax deduction. However, the practice of donating a *set* percentage annually is not widespread. In fact, estimates are that of the 5 million corporations in the United States, only 35 percent dedicate *any* funds to nonprofit organizations.

At the beginning of the twenty-first century, the Bush administration backed a change in legislation to increase the corporate profits write-off from 10 percent to 20 percent. Even if passed, the current upper limit of 10 percent of deductions has never been approached. For example, when the limit was 5 percent, the average pretax profits donated was just over 2 percent. When the limit was raised to 10 percent, the average declined to around 1 percent and has remained below 2. Current efforts to allow 20 percent will likely have little if any impact on increasing this percentage. In fact, if history is any indicator, charitable corporate write-offs could even decrease. Many large corporations set an amount such as 1 percent of pretax profit. Since corporate profits are currently at record levels, the corporate marketplace is growing and warrants your investigation.

It is interesting to note that corporate philanthropic contributions are not required to be reported to stockholders in an itemized format. Stockholders are not *entitled* to a list of recipient organizations and the associated amounts of grant support. Only the IRS receives such a list with the corporate tax return, and it is not at liberty to share it with anyone.

Table 24.1 shows the funding priorities of corporate contributions programs. Health and human services receives 44 percent, followed by international support at 19 percent, and education at 14 percent. Although the category terms differ somewhat, the funding priorities of corporate contributions programs are much different than those of the next group—corporate foundation grants.

Corporate Foundations Grants

In this grants investment mechanism, companies designate a portion of their entitled write-off of pretax profits to be transferred to a foundation (usually named after the corporation) from which grants are paid. The main reason for initiating a corporate foundation is to stabilize a corporation's philanthropy

TABLE 24.1

FUNDING PRIORITIES OF CORPORATE CONTRIBUTIONS PROGRAMS

Health and Human Services	44%
International	19%
Education	14%
Civic—Community	8%
Culture—Arts	4%
Environment	1%
Other	10%

program. Corporate foundations lead to a more uniform and stable approach to corporate social philanthropy than giving programs that rely solely on a percentage of company profits each year. Programs tied to company profits are subject to the seesaw effect, because profits can vary widely from year to year. Funds from the corporate foundation corpus can be moved to grants in lean profit years.

Many corporations maintain both a corporate contributions program *and* a corporate foundation. This allows the company some flexibility in making grants. For example, if profits are down one year, the corporate contributions program can be supported by expending some of the assets that have built up in the foundation. The corporation can level out the highs and lows of its corporate contributions over periods of high, low, and no profits and still attain some level of support for its favorite nonprofit organizations. While all foundations are required to pay out a minimum of 5 percent of their assets, corporate foundations have historically paid out a much higher percentage, especially in the years marked by recession or low corporate profits.

Like the other types of foundations discussed in chapter 19, corporate foundations must list the benefactors of their grants and make their tax returns available for public viewing. This requirement can become a problem for corporations when their stockholders object to the types of organizations or specific projects that the corporate foundation supports. In addition, the public scrutiny to which the corporate foundation is subject allows for social activists and leaders of particular causes to research the foundation's giving pattern and arrange for demonstrations, which could result in negative public relations. To avoid such problems, many corporations make only noncontroversial grants (for example, a grant to the United Way) through their foundation; they make all other grants through their corporate contributions program that does not require public disclosure.

Since corporate foundations are an extension of a profit-making company, they tend to view the world and your proposal as any corporation would. They must see a benefit in all of the projects they fund. Many of these corporate foundations fund grants only in communities where their parent corporations have factories or a special interest. Table 24.2 shows the largest recipients of corporate foundation grants. Proposals related to public society benefit are the top recipients of corporate foundation grants (26.7 percent), followed by education (25.5 percent). Note that while international support was the second highest recipient of *corporate contributions programs* at 19 percent, it falls to sixth place in *corporate foundation* support (2.6 percent). For the most part, every grant made by a corporate foundation must benefit either the corporation or its workers or enhance the corporation's ability to attract high-quality personnel to the community in which it operates. Since we are rapidly becoming a global economy, the "community" is changing to an international one.

Corporate Marketing

While it is estimated that 25 percent of corporate support to nonprofits comes in the form of donated products, this figure is probably deceptively low. Corporate support in the form of products is likely to be far greater than the reported levels, but data on this marketing mechanism are difficult to collect and analyze. Much is simply not reported and thus is impossible to track.

Many corporate contributions of products may not be recorded as gifts per se because they are being used in a product positioning effort that the company believes will result in future sales. In essence, these product gifts could be questioned by the IRS because they do not qualify as true gifts; some *quid pro quo* (or this-for-that) is involved in these transactions, but the company writes off the associated costs before net earnings are ever calculated to avoid any problems.

TABLE 24.2

CORPORATE FOUNDATION GRANTS BY RECIPIENT CATEGORY

Public—Society	26.7%
Education	25.5%
Human Service	18.8%
Health	11.3%
Environment	2.9%
International	2.6%
Religion	0.6%
Other	0.1%

Corporate Research Contributions and Grants

Corporations have traditionally supported colleges, universities, and nonprofit organizations' attempts to apply science to further the development of new technologies, patents, and breakthroughs in their fields of interest. Some corporations also contribute to nonprofit organizations based on the nonprofit's ability to contribute to the testing, improvement, or creation of a new product. The litmus test as to whether the support provided is really a grant is whether the nonprofit that is involved in the receipt of corporate support is acting as a free agent or is a captive contractor for the corporate sponsor of the proposed work.

To be considered a true corporate grant, the results of the research must be published and shared for the "greater good" of the field. If the work is to be prescribed by the corporation, and/or the freedom to publish the resulting data is restricted, and any patents derived are the sole ownership of the corporation, the corporation's support will not be viewed by the IRS as a grant, but rather as a fee for services rendered or a corporate contract. If the support is viewed as a corporate contract, it is not allowed to be written off as a charitable contribution. However, it could be considered as a research or marketing cost and as such could be deducted before the company arrives at its net earnings before taxes.

While you do not need to be concerned with how the company deducts these costs from its balance sheet, it is crucial to both you and your institution/organization to clarify the intellectual property rights (copyrights, patents, and so forth) before entering into any research-related agreement.

Review your proposed project and consider how it provides your prospective corporate grantor with what it values. Then, based on these variables, determine which corporate grant making mechanism best fits your project (see exhibit 24.1). Compare the corporate self-interest variables in the column on the left of the exhibit to the four basic mechanisms for corporate support presented in the top row of the exhibit.

Corporate Funding and Ethical Issues

Most researchers are aware of the traditional hierarchy of grant support. By tradition, government, peer-reviewed grants have been viewed as the most prestigious, followed by foundation grants (not always peer reviewed and subject to foundation board bias), and finally, corporate grants (reviewed by a biased corporate grants committee looking for a return on its investment). However, the traditional ways of looking at corporate grants for research and corporate involvement with colleges and universities have changed dramatically over the last decade. One reason for this change has to do with the government's cuts in research. The cuts have encouraged, if not forced, universities to partner with the corporate world to collaborate, transfer technology, and develop intellectual property. Sheldon Krimsky, in his book *Science in the Private Interest: Has the Lure of Profits Corrupted the Virtue of Biomedical Research?* questions whether

Analyze how your project fulfills various corporate self-interests, and then compare these interests to the funding criteria of the four basic corporate grant-making mechanisms to determine which vehicle best fits your project.

Corporate Self-Interest	Corporate Contributions Program Grants	Corporate Foundation Grants	Corporate Marketing Contributions & Grants	Corporate Research Program Contributions & Grants
Ability to Attract High Quality Personnel				
Benefits Workers and/or Their Families				
Benefits Overall Community Where Parent Corporation Has Factory or Special Interests				
Positions Product in Such a Way That It Results in Future Sales				
Product Development – Tests, Improves, or Creates a New Product				
Research – Furthers Knowledge in Corporation's Field of Interest				
Other:				

CORPORATE GRANTS SUPPORT WORKSHEET

EXHIBIT 24.1

universities should be turned into instruments of wealth rather than protected enclaves whose primary roles are as sources of enlightenment.[1] The traditional assumption that research findings that come from the ivory tower of higher education are true and not biased or corrupt has been challenged by science selling findings to the highest bidder.

There exists a tremendous pressure to trade off the values of higher education as the costs for supporting research soar and the government cuts its funding for peer-reviewed research and continues to support earmarked noncompetitive grants. Not only has Congress pushed the bounds of ethical standards related to research, it has left the university and the researcher little choice but to surround themselves with corporations that have never been the bastion of ethical standards.

The big question now is how much financial gain will the researcher get by proving what the company wants. In fact, the incentives given by companies in stock and whether the company is owned by the researcher have now become the operant questions from which to judge the research findings.

Corporate support for research presents problems all across the nonprofit sector because the profits from potential products are so high. How far can this corporate interest in research take us? Several universities have auctioned off exclusive rights to their intellectual resources and their reputations to corporate bidders as a result of budget cuts. They pledge to maintain scientific ethics, but would they really do research that questioned their corporate partners' products? The lines are so blurred that some universities have actually warned their researchers that they could be sued if their research cost their corporate sponsors to lose profits.

The bottom line is that researchers must be very careful when dealing with corporate grants. They come at a price. Being forewarned is being forearmed.

NOTE

1. Sheldon Krimsky, *Science in the Private Interest: Has the Lure of Profits Corrupted the Virtue of Biomedical Research?* (Maryland: Rowman & Littlefield Publisher, Inc., 2004), p. 2.

CHAPTER 25

Researching Potential Corporate Grantors

How to Find the Corporate Funding Source That Is Best Suited to Fund Your Project

To be a successful corporate grantseeker, you will need to gather accurate information on your prospective corporate grantors before you approach them. The corporate research form (exhibit 25.1) outlines what information you will need to collect. The biggest mistake you can make with this marketplace is to send the same proposal to all the companies in your area. Research results in your ability to create targeted, tailored, winning proposals.

How you research the corporate marketplace depends on many factors, including the type of corporate grants mechanism you are pursuing. You must ask why a corporation would value your proposal. If your project is related to products, product positioning, product development, or research, you can cast a wide corporate net. In fact, you can move beyond local boundaries and look all across the country for the corporations best suited to fund your project.

To do so, you must first determine which major corporations could possibly be affected by your project. Develop a list of the products and services (the key words) that could be related to your project, and then access the *US NAICS (North American Industry Classification System—United States) Manual* at your university or public library. This publication references companies by the types of goods they produce. By searching the *US NAICS Manual*, using your key words, you can discover the names of the corporations that might be interested in your project. For example, if your project uses innovative ways to educate people with visual impairments, you might use the *US NAICS Manual* to locate

The following form outlines the data you need to collect in order to make a decision to seek funding from this grant source. Your attempts to collect as much of this information as possible will prove rewarding. (When feasible, record the source of the information and the date it was recorded.)

Name of Corporation: _____

Name of Corporate Foundation: _____

Name of Corporate Contributions Program: _____

Address: _____

Phone: _____ Fax: _____ Email: _____

Web site: _____

Contact Person: _____

Title: _____

Any Links from Our Organization to Contact Person: _____

_____

Corporation's Areas of Interests:

_____

_____

_____

Eligibility Requirements/Restrictions:

a. Activities Funded/Restricted: _____

_____

b. Organizations Funded/Restricted: _____

_____

c. Geographic Funding Preferences/Restrictions: _____

_____

d. Other Requirements/Restrictions: _____

_____

_____

_____

_____

Information Available	In Possession Of	
IRS 990-PF Tax Return (Year)	_____	(Corporate Foundation Only)
Guidelines	_____	
Newsletters	_____	
Annual Report	_____	
_____	_____	
_____	_____	

CORPORATE RESEARCH FORM

EXHIBIT 25.1

Contributions Committee Members/Board of Directors/Foundation Officers:

_____

_____

_____

_____

Deadline(s): _____

Application Process/Requirements:

_____

_____

_____

Financial Information

Fiscal Year: _____
Corporate Sales: $_____
Parent Company: _____
Corporate Sites: _____
# of Employees: _____
Credit Rating: _____   Source: _____
Private or Publicly Held: _____
If Publicly Held: Stock Price $_____   Dividend: $_____
Products Produced/Distributed: _____

For Corporate Foundations:

Asset Base: $_____
Are there current gifts to build the asset base?   Yes _____   No_____
If yes, how much? $_____

Total number of grants awarded in ____: _____
Total amount of grants awarded in ____: $_____

High Grant: $_____
Low Grant: $_____
Average Grant: $_____

In our interest area there were _____ grants, totaling $_____
High grant in our interest area: $ _____
Low grant in our interest area: $ _____
Average grant in our interest area: $ _____

Grants Received Versus Grants Funded
Number of proposals received in ____ : _____
Number of proposals funded in ____ : _____

Sample Grants in Our Area of Interest:

 Recipient Organization_____   Amount

_____   _____

_____   _____

CORPORATE RESEARCH FORM *(continued)*

EXHIBIT 25.1

companies that manufacture equipment for the blind or the latest telecommunications equipment that could be used in your solution.

Please note that while the North American Industry Classification System (NAICS) has replaced the U.S. Standard Industrial Classification (SIC) for statistical purposes, you will find that some publications still refer to SIC codes. Like the NAICS, the SIC is a system for classifying establishments by type of economic activity. Although the principles of the systems are the same, NAICS codes may vary considerably from the SIC codes.

You will also want to find out if there are any major industry specific associations or membership groups that fund research or projects in your field. For instance, the Society of Manufacturing Engineers funds beneficial research in its field, and there are many more like it.

While you should look outside of your local area for corporate grantors when your project is related to research and product development, remember that most corporations give where they live. Therefore, you may find that targeting corporations that are hundreds or thousands of miles away is not productive unless they have a vested interest in your project or research.

Checking with your grant office and development office is always recommended when dealing with corporations, and it is absolutely essential when contacting companies close to home. Corporate people assume that anyone who submits a proposal or contacts them has the approval of the institution or organization he or she represents, and you risk negative positioning if the right hand does not know what the left is doing. This does not mean that you should not consider local corporations, but do your research and make a case to your organization as to why you and your project should be allowed to proceed to submittal with each target corporation.

There are several great sources of information on corporate support. The Foundation Center, in particular, is a good resource for information on corporate foundation grants. Its publication, the *National Directory of Corporate Giving*, provides information on 3,000+ company-sponsored foundations, 1,400 corporate-giving programs, and 7,500+ selected grants. It is available in print edition and online. The online version, *Corporate Giving Online*, is updated weekly and provides immediate access to detailed company profiles, company-sponsored foundation descriptions, key facts on direct corporate-giving programs, and summaries of recently awarded grants. It also offers three ways to search—by company, by grant maker, and by grants. The *Corporate Giving Directory*, published by Information Today, Inc., is another good source. It provides profiles on 1,000 of the largest corporate foundations and corporate direct-giving programs in the United States, representing nearly $5.6 billion in cash and nonmonetary support annually. (See the List of Resources for ordering information.) In addition, the annual 990-PF tax returns for corporate foundations can be accessed through the Foundation Center's regional and cooperating collections and on the web (see chapter 20).

Corporate funders can also be found through the Internet, especially since many companies now maintain a presence on the web. There are several helpful portal sites available, including

- http://lnp.foundationcenter.org/finder.html (the Foundation Center's web site),
- http://www.cafonline.org (the U.K.–based Charities Aid Foundation's CCInet), and
- http://www.fundsnetservices.com/ (Fundsnet Services Online).

While it makes sense to check out these web sites and the corporate grant resource books available in your local public library and at the Foundation Center's regional collections, another important source for data is your local chamber of commerce. Your chamber of commerce can provide you with a list of local corporations and information on number of employees, total value of payroll, and products and services provided. You can obtain this list by visiting or phoning your chamber, and in some instances, off of its web site.

This list is most valuable as you begin to target your local grantors and develop your strategy on why they should be interested in your proposal. For example, when I was an associate professor at the University of Alabama, Birmingham, I asked for and received a list of the area's largest employers from the local chamber of commerce (see exhibit 25.2). By reviewing the information on the list, I discovered the following facts:

- The university I was employed by was the area's largest employer.
- Of the top ten largest employers, only three were profit-making corporate prospects.
- Seventy percent of the ten largest employers were nonprofit organizations and in competition with me for corporate support.
- Seventy percent of the next group (10–20) were profit making, but had only 19,890 employees in total compared to the nonprofits' 87,556 employees.

In addition to having to deal with the harsh reality of these facts, I also had to come to terms with the fact that hundreds of local nonprofits were targeting this corporate group, that the rest of my university had designs on the same local corporations that I did, and that I would have to plead my case for approval to submit a proposal to a development team comprised of representatives from colleges and departments other than mine.

If your institution or organization is not in a large metropolitan area, and there is no chamber of commerce, contact your nearest economic development agency, industrial park headquarters, or business incubator. One of these groups should have the data you need to uncover the corporations in your geographic area.

Top Employers
Birmingham–Hoover Metropolitan Area
Top Twenty Employers

	Company	Employees
1.	University of Alabama at Birmingham	18,750
2.	BellSouth	5,485
3.	Baptist Health System, Inc.	5,000+
4.	Birmingham Board of Education	5,000
5.	City of Birmingham	4,989
6.	Jefferson County Board of Education	4,800
7.	Jefferson County Commission	3,875
8.	AmSouth Bancorporation	3,785
9.	Bruno's Supermarkets, Inc.	3,477
10.	Children's Health System	3,200
11.	Wachovia	3,094
12.	Alabama Power Company	3,000
13.	Blue Cross-Blue Shield of Alabama	3,000
14.	Drummond Company, Inc.	2,900
15.	Brasfield & Gorrie, L.L.C.	2,800
16.	St. Vincent's Hospital	2,800
17.	United States Postal Service	2,800
18.	Compass Bancshares	2,696
19.	Brookwood Medical Center	2,600
20.	American Cast Iron Pipe Company	2,400

CHAMBER OF COMMERCE LIST

EXHIBIT 25.2

Once you have identified your distant and nearby potential corporate funding sources, the Internet and your public library or local college library will have several resources to help you gather more information to determine your best prospects for funding.

The following web sites are a good place to start researching corporate information. In general, they will provide basic information about the company itself such as areas of company operations, products and services, corporate officers, and fiscal data.

- http://www.sec.gov/edgar/searchedgar/webusers.htm (EDGAR database that contains information on companies whose stocks are traded publicly);

- http://biz.yahoo.com/i (Yahoo! Finance Company and Fund Index, a searchable database with information on more than 9,000 public companies in the United States);

- http://www.hoovers.com (Hoover's Online, a comprehensive subscription-based site that provides information on public and private companies in the United States and abroad);

- http://www.internet-prospector.org/company.html (Internet Prospector's Corporations Page, which provides links to corporate directories and other sources of business information);
- http://www.lambresearch.com/CorpsExecs.htm (the Companies and Executives section of David Lamb's Prospect Research Page).

Several of the Dun & Bradstreet or Standard & Poor's products and publications will provide the basic information you will need on profitability, board members, and so on.

The D & B Million Dollar Database is the online equivalent to the well-known *Million Dollar Directory*. It is a subscription-based database that provides basic data on U.S. companies, such as addresses, ticker symbols, key officers, number of employees, sales, and so on. It also provides brief, searchable executive biographies and titles, listings of international offices of U.S. companies, and the ability to download to spreadsheet or print out lists of companies. It covers companies with at least $9 million in sales or 180+ employees. The database is updated monthly, with company data updated every 60 days. Also available online, on a subscription basis, is the *D & B North American Million Dollar Database* that provides information on U.S. and Canadian leading public and private businesses, and the *D & B International Million Dollar Database* that provides information on international companies. (See the List of Resources for ordering information.)

Exhibit 25.3 has been taken directly from Dun & Bradstreet's web site (http://www.dnbmdd.com/mddi/sample.aspx) and is an example of what an entry in the *D & B Million Dollar Database* looks like.

Standard and Poor's Register—Corporate (File 527) is a database that provides information on over 100,000 public and private corporations worldwide, including current address, financial and marketing information, and a listing of officers and directors with positions and departments. Most of the companies covered have sales in excess of $1 million per year. The database's print counterpart is *Standard & Poor's Register of Corporations, Directors, and Executives, Volume 1.* When available, additional information on officers and directors is included in *Standard & Poor's Register—Biographical* database (File 526). This database's print counterpart is *Standard & Poor's Register of Corporations, Directors, and Executives, Volume Two.* Further information on companies can be found in Standard & Poor's Corporate Descriptions (File 133). These databases are all available online through Dialog, a service of The Dialog Corporation (see the List of Resources for ordering information). In addition, most university and public libraries will have access to Dialog databases for a fee, and some will have hard copies of the publications for free use. Exhibits 25.4 and 25.5 have been taken from Dialog's web site and are, respectively, sample records of *Standard & Poor's Register—Corporate Database* and *Standard & Poor's Register—Biographical Database.*

Gorman Manufacturing Company

Marked for Output	[ ]
D&B D-U-N-S Number	80-480-0217
Company Name(s)	Gorman Manufacturing Company
Trade Styles	
Street Address	492 Koller St.
City	San Francisco
State/Province	CA
Zip Code	94110
County	San Francisco
Phone Number	(415) 555-0000
Sales	$10,600,000
Employees Here	100
Employees Total	105
Location Type	SINGLE LOCATION
Line of Business	COMMERCIAL PRINTING
Primary SICs	27520000 COMMERCIAL PRINTING, LITHOGRAPHIC
Secondary SICs	
Primary NAICS	
Secondary NAICS	
Ownership/Control Date	1965
Metropolitan Area	SAN FRANCISCO-OAKLAND, CA
State of Incorporation	CA
Import/Export	IMPORTER
Public/Private	PRIVATE
Ticker Symbol	
Bank	FIRST SECURITY NAT BANK OF NEV
Accountant	ABC ACCOUNTING
CEO	Leslie Smith, President
Executives	Mr. Kevin J Hunt, Sec-Treas
Other Officers	Robert F Woods
Executive Biographies	

LESLIE SMITH YEAR OF BIRTH: 1926 Graduated from the University of California, Los Angeles, in June 1947 with a BS in Business Management. 1947-1965 general manager with Raymor Printing Co., San Francisco, CA. 1956 formed subject with Kevin Hunt.

KEVIN J HUNT YEAR OF BIRTH: 1925 Graduated from Northwestern University, Evanston, IL in June 1946. 1946-1965 general manager for Raymor Printing Co., San Francisco, CA. In 1965 formed subject with Leslie Smith.

SAMPLE ENTRY FROM THE *D & B MILLION DOLLAR DATABASE*

EXHIBIT 25.3

As you can see from the sample in exhibit 25.5, the information provided in the entries in the biographical database includes the age, the educational background, and the residence of the corporate executive, as well as his or her other corporate affiliations and activities. This biographical information is very valuable in that it can be used with your grants advisory committee to uncover links

Dialog (R) File 527: S&P Register – Corp.
(c) 2003 McGraw-Hill Companies Inc. All rts. reserve

0018401

Company	CHEMDESIGN CORP.
Parent Company	(Subsidiary of Bayer AG)
Street Address	310 Authority Dr.
City, State, Zip Code	Fitchburg, MA USA 01420
Telephone	(978) 345-9999
Business	Manufacturing, Manufactures, devel. & sells fine chemicals on a custom basis
NAICS codes	325998; 325110
NAICS descriptions	All Other Miscellaneous Chemical Product Manufacturing; Petrochemical Manufacturing
Year Started	1982
Sales	$61.00 Mil
Employee Total	395
Market Territory	NATIONAL, INTERNATIONAL
Special Feature	THIS IS A SUBSIDIARY A PUBLIC COMPANY
Stock Exchange	NYS
Ticker Symbol	XYZ
Accounting Firm	Deloitte & Touche Boston MA
Bank	Citibank
Law Firm	Miles & Stockbridge

EXECUTIVES AND DIRECTORS

Chrm, Pres & Chief Exec Officer	Archibald, Nolan D.
Exec V-P	Stevens, William E.
Exec V-P (Worldwide Inf Serv)	Barcus, James F. Jr.
Sr. V-P (Power Tools Group)	Sherman, George M.
Sr V-P (Household Products Group)	Heiner, Dennis G.

OTHER DIRECTORS:

Battle, William C.	Bolton, John E.
Decker, Alonzo G. Jr.	Franklin, Barbara H.
Krikorian, Robert V.	Muncaster, J.D.
Pugh, Lawrence R.	Storrs, Thomas I.
Voell, Richard A.	Watkins, Judy

SAMPLE RECORD *STANDARD & POOR'S REGISTER—CORPORATE DATABASE*

EXHIBIT 25.4

and expand corporate relationships. For example, in the sample entry we can see that James H. Yocum graduated from Harvard University. Therefore, if you have an advocate or grants advisory committee member who is a graduate of Harvard, you will be wise to take that individual with you when you make preproposal contact.

In addition to these references, your library should also have *Who's Who in America* and other books on outstanding individuals in your geographic area.

```
Dialog (R) File 526:  S&P Register – Biographical
(c) 1997 McGraw-Hill Companies Inc. All rts. reserve

0067511

NAME:                          YOCUM, JAMES H.
BIRTH:                         Reading, PA  (1926)
RESIDENCE ADDRESS:             920 Centre Ave.
                               Reading, PA  19601
UNDERGRADUATE COLLEGE:         Harvard Univ. (1948)
GRADUATE COLLEGE:              Harvard Univ. (Grad. Sch. of Bus. Admin.)
GRADUATE YEAR:                 1952
PRIMARY COMPANY AFFILIATION:   Exec. V-P, Treas & Dir
                               Penn Square Management Corp.
                               P.O. Box 1419
                               Reading, PA  19603
POSITION(S):                   Vice President – Executive
                               Treasurer
                               Inside Director
DEPARTMENT(S):                 Finance
                               Administration
SECONDARY AFFILIATIONS:        Penn Square Mutual Fund, Trustee
                               Yocum Brothers, Inc., V-P, Secy & Dir
                               Hamilton Bank, Reg Dir
                               U.S. Merchant Marine Academy Alumni
                               Assn., Pres
FRATERNAL ORGANIZATIONS:       Free & Accepted Masons
```

SAMPLE RECORD STANDARD & POOR'S REGISTER—BIOGRAPHICAL DATABASE

EXHIBIT 25.5

The more you know about the people you will be approaching for a grant, the more prepared you will be to create a powerful appeal that motivates the grantor to award you funds. Corporate leaders have much more written about them than federal bureaucrats, and your local librarian can show you how to use free resource tools to learn more about corporate grant prospects. Check the List of Resources in the back of this book for commercially available materials that you will find helpful in your search for corporate funding sources.

Profits are the bottom line in corporate philanthropy. If there are no profits there is little incentive to donate money to reduce taxes. Since corporate contributions depend on a company's profitability, your corporate research should include information on revenue. There are several ways to obtain accurate data on profitability. You can

- access a corporation's web site to learn about its new products and plans.
- track a corporation's stock prices on the DOW, NASDAQ, or AMEX.
- include a stockbroker on your advisory group to help you monitor corporate profits.

- include a corporate executive on your advisory group who subscribes to Dun & Bradstreet's financial services and ask him or her to request a Dun & Bradstreet report on your prospective corporate grantor. This report will rate the fiscal stability of the company and give you a sense of the company's ability to support your proposal. (A corporate person will also understand the values of corporations and may have linkages to companies you are interested in pursuing for grant support.)

- purchase a few shares of stock in each publicly held company in your area. If you receive a dividend check, you will know the company made money! Using this technique you will also receive corporate reports, proxy statements, and up-to-date information on top corporate administrators and board member changes. You might even make some money, and if you get rejected by a corporation you can always sell its stock for revenge!

Doing your homework on corporate grantors can be more frustrating than researching federal or foundation sources. You will find much less information available on corporate grants awarded by companies that do not use a foundation to make their grants, and the information you do find will be much less reliable. The reason for the lack of sound data on corporate giving is that there are no laws allowing public review of corporate contributions programs. Companies must record their corporate charitable contributions on their Internal Revenue Service tax return, but no one, not even a stockholder, has the right to see the return.

Except for the portion of corporate grants that is awarded through corporate foundations, corporate data are not subject to validation, and hence the reporting is not always accurate. The data on corporate giving are derived from self-reported, voluntary responses to surveys and questionnaires. Even the corporate contributions data reported to *Giving USA* (published by the Giving USA Foundation) are based on a voluntary survey conducted by the Conference Board, a nonprofit organization with a reputation for keeping corporate responses confidential.

Irrespective of the difficulties in obtaining accurate corporate granting information, the corporate research strategies recommended in this chapter will at least provide you with the ability to gather the name, the address, the email address, the fax and/or phone number of the corporate contact person; information you will find necessary to take the next step in your grant-winning strategy step—contacting a corporate grantor before submission.

CHAPTER 26

Contacting a Corporate
Grantor Before Submission

Just as with private foundation grantseekers, corporate grantseekers who discuss their projects with the appropriate corporate funding officials before submitting their proposals increase their success rates dramatically. A fivefold increase in success was found when preproposal contact was made with private foundation funding sources. Experience leads me to believe that the impact of preproposal contact on success rate is much higher in the corporate marketplace, and could approach a tenfold factor.

Often it is difficult for grantseekers to make preproposal contact with corporate grantors. This is because it takes more time to make profits than it does to grant the 1 percent of net earnings before taxes that most corporations award. In a sense, it costs the corporate grantor even more money to make grants when its time would be better spent on making more profits.

Corporate webbing and linkages become critical here (see chapter 7). It pays to figure out who may know whom, and who would be willing to make an appointment or open a door for you. If you do not have a linkage to any of your prospective corporate grantors, consider creating one by inviting selected corporate representatives to take part in your advisory group, or by hosting an open house or public forum.

Your initial point of contact may not always be the individual listed in your research as the corporate foundation contact or the chair of the corporate contributions committee. Your initial contact person could be a salesperson for the corporation, parents of your students who are employed by the corporation, clients of your organization who work for the company, and so on. Many corporations pay special attention to proposals that can be linked to employees that are volunteers of the prospective grantee's organization.

One big difference between private foundation grantors and corporate grantors is that the corporate grantor has an office or a facility. Even so, corporate grantors have a multitude of responsibilities and cannot spend unlimited amounts of time with grantseekers. Therefore, it is imperative that you follow the formal instructions your research uncovers. If you uncover a name, and an email address and/or a phone number, assume that you can contact the person listed. If your research states no contact except by letter or application, then follow those instructions. However, *informal* contact through an advisory committee member, advocate, or linkage is still advised. In these instances, the important thing is that *you* are not the one making the contact. If your advisory committee member, advocate, or linkage can orchestrate a conference call or preferably a face-to-face meeting, go with him or her. If you are instructed to request current guidelines or an application package, you can use the sample corporate inquiry letter/email shown in exhibit 26.1. If the instructions call for a letter proposal or letter of inquiry and do not allow for formal preproposal contact, go to chapter 27.

Contact by Telephone

If contact by telephone is allowed or encouraged, call to discuss how your project relates to the corporation's interests. Let the person to whom you are speaking know that you have done your homework. If it is a corporate foundation, use the information you obtained from its tax return (IRS form 990-PF) to show your knowledge of its past granting interests. If the corporate grantor seems interested in your project, do not be afraid to inquire about the possibility of a face-to-face meeting. If a visit is out of the question, then discuss the same issues over the phone as you would in person.

The Visit

While often the most anxiety producing, a face-to-face visit is usually the best way to discuss your project and to gauge the interest of the corporate grantor.

Who Should Go? It is advisable for you to take either an advocate, linkage, or an advisory committee member with you. A good listener who can summarize and reflect back what you believe is the grantor's position is a good choice. Successful corporate people are skilled at making sales calls, and they will expect you to be skilled when asking for their money. You do not want to appear as a fast-talking used-car salesman, but your approach should be well rehearsed and professional, and your appearance should be conservative, reflecting that of the corporate official's as closely as possible. Remember, corporate people do dress for success.

Materials to Bring. Your proposal development workbook (Swiss cheese book) will be a great confidence builder, since you will most likely be able to

Name
Title
Address

Dear _____ :

We at (nonprofit organization) are developing a project that deals with (problem) and
provides benefit to [or in] (target population). Our research indicates that this area is an
important concern of the (name of corporation or corporate foundation).

[Choose from the following paragraphs]

(Name and title) from our organization is planning a trip to (corporation's geographic
location) and would appreciate being able to talk with you regarding an exciting project
that we feel would be of mutual benefit. I will be contacting you soon to discuss this
further.

[Or]

We would like to explain our innovative solution in a full proposal, and request that you
send or email us a request to apply or your application guidelines/form.

Thank you for your cooperation.

Name/Title
Organization
Address
Email

SAMPLE INQUIRY LETTER/EMAIL TO A CORPORATION

EXHIBIT 26.1

open it right to the areas of question. Also bring a short video or a CD that you
can play on your laptop to document the need and the unique qualities you and
your institution bring to the solution. Use your battery to power your short two-
to three minute presentation so you do not require any plugs or adapters. If the
corporate representative asks you to join his or her colleagues in a conference
room, you may need to set up a PowerPoint presentation on the corporation's
equipment. Make sure you know how, and have an extra CD-ROM to use with
the corporation's data projection system.

What to Discuss with a Corporate Grantor. Review the following topics of
discussion and tailor them to your particular situation and prospective corporate
funding source. Remember that the purpose of these discussions is to verify the
information you gathered through your research and to gain more insight into
how to produce a proposal that the prospective grantor will find impossible not
to fund.

1. Discuss the need for your project/research and then introduce your solutions. Briefly explain the various approaches you are considering to solve

the problem, and then ask if any one approach is preferred over the others. Asking for the corporation's input is often a good way to start.

2. Verify all information you have on the corporation's granting programs and patterns. Show the corporation's representatives that you have looked at their annual reports, or corporate foundation tax returns, by the comments you make and the questions you ask. For example, "I can see from my research that this area is important to your corporation because it represents 50 percent of all your granted projects. My research indicates that your board is very educated and sophisticated in this field. Will they be the group that reads and selects the proposals for approval?"

Corporate Grantor Report Form

Whether you, your advocate, linkage, advisory member, or staff person makes contact with the prospective grantor, make sure that *who* was contacted and *what* was discussed is documented. Complete a corporate grantor report form (exhibit 26.2) after each contact with a corporate funding source whether the contact was made in person, over the phone, or through an email.

Complete one of these forms after each contact with a corporate grantor.

Funding Source: _____
Funding Source Address: _____

Funding Source Contact Person: _____
Telephone Number: _____ Fax:_____ Email: _____
Contacted On (Date): _____
Contacted By (Name): _____
Type of Contact: Phone _____ Visit _____ Other (Explain) _____

Objective of Contact: _____
_____
_____

Results of Contact: _____
_____
_____
_____

Follow-up: _____
_____
_____

CORPORATE GRANTOR REPORT FORM

EXHIBIT 26.2

CHAPTER 27

Applying for Corporate Funds

Many of the corporate grantors you will approach for funding have had experience developing applications for use with government grant programs they are eligible for, and with contract and procurement programs as bidders and contractors. They strive to put together succinct and well-written proposals, sales and marketing materials, and presentations for their sales prospects. They value email and correspondence that is effectively written. Of all the grantor types, they are probably the most critical and demanding audience you will encounter in your grants quest.

Construct your corporate proposal as outlined in this section, and have a quality circle or mock review of your proposal performed by corporate individuals from your advisory group. While you have chosen to make the nonprofit world your base of operation, you must recognize that your value glasses are different from those who have chosen the for-profit world as their primary frame of reference and that you must adjust your proposal writing style accordingly.

When I asked a corporate vice president what the biggest mistake was in proposals from the nonprofit world he said, "The vocabulary." When I asked him to clarify, he said that nonprofits should never use the "g" word. I asked him if he meant "g" for grants and he said, "No, 'g' for 'give.'" Proposal writers had repeatedly asked his company to *give* them funding. He suggested to me that they use the "I" word, or "invest" instead. Considering what you learned about corporate self-interest in chapter 24, this should make sense to you. To be successful in the corporate grants marketplace, you must be able to convince the prospective grantor that it will get a *return on its investment* if it funds your project.

The fact that only a few of the larger corporations have staff members dedicated to contributions or community relations, and that most do not rely on outside readers or peer reviewers to evaluate submitted proposals, means your proposal will probably be read by individuals on the corporate foundation board or the corporate board, research and development types, salespeople, and/or marketing representatives. Corporate contributions' committees are often comprised of a mix of these types of individuals.

As with the private foundation marketplace, you will fail miserably if you take the "one size fits all" approach and blanket the corporate community with the same proposal that starts with, "We want _____. Please send money." To make matters worse, the corporations you approach with this method are likely to never forget the poorly developed, mass-produced proposal you submitted to them.

The successful corporate letter proposal follows the same basic order as the proposal to a private foundation. The main components are as follows:

- an introductory paragraph stating the reason for writing,
- a paragraph explaining why this grantor was selected,
- a needs paragraph,
- a solution paragraph,
- a uniqueness paragraph,
- a request for funds paragraph,
- a closing paragraph,
- signatures, and
- attachments, if allowed.

Many corporations specify a proposal format and rules on such things as number of pages on their web sites. If they specify a short, one-page letter proposal or letter of intent but provide little in the form of guidance, use the proposal format suggested above. However, instead of addressing each component in a full paragraph, use just a sentence or two. The key is to identify the problem and how you will close the gap between what is and what should be together.

INTRODUCTORY PARAGRAPH

If you have a linkage to the corporation, use it here. For example,

> When this exciting project to increase the technology skills of educators was discussed with John Smith, the vice president of your corporate board, he suggested we ask the Jones Corporation to consider a role in increasing teacher competencies.

You could also mention a volunteer connection in your opening paragraph. This is a particularly good idea since many corporations will not invest in a local nonprofit organization unless their employees are voluntarily involved with it. Consider using your introductory paragraph to refer to the commitment of their employees to your cause. For instance,

> Will Olsen, your Region Four supervisor, and I have discussed Oak Computer's role in increasing the performance of our students through the use of applied technology. As chairperson of our school advisory committee, Mr. Olsen has donated over 100 hours of time and has been instrumental in making our computer lab a reality.

In the case of a research-related project, you might refer to an employee linkage who has served on your advisory committee, given a talk or lecture to your staff or students, served as a mentor, or allowed students to shadow workers to gain insight into the corporate marketplace.

Always check with your linkages before submitting your letter proposal, and provide them with a draft copy of the section that refers to them to be sure that they are agreeable. If you do not have a linkage to whom you can refer in the opening paragraph, start your letter proposal by focusing on the grantor.

WHY THE GRANTOR WAS SELECTED

This paragraph presents you with another opportunity to express your knowledge about the grantor. The purpose of this section of your letter proposal is to establish that the similarities between what it, the grantor, values and what you value are why you selected it. Align your organization with the values of the grantor by saying something such as the following:

> As the Jones Corporation has become an international leader in innovative technology related to energy conservation, the Jonathan Smith Laboratory has dedicated its research to the same field of study.

If it is a corporate foundation, you have access to its IRS return (990-PF) and should use it. Unfortunately, corporate contribution grants cannot be tracked. Therefore, you will have little, if any, research with which to work.

NEEDS PARAGRAPH

This section of your corporate proposal must establish that you have a command of the knowledge in the field. You must convince the reader/reviewer that you know what exists now in your field of expertise and that you know what needs to happen to close the gap between what is and what should be. The gap provides the reason why your proposal cannot be rejected. If the corporate grantor is truly interested in the area and in contributing toward solving the problem, then that corporate grantor must keep reading your proposal and ultimately fund your project.

The following example illustrates the proposal writer's expertise in the field and identifies the gap.

The problem is simple, the solution is not. Current accepted theory used to explain the energy expended in the X reaction does not account for Y. The inability to predict Y costs our energy conservation effort billions of dollars in the United States alone.

Make sure that you do not mention your proposed solution or your organization in the needs section of your letter proposal except if you need to make reference to your own studies or findings. One way to ensure that you do not make this mistake is to include a transition sentence or two that enables you to move smoothly from the problem to your solution. For example, "What must be done to address and close this gap? We propose a solution!"

SOLUTION PARAGRAPH

The purpose of this paragraph is to provide a short summary of the methodology that will be employed to solve the problem.

Corporate executives are accustomed to using spreadsheets to analyze the steps and costs involved in planning and evaluating just about everything they do in the corporate world. Therefore, if space allows (you need to be able to submit at least three pages) it is a good idea to include a one-page project planner/spreadsheet (see chapter 13) as page 2 of your corporate proposal. Refer to this project planning aid as a one-page summary of your more detailed plan. Make mention that you have several more pages of project planners that detail the methods summarized on the page included in your letter proposal and that you would be happy to provide them upon request. Remember that corporate people are likely to ask for more detail, might visit you, and could ask you to come to them. While they may not designate a specific amount of time to grants, they do have an office and a travel budget.

UNIQUENESS PARAGRAPH

The corporate grantor wants to be assured that you, your organization/institution, and your project are the right investment choice for it. Most nonprofits reflect on their organizations' missions and history when creating this section. While this may work with private foundations to demonstrate commitment to the field of interest, corporate grantors want facts, data, statistics, and examples of winning characteristics. While they will probably want to know that you have been a grant winner before, what really matters to them is the breakthroughs your institution, program, or lab have made in the field, and the competency and productivity of your staff. If your key personnel are exceptional, tell them so. While you may have written the proposal, you will probably not be the individual to sign it. Therefore, it is okay to refer to yourself in this paragraph as the qualified leader to carry out the plan.

Think of this paragraph as part of a corporate marketing brochure. For example, what convinces you to buy a particular product from one company over another? It is probably that company's credibility, the proof that it stands behind its product, and its commitment to quality! These are the same attributes that corporate funding sources want to see in their grantees.

REQUEST FOR FUNDS PARAGRAPH

As in all proposals you must ask for the money. If you are targeting a corporate foundation, you have access to its 990-PF IRS tax return and can use the data provided on that form to decide how much to request. However, it is difficult to know how much to request from a corporation that awards grants through a contributions program due to the lack of available public information. If are unable to decipher an appropriate amount through preproposal contact, you will have to guess. As you learned in chapter 8, most grantseekers think that corporate grants account for $60 to $75 billion dollars per year, when it is actually $12.8 billion. With this in mind, you might want to scale down your request. Anything over $100,000 is a very large corporate commitment.

If you are forced to divide your project into several fundable pieces, explain that in this paragraph. Also name-drop any of the grantors who have already granted you funds. You and your project are a junk bond until someone else with a good reputation buys in. Then you become a blue-chip stock.

Your project planner should help the corporate decision maker evaluate the appropriateness of your request. If you must present a budget, avoid dedicating a whole page to this purpose. Use a paragraph form budget instead and refer to the column totals on your project planner.

You can refer to the return for its investment by dividing the total cost by the number of people the project will serve. In a research proposal, compare the requested amount to the benefits that may occur as a result of answering the research question and closing the gap in the field or knowledge, and suggest what this may lead to in the future. Both of these approaches are quite successful with corporate grantors.

Corporate grantors will also want to know how you intend to continue a program or project that you will use their grant to initiate. How much will it take to continue this project, and how do you intend to procure that money? For example, the Boeing Corporation states on its corporate web site that Boeing's philanthropic strategy is to contribute toward sustainable growth and self-sufficiency for the organizations with which it partners. That principle guided $102.4 million in contributions in 2005.

CLOSING PARAGRAPH

Do not start this paragraph off by stating that you would like to meet with the grantor; the grantor already knows you would. Instead, invite the grantor to meet

Michael Casper, President
Garner Corporation
1374 Chichester Highway
Appleton, OH 25891

Dear Mr. Casper:

I would like to take this opportunity to invite you to join our school district in initiating an exciting new program. We know your company is particularly interested in education because you generously support elementary and secondary schools, are an enthusiastic partner in the Adopt-A-School Program, and encourage your employees, like Stefan Pelon and Vicki Thames, to volunteer at our local schools.

As a matter of fact, Mr. Pelon and Ms. Thames are currently involved in helping our district address the problem of declining math and science skills and the growing inability of our students to transfer these skills from the classroom to the workplace. Our students rank _____ in the country and score in the ____ percentile on standardized math tests, but we are not the only ones to recognize the problem.

A ____ study conducted by the Educational Testing Center showed that American 13-year-olds placed 14th among 15 industrialized countries on standard math tests.

A ____ Scans Report indicated that the average American high school junior spends 30 hours a week on school work; the average Japanese junior spends 60.

Although there is some evidence that our students' mathematical scores are improving, the demand for mathematical skills is not remaining constant. It is growing, and we have already graduated individuals with inadequate skills.

You may have read about the Will-Burt Corporation of Orrville, Ohio (*Profile*, August ____). They recently found themselves in a terrible situation. Their company employees were producing inferior products. In fact, they had a 35 percent rejection rate, massive product recalls, and 2,000 hours per month of "re-work." Their employees' lack of basic math skills was found to be one of the main culprits. After setting up a school in the plant to teach math skills, the company's rejection rate decreased to 2 percent, but the Will-Burt Corporation discovered that while remedial training was an effective solution, it was also a costly one.

It is estimated that over $25 billion is spent annually on remedial training in this country! We must do better. Our schools must provide our students with the skills necessary to meet future challenges. An April ____ article in *INC.* magazine reported that even today's modern corporations want employees who can and will think about

SMALL LETTER PROPOSAL TO A CORPORATION

EXHIBIT 27.1

with you and your key personnel and to visit your institution, organization, laboratory, and so on. Be sure to express your desire to provide any additional information and request that the prospective grantor contact you (or the individual responsible for the project) to provide that information and/or to answer any questions.

innovation, quality service, and using advanced techniques such as statistical process control.

Our school district has been developing several solutions to deal with declining math and science skills, including parental involvement in education, less television, and more valuable homework. However, we also need to apply new techniques – techniques we cannot afford in our regular budget. For example, we know that individualized instruction and self-paced learning materials could make a big difference if we only had the funds to provide for and purchase these resources.

Our parents advisory committee, teachers, staff, and volunteers are very excited about implementing SUCCESS-MAKER, a computer-assisted learning program designed to help teachers develop an individualized instructional approach that will allow

- remedial students to catch up,
- average students to excel, and
- gifted students to leap beyond.

The SUCCESS-MAKER elementary package in math is particularly interesting to us. It would allow our teachers to place students on computers to improve skills in number concepts, computation, problem solving, and math applications in science. The students' progress would be continually recorded and a report would be developed for the student, teacher, and parents. Our objective would be to increase our district's math competency by ___ percent. Other districts that have used this approach have not only documented an improvement in skills but also significant increases in parental involvement.

Our district is ready to accept the challenge that SUCCESS-MAKER offers. Our teachers have already volunteered their time for in-service training, and our district has dedicated $____ in resources to support the project. Everything is ready, but we need you.

A grant of $____ from the Garner Corporation equates to an investment of $____ per student who will benefit. I have enclosed a spreadsheet [or project planner] that outlines exactly how your funds will be put to use. I am sure you will agree that we need to move now before another group of students becomes another group of American workers needing remedial training. Your support will be an important catalyst in ensuring the strength of our country's future workforce and the growth of companies such as the Garner Corporation.

We think of this project as an investment with a tremendous return, and we hope you will, too. We promise to stand accountable and to share all results of the program with you and your company. Please contact my office or [name] at [phone number] with any questions you may have. If you would like, we can provide you with support materials and a videotape that describes SUCCESS-MAKER in greater detail and includes comments from educators who have used this approach.

Sincerely,
Ellie Jade, Ed.D.
Superintendent, Friendship Heights School District

SAMPLE LETTER PROPOSAL TO A CORPORATION *(continued)*

EXHIBIT 27.1

SIGNATURES

Corporate people expect your proposal to be signed by an administrator or officer who holds rank and responsibility within your organization/institution. This is

How to Apply

The grant application process begins with the submission of a simple-to-use online questionnaire. To get started, you need to identify the region in which your program will be administered by going to the Grants Contacts page, where you can locate your state contact. From there, click on the application link associated with your state to begin the online questionnaire.

Questions on the application will include:

A brief description of your organization's:
- Mission
- Recent achievements
- Program focus and population served
- Program/project description
- Program/project budget
- Program/project evaluation methods and project outcomes
- Geography to be served

Your contact information

If your organization has been previously funded, add a description of how the grant funds were used and the grant's impact on the communities you serve.

In addition, you will be asked to provide the following documents:
- The current operating budget, program budget (if applicable), principal funding sources and levels
- The organization's most recent annual report and audited financial statements
- A list of board members and their affiliations

The following guidelines are used in evaluating the proposal:
- Alignment with our three focus areas of philanthropic giving
- Demonstration of effective organizational, programmatic, and financial objective setting and management
- Evidence of broad-based support, with an accounting of funds received from public and private sources
- Description of the target population to be served
- Evidence that the service is a response to a valid need, is superior to other competing services, and/or encourages collaboration with other organizations for maximum leverage
- Documentation of previous program success or substantial reasons to expect such success in the future.

Grant limitations
Grant contacts

JPMorgan Chase Grant Guidelines

EXHIBIT 27.2

viewed by the corporate grantor as an institutional commitment and endorsement. More than one signature is okay, including the signature from your consortia partner(s), which can be impressive to them.

ATTACHMENTS, IF ALLOWED

While most corporations do not *encourage* attachments, they may be *allowed* in proposals for research grants. In these instances, project planner spreadsheets detailing your protocol are recommended over text.

Corporate application instructions for other types of grants (nonresearch) will usually restrict the use of any attachments. For example, when applying for a $300,000 grant from the BellSouth Foundation, the application instructions received by my institution specifically stated that letter proposals were restricted to five double-spaced pages of 12 to 13 characters per inch and that no attachments were allowed. The guidelines also stated that the Foundation would request further information from a select group of applicants from which one-half would be funded. We eventually received a letter stating that our proposal had made the first cut and that of the total 200 applicants, we were one of the 20 under consideration. Along with that letter came a list of ten questions that the reviewers had regarding our proposal. We were required to answer these questions, limiting our responses to a total of three double-spaced pages. Our $300,000 successful grant consisted of eight double-spaced pages (four single-spaced pages).

Review the sample corporate proposal in exhibit 27.1. This sample includes the main components of a letter proposal outlined in this chapter. While you are encouraged to develop your own style, you should still include these integral parts in any letter proposal you submit. Even when provided with an online application and specific corporate contributions guidelines like those in exhibit 27.2, try to incorporate the concepts suggested in this chapter into your proposal. For instance, in the needs section, you should work in the fact that through your research you are aware of the company's strong commitment to resolving this problem. And, after the section outlining your solution, you could slip in a few sentences explaining to the prospective corporate funding source why you are a unique grantee, and the best choice to implement the solution.

CHAPTER 28

Proposal Submission, the Decision, and Follow-Up
Corporate Grantors

Before submitting your proposal to a corporate grantor, put it through a quality circle (see chapters 14 and 23) that resembles the actual review process as closely as possible. The purpose of this exercise is to get an unbiased first impression of your proposal from individuals who view it from the perspective of enlightened, corporate self-interest.

Ask two or three of your colleagues and two of your advisory committee members from the corporate world, or a professor from your local college's business school to participate. Encourage everyone to role-play being corporate executives. Unless you have information otherwise, inform all of the participants that the real reviewers will be corporate executives who read your proposal in less than five minutes. They should also be made aware that the real reviewers (the corporate executives) will most likely not follow any specific scoring or rating system and will not provide any comments to the applicants. Therefore, the applicant really needs their feedback. Ask your quality circle participants to designate those areas of the proposal they think a corporate executive would like with a plus sign (+) and those areas they think they (the corporate executives) would dislike with a minus sign (−). Discuss suggestions for improving or highlighting the positive sections and for rewriting the negative sections. The whole exercise should take less than one hour.

SUBMISSION

Many of the larger corporate grantors now allow online application and submittal. For the smaller corporations you will likely be sending a print copy of your proposal to the contact person listed in your research. Even when you apply and submit online, print your proposal out to be certain the font and/or graphics are not altered, and send a hard copy of your proposal to the funding source just in case it does not receive the electronic version. Submit the proposal a few days before the deadline using the United States Postal Service, United Parcel Service, or FedEx. When mailing your proposal, require a proof of receipt, and send it via a carrier that can guarantee next-day delivery.

Send copies of your final proposal to your corporate linkages so that they know you finally submitted your proposal and are aware of exactly what you requested. Thank them for the assistance they provided up to this point and for the assistance they may provide in the future to help get your submitted proposal funded.

THE DECISION

Corporate grantors may provide an outcome only to those to whom they award grants. They may fail to notify those they reject. In any case, your research will provide you with the dates that the corporate board meets, and from these dates you can approximate when you should hear from the grantor.

Rejected

If you do not hear by six months after the deadline date, your proposal was probably rejected. If you do receive a rejection letter, you may also receive little in the way of constructive criticism, redirection of your efforts, and/or reapplication rules. Some corporate grantors do not allow you to resubmit immediately. For example, I was once told by a corporate foundation that I could not resubmit for three years. Other grantors may advise you never to resubmit due to new restrictions and/or changes in their priorities and philosophy. Learn what you can from the grantor, your advocates, and/or your linkages and reapply when it is allowable and advisable.

Always send a thank-you letter that acknowledges the time the funding source invested in the selection process, and express your gratitude for its foresight in dedicating profits to impacting these problems and its areas of interest.

Awarded

If your proposal is funded, send the same thank-you letter as outlined above, but include an invitation to visit your institution/organization to see the important work you are conducting and the unique qualities you mentioned in your proposal. You should also request any comments the grantor may have that would help you improve on a future proposal to it or another corporation. However, do not expect a response.

FOLLOW-UP

Whether you are successful or not in your corporate grants quest, try to maintain professional contact. Like you, corporate decision makers are trying to keep up on the advances in your mutual field of interest. Send them an interesting article that your research uncovers, or even an article of yours that is scheduled for publication. Let them know you are alive between the deadline dates. Seek them out at conferences and meetings, and ask them questions about their next grant opportunities.

Persistence and the maintaining of a professional interest in their area of concern will pay off. You will improve your relationship with them and have chances to learn of their upcoming grant priorities. Just remember that being persistent is different from being a pest! Keep your relationship focused on the need for your projects and research, and their opportunities for involvement.

The best approach to grantseeking is to develop a long-term and mutually beneficial relationship among you, your organization, and the grantor. This relationship should be based on honesty and a sincere concern for the grantor's needs. Saying thank you is a crucial element in building such a relationship.

Thank you for purchasing this book, and I am confident that you will be rewarded for practicing the strategies outlined.

LIST OF
RESOURCES

You may wish to look at copies of these recommended grant tools before you purchase them. Many of the resources listed include locations where you can find the materials and get assistance from helpful staff. Many institutions have developed joint or cooperative grants libraries to reduce costs and encourage consortium projects.

The list of resources is divided into the following sections:

- Government Grant Research Aids
- Foundation Grant Research Aids
- Corporate Grant Research Aids
- Government, Foundation, and Corporate Grant Resources
- Electronic Resources

GOVERNMENT GRANT RESEARCH AIDS
Tips

1. Each congressional district has at least two federal depository libraries. All the government publications listed below are available in print copy at federal depository libraries. To locate a library near you, visit http://www.gpoaccess.gov/libraries.html.
2. Many federal agencies have newsletters or agency publications. You can ask to be placed on their mailing lists to receive these publications (see chapter 11).
3. Contact federal programs to get the most up-to-date information.

4. All of the government grant publications listed here are available through your congressperson's office.

Government Publications

Catalog of Federal Domestic Assistance (CFDA)

The *Catalog* is the government's most complete listing of federal domestic assistance programs, with details on eligibility, application procedures, and deadlines, including the location of state plans. It is published at the beginning of each fiscal year, with supplementary updates during the year. Indexes are by agency program, function, popular name, applicant eligibility, and subject. Access is free online at http://www.cfda.gov. A hard copy is also at federal depository libraries.

Congressional Record

The *Congressional Record* covers the day-to-day proceedings of the Senate and the House of Representatives. Access is free online at http://www.gpoaccess.gov/crecord/index.html. A hard copy is also at federal depository libraries, or for purchase at the Government Printing Office's (GPO's) online bookstore at http://bookstore.gpo.gov.

Superintendent of Documents

P.O. Box 271954

Pittsburgh, PA 15250-7954

(866) 512-1800 or (202) 512-1800 in the DC metro area

Federal Register

Published five times a week (Monday through Friday), the *Federal Register* supplies up-to-date information on federal assistance and supplements the *Catalog of Federal Domestic Assistance (CFDA)*. The *Federal Register* includes public regulations and legal notices issued by all federal agencies and presidential proclamations. Of particular importance are the proposed rules, final rules, and program deadlines. An index is published monthly. It is available for free at http://www.gpoaccess.gov/fr/index.html. A hard copy is also at federal depository libraries.

United States Government Manual

This is the official handbook of the Federal Government and provides comprehensive information on the agencies of the legislative, judicial, and executive branches. It is available online for free at http://www.gpoaccess.gov/gmanual/index.html. A print copy can be purchased from the U.S. Government Online Bookstore at http://bookstore.gpo.gov. It can also be located in federal depository libraries.

Other popular government web sites:

National Endowment for the Humanities, www.neh.gov.

National Institutes of Health, www.nih.gov.

National Science Foundation, www.nsf.gov.

Department of Education, www.ed.gov.

Department of Housing and Urban Development, www.hud.gov.

Commercially Produced Publications

Federal and Foundation Assistance Monitor

This bi-monthly newsletter is available online and in print, and features a comprehensive review of federal funding announcements, private grants, and legislative actions.

Price: $427.00 softcover

Order from:

CD Publications

(301) 588-6380 or (800) 666-6380

http://www.cdpublications.com/pubs/federalassistance.php

Federal Directory

The *Directory* includes names, addresses, and phone numbers of federal government agencies and key personnel.

Price: $425.00 print version

Order from:

Carroll Publishing

4701 Sangamore Rd.

Suite S-155

Bethesda, MD 20816

(800) 336-4240

Federal Yellow Book

This directory of the federal departments and agencies is updated quarterly.

Price: $450.00

Order from:

Leadership Directories, Inc.

104 Fifth Avenue, 3rd Floor

New York, NY 10011

Phone: (212) 627-4140

Fax: (212) 645-0931

Or order online at http://www.leadershipdirectories.com

Guide to Federal Funding for Governments and Nonprofits

This two-volume loose-leaf manual offers access to funding details on more than 750 federal aid programs. Included in your subscription is online access to a federal grant deadline calendar.

Price: $399.00

Order from:

Thompson Publishing Group

Subscription Service Center

P.O. Box 26185

Tampa, FL 33623-6185

(800) 677-3789

http://www.thompson.com/fits36

Washington Information Directory, 2005/2006

This directory is divided into three categories: agencies of the executive branch, Congress, and private or "nongovernmental" organizations. Each entry includes the name, address, telephone number, and director of the organization, along with a short description of its work.

Price: $140.00 print edition; call for online pricing

Order from:

Customer Service and Order Dept. WEB2

1255 22nd St., NW, Suite 400

Washington, DC 20037

Phone: (866) 427-7737 or (202) 729-1900 in the DC metro area

Fax: (202) 729-1923

http://www.CQpress.com

FOUNDATION GRANT RESEARCH AIDS

Many of the following research aids can be found through the Foundation Center Cooperating Collections Network. If you wish to purchase any of the following Foundation Center publications, contact

The Foundation Center

79 Fifth Avenue

New York, NY 10003-3076

Phone: (800) 424-9836

Fax: (212) 807-3691

http://www.fdncenter.org/marketplace

The following five directories can all be ordered by mail or fax (no telephone or credit card orders accepted) from:

Research Grant Guides, Inc.

P.O. Box 1214

Loxahatchee, FL 33470

Fax: (561) 795-7794

Directory of Building and Equipment Grants, 7th edition

Profiles on 900 foundations that provide support for buildings, equipment, and/or renovations.

Price: $89.00

Order from: Research Grant Guides, Inc.

Directory of Computer and High Technology Grants, 5th edition

Includes 875 foundation profiles to help you search for funds for computers and software.

Price: $89.00

Order from: Research Grant Guides, Inc.

Directory of Grants for Organizations Serving People with Disabilities

Profiles of 700 foundations with specific interests in this area.

Price: $89.00

Order from: Research Grant Guides, Inc.

Directory of Operating Grants, 8th edition

Profiles on 1,000 foundations receptive to proposals for operating grants (salaries, rent, overhead, and so forth).

Price: $89.00

Order from: Research Grant Guides, Inc.

Directory of Program Grants, 3rd edition

900 profiles of foundations interested in programs and projects that help meet community needs.

Price: $89.00

Order from: Research Grant Guides, Inc.

The Foundation Directory, March 2007, 2,730 pages

The most important single reference work available on grant-making foundations in the United States, this directory includes information on foundations having assets of more than $2 million or annual grants exceeding $200,000. Each entry includes a description of giving interests, along with address, telephone numbers, current financial data, names of donors, contact person, and IRS identification number. Six indexes are included: index to donors, officers, and trustees; geographic index; types of support index; subject index; foundations new to edition index; and foundation name index. The index to donors, officers, and trustees is very valuable in developing links to decision makers.

Price: $215.00

Order from: The Foundation Center

The Foundation Directory Part 2, March 2007, 2,148 pages

This directory provides information on 10,000 mid-size foundations.

Price: $185.00

Order from: The Foundation Center

The Foundation Directory Supplement, September 2007

The *Supplement* updates the *Directory*, so that users will have the latest addresses, contacts, policy statements, application guidelines, and financial data.

Price: $125.00

Order from: The Foundation Center

Foundation Grants to Individuals, 15th edition, 1,117 pages

This directory provides a comprehensive listing of over 4,300 independent and corporate foundations that provide financial assistance to individuals.

Price: $65.00

Order from: The Foundation Center

The Foundation 1,000, October 2006, 3,030 pages

The 1,000 largest U.S. foundations are profiled by foundation name, subject field, type of support, and geographic location. There is also an index that allows you to target grant makers by the names of officers, staff, and trustees.

Price: $295.00

Order from: The Foundation Center

Foundation Reporter, 2007, 38th edition

This annual directory of the top 1,000 private foundations in the U.S. supplies descriptions and statistical analyses.

Price: $535.00 print, first time standing order

Order from: Information Today's online store at

http://infotoday.stores.yahoo.net/foundrep38ed.html

Grant Guides

There are a total of 12 Grant Guides available in a variety of subjects including arts, culture, and the humanities; children and youth; elementary and secondary education; environmental protection and animal welfare; foreign and international programs; higher education; libraries and information services; mental health, addictions, and crisis services; minorities; people with disabilities; religion, religious welfare, and religious education; and women and children.

Price: $75.00 each

Order from: The Foundation Center

Guide to Funding for International and Foreign Programs, 8th edition, May 2006, 629 pages

This guide includes over 1,500 funding sources that award grants to international nonprofit institutions and projects, as well as over 8,700 grant descriptions.

Price: $125.00

Order from: The Foundation Center

Guide to Grantseeking on the Web, September 2003, 852 pages

Includes information on hundreds of grant-maker web sites and a variety of related nonprofit sites of interest.

Price: $29.95

Order from: The Foundation Center

Guide to U.S. Foundations, Their Trustees, Officers, and Donors, May 2007, 7,929 pages

This three-volume guide includes information on over 400,000 decision makers.

Price: $395.00

Order from: The Foundation Center

National Guide to Funding in Health, 9th edition, May 2005, 2,892 pages

This guide includes over 11,500 sources for health-related projects and institutions and over 21,000 grant descriptions.

Order from: The Foundation Center

National Guide to Funding in Religion, 8th edition, May 2005, 1,892 pages

This guide includes nearly 9,000 grant makers, as well as more than 14,000 selected grant descriptions.

Price: $175.00

Order from: The Foundation Center

National Guides from the Foundation Center are also available in the following areas:

AIDS, $125.00

Libraries and Information Services, $125.00

Private Foundation IRS Tax Returns

The Internal Revenue Service requires private foundations to file income tax returns each year. Form 990-PF provides fiscal details on receipts and expenditures, compensation of officers, capital gains or losses, and other financial matters. Form 990-AR provides information on foundation managers, assets, and grants paid or committed for future payment.

The IRS makes this information available on aperture (microfiche) cards that may be viewed for free at the reference collections operated by the Foundation Center (New York, San Francisco, Washington, D.C., Cleveland, and Atlanta) or at the Foundation Center's regional cooperating collections. You may also obtain this information online at

- http://foundationcenter.org/findfunders/990finder/,
- http://www.guidestar.org, and
- http://www.grantsmart.org.

Directories of State and Local Grant Makers

Visit the Foundation Center cooperating collection (see chapter 20) closest to you to determine what directories are available for your state and surrounding region. The following regional guides are available through the Foundation Center:

- *Guide to Greater Washington D.C. Grantmakers* on CD-ROM, $75.00
- *Directory of Missouri Grantmakers* on CD-ROM, $75.00
- *Guide to Ohio Grantmakers* on CD-ROM, $125.00
- *New York Metropolitan Area Foundations: A Profile of the Grantmaking Community*, $24.95
- Visit the Rural Information Center at www.nal.usda.gov/ric/ricpubs/funding/fundguide.html#fdatabase for a comprehensive listing of available state directories. Please note that some directories are updated on a regular basis, but many are not.

Other popular foundation-related web sites:

The Council on Foundations—www.cof.org

Philanthropy News Network Online—www.pnnonline.org

The Foundation Center's homepage—www.fdncenter.org

CORPORATE GRANT RESEARCH AIDS

Corporations interested in corporate giving often establish foundations to handle their contributions. Once foundations are established, their Internal Revenue Service returns become public information, and data are compiled into the directories previously mentioned under Foundation Grant Research Aids.

Corporate contributions that do not go through a foundation are not public information, and research sources consist of

- information volunteered by the corporation,

- product information, and
- profitability information.

The 2005 Corporate Contributions Report

The results of this annual survey include a detailed analysis of beneficiaries of corporate support, but do not list individual firms and specific recipients.

Price: $125.00 for associates; $495.00 for nonassociates

Order from:

The Conference Board

845 Third Avenue

New York, NY 10022

Phone: (212) 759-0900, general information

Phone: (212) 339-0345, customer service

Fax: (212) 980-7014

http://www.conference-board.org/publications

Corporate Giving Directory, 2007, 29th edition

This directory provides detailed entries on 1,000 company-sponsored foundations.

Price: $562.50 for first time standing orders

Order from:

Information Today

143 Old Marlton Pike

Medford, NJ 08055-8750

(609) 654-6266

http://books.infotoday.com/directories/corporategivingdirectory.shtml

Dun & Bradstreet's (D & B) Million Dollar Database

This is a subscription-based database that provides basic data on U.S. companies, such as addresses, ticker symbols, key officers, number of employees, and sales. It also provides brief, searchable executive biographies and titles, listings of international offices of U.S. companies, and the ability to download to spreadsheet or print out lists of companies. Also available online from Dun & Bradstreet is the D & B North American Million Dollar Database that provides information on U.S. and Canadian public and private businesses, and the D & B International Million Dollar Database that provides information on international companies.

Call company for pricing.

The D & B Corporation

103 JFK Parkway

Short Hills, NJ 07078

(800) 234-3867, customer service

http://www.dnb.com/

The National Directory of Corporate Giving, 12th edition, August 2006, 1,527 pages

Information on over 3,000 corporate foundations, plus an additional 1,400 direct-giving programs, is provided in this directory. An extensive bibliography and seven indexes are included to help you target funding prospects.

Price: $195.00

Order from:

The Foundation Center

79 Fifth Avenue, Dept. FJ

New York, NY 10003-3076

Phone: (800) 424-9836 or in New York State, (212) 807-3690

Fax: (212) 807-3677

www.fdncenter.org

North American Industry Classification System Manual, 2002

Developed for use in the classification of establishments by type of activity in which they are engaged.

Price: printed version $49.00, $32.50 hardcover; CD-ROM version with search and retrieval software $60.00

Order from:

National Technical Information Service

5285 Port Royal Rd.

Springfield, VA 22161

(888) 584-8332 or (703) 605-6000

http://www.ntis.gov

Standard & Poor's Register—Biographical (File 526)

This database provides additional information on officers and directors. Both of these databases are available online through Dialog.

Order from:

Dialog Corporation

11000 Regency Parkway, Suite 10

Cary, NC 27511

Phone: (800) 334-2564

Fax: (919) 468-9890

http://www.dialog.com

The print counterparts to these databases are available from the Standard & Poor's Corporation. Call customer service for pricing.

Standard & Poor's Corporation

55 Water St.

New York, NY 10041

(800) 523-4534

Standard & Poor's Register—Corporate (File 527)

This database provides information on over 100,000 public and private corporations worldwide, including current address, financial and marketing information, and a listing of officers and directors with positions and departments.

Who's Who in America 2007, 61st edition

Known for its life and career data on noteworthy individuals. The 2007 edition chronicles American leadership with 110,000 of the nation's most noteworthy people. Available in hard copy and on the web.

Price: $710.10 for print version, first-time orders

Order from:

Order Dept.

Marquis Who's Who

P.O. Box 31

New Providence, NJ 07974

Phone: (800) 473-7020

Fax: (800) 836-7766

http://www.marquiswhoswho.com

Other corporate-related web sites:

Hoovers—www.hoovers.com

Busines Journal's Book of Lists—www.bizjournals.com

Securities and Exchange Commission (SEC)—www.sec.gov

GOVERNMENT, FOUNDATION, AND CORPORATE GRANT RESOURCES

Many of the following research aids can be purchased from Greenwood Publishing Group online at http://www.greenwood.com, or by phone at (800) 225-5800.

Directory of Biomedical and Health Care Grants, 2006, 20th edition

This directory provides information on biomedical and health care–related programs sponsored by the federal government, corporations, professional associations, special interest groups, and state and local governments. Published annually.

Price: $89.50

Order from: Greenwood Publishing Group

Directory of Grants in the Humanities, 2005/2006, 19th edition

Current data on funds available to individual artists and art organizations from corporations, foundations, and professional associations as well as from the NEA (National Education Association), NEH (National Endowment for the Humanities), and state and local arts and humanities councils.

Price: $89.50

Order from: Greenwood Publishing Group

Directory of Research Grants, 2006

Information on government, corporate, organizational, and private funding sources supporting research programs in academic-, scientific-, and technology-related subjects is included. Published annually.

Price: $145.00

Order from: Greenwood Publishing Group

Funding Sources for K–12 Education, 2005, 7th edition

Descriptions of programs that offer funding opportunities for classroom instruction, teacher education, art in education, general operating grants, and equipment from federal, state, corporate, and foundation sources.

Price: $60.00

Order from: Greenwood Publishing Group

Giving USA 2007

Annual report on philanthropy for the year 2006.

Price: $75.00

Order online, by phone, or by fax from:

The Giving Institute

http://www.givinginstitute.org

Phone: (847) 375-4709

Fax: (866) 607-0913

How to Evaluate and Improve Your Grants Effort, 2nd edition

Provides information on the roles and responsibilities of an effective grants office. Particularly useful for those in the process of setting up a new grants office or evaluating an existing one.

Price: $43.16

Order from: Greenwood Publishing Group

ELECTRONIC RESOURCES

There is a wealth of information available through online databases (free and subscription) and CD-ROMs. Check with your librarian and your grants office to locate those electronic resources to which you may already have access.

Grants.gov

This is the central storehouse for information on over 1,000 federal grant programs and access to $400 billion in annual awards. Access is free online at http://www.grants.gov.

FedBizOpps (Federal Business Opportunities)

A government database listing notices of proposed government procurement actions, contract awards, sales of government property, and other procurement information over $25,000. Available free online at http://www.fedbizopps.gov/.

Community of Science (COS) Funding Opportunities

COS Funding Opportunities database is a comprehensive source of funding information available on the web. It contains more than 22,000 records worth over $33 billion.

Price: COS Funding Opportunities is included with fee-based membership in the Community of Scholars. Other institutions may purchase access to COS Funding Opportunities for a fixed annual subscription fee. Subscription pricing is determined by the amount of external research funding your institution manages. Visit http://www.cos.com for further information.

Congressional Information Service Index (CIS Index)

CIS Index covers congressional publications and legislation from 1970 to date. Hearings, committee prints, House and Senate reports and documents, special publications, Senate executive reports and documents, and public laws are indexed. *CIS Index* includes monthly abstracts and index volumes. CIS publications are available in print, microfiche, and microfilm formats. Pricing information is available from customer service.

LexisNexis Academic and Library Solutions

4520 East West Highway

Bethesda, MD 20814

(800) 638-8380, customer service

http://www.lexisnexis.com/academic/CISPubs/

DIALOG OnDisc Grants Database

DIALOG OnDisc Grants Database lists approximately 8,900 grants offered by federal, state, and local governments; commercial organizations; professional associations; and private and community foundations. Each entry includes a description, qualifications, money available, and renewability. Full name, address, and telephone number for each sponsoring organization are included as available.

Price: $850.00 includes bimonthly updated CD-ROM

Foundation Center Databases/CD-ROMs

The Foundation Center offers several grant-related electronic resources. For further information on these products visit http://www.fdncenter.org/marketplace or call (800) 478-4661.

Foundation Directory Online Subscription Plans

The Foundation Center has several different online subscription plans, including *The Foundation Directory Online Professional, The Foundation Directory Online Platinum, The Foundation Directory Online Premium, The Foundation Directory Online Plus,* and *The Foundation Directory Online Basic.* The basic subscription allows you to search the nation's largest 10,000 foundations including the names of over 60,000 trustees, officers, and donors starting from $19.95 per month or $195.00 per year. Contact the Foundation Center for information and pricing for the other plans.

FC Search: The Foundation Center's Database on CD-ROM

This CD-ROM provides information on over 88,000 U.S.–based foundations, corporate givers, and grant-making public charities. It also contains a database of 350,000 recent grants. It costs $1,195 for a single user disk. This price includes a free Fall Update disk and one user manual. Contact the Foundation Center for network prices.

Other CD-ROMs available through the Foundation Center include

- *Corporate Giving Online*
- *Foundation Directory on CD-ROM*—$295 for the single user disk
- *Foundation Directory 1&2 on CD-ROM*—$495 for the single user disk
- *Foundation Grants Index on CD-ROM*—$165 for the single user disk

GrantSelect

This database is available on the World Wide Web; it provides information on more than 10,000 funding opportunities. Grantseekers can subscribe to the full database or to any one of seven special segments offered: children and youth, health care and biomedical, arts and humanities, K–12 schools and adult basic education, community development, international programs, and operating grants. An email alert service that notifies grantseekers of any new funding opportunities within their area of interest is also available.

For pricing information, visit http://grantselect.com/.

For questions on registration, pricing, and information for consortia, email Sales@grantselect.com.

For questions about the content of GrantSelect, email louschafer@grantselect.com.

For further information, call GrantSelect at (812) 988-6400.

For questions about the content, emailgrantsadmin@oryxpress.com.

BIG Online

This is a membership-based keyword and field searchable database with detailed information and profiles on 25,000 American and Canadian foundations, corporate donors, matching gift programs, in-kind donations, and government grant makers. For information call BIG Online at (888) 638-2763 or email info@bigdatabase.com.

Illinois Researcher Information Service (IRIS)

The *IRIS* database of funding opportunities contains records on over 9,000 federal and nonfederal funding opportunities in all disciplines. It is updated daily.

Price: *IRIS* is a subscription service. It is available to colleges and universities for an anual subscription fee. For more information on the subscription policy and/or an *IRIS* trial period, contact

Illinois Researcher Information Service (IRIS)

University of Illinois at Urbana-Champaign

128 Observatory

901 South Mathews Avenue

Urbana, IL 61801

(217) 333-9893

http://www.library.uiuc.edu/iris/.

The Sponsored Programs Information Network (SPIN)

This is a database of federal and private funding sources. Price depends on the institution's level of research and development expenditures.

For pricing, more information, or to order, contact

InfoEd International

(800) 727-6427

http://www.infoed.org/

DAVID G. BAUER ASSOCIATES, INC. ORDERING INFORMATION

Order the following grantseeking and fundraising materials directly from David G. Bauer Associates, Inc. Prices do not include shipping charges and are subject to change without notice.

Call toll-free (800) 836-0732, Monday–Friday, 9–5 Pacific Standard Time

GRANTSEEKING MATERIALS

Creating Foundations for American Schools—Techniques for creating and using school foundations. $49.95.

The Principal's Guide to Winning Grants—Strategies principals can apply to support grantseeking at their schools. $36.00.

Project Planner—Pad of 25 worksheets for developing work plans and budget narratives. $8.95 per pad; 10 or more pads, $7.95 each.

Proposal Organizing Workbook—Set of Swiss cheese tabs. $9.95 per set; 10 or more sets, $8.95 each.

Successful Grants Program Management—Practical tool for the superintendent or central office administrator to assist in developing a district-wide grants support system. $36.00.

The Teacher's Guide to Winning Grants—A systematic guide to grantseeking skills that work for classroom leaders. $35.00.

Technology Funding for Schools—Techniques schools can use for obtaining funding for their technology-related goals. $41.00.

FUND-RAISING MATERIALS

Donor Pyramid—Threefold visual depicting various levels of donor activities and volunteer involvement. $9.95 each; 10 or more, $8.95 each.

Fund Raising Organizer—Pad of 25 spreadsheets for planning and analyzing fund-raising events. $8.95 per pad; 10 or more pads, $7.95 each.

Fund Raising Organizer Activity Cards—Pack of 25 cards that summarize resource allocation, costs, and net funds. $3.95 per pack; 10 or more packs, $2.95 each.

The Fund Raising Primer—112 pages that provide basic information on various fund-raising strategies. $24.95.

VIDEO PROGRAMS

David G. Bauer Associates, Inc. has three video programs available:

- *Winning Grants*
- *How To Teach Grantseeking to Others*
- *Strategic Fund Raising*

For more information, call (800) 836-0732.

IN-HOUSE SEMINARS AND CONSULTING

David G. Bauer gives seminars at your institution or organization to increase your faculty, staff, and/or board member's skills and interest in the following areas: federal grantseeking, foundation and corporate grantseeking, using quality circles to improve your proposals, team building, fund-raising, evaluating your grants and/or fund-raising system, and motivation/productivity. David G. Bauer also provides a unique faculty development program aimed at increasing the grants success rates of faculty at colleges and universities throughout the United States. For more information on these services, call (800) 836-0732.

INDEX

About the Author

DAVID G. BAUER is highly sought after as a speaker on grantseeking. He is president of David G. Bauer Associates, Inc., a consulting firm created in 1981 to provide educationally based grantseeking and fund raising seminars and materials. Bauer has taught more than 30,000 individuals the keys to grantseeking and fund raising. He has served as the director of development for the Center for Educational Accountability and Associate Professor at the University of Alabama at Birmingham School of Education. David Bauer is also author of ten books on winning grants and administering grants programs, some having appeared in several editions. He has developed several videotape series and two software programs in this field as well.